Nathaniel Hawthorne
The scarlet letter

COLUMBIA CRITICAL GUIDES

Nathaniel Hawthorne

The Scarlet Letter

EDITED BY ELMER KENNEDY-ANDREWS

Series editor: Richard Beynon

COLUMBIA UNIVERSITY PRESS   NEW YORK

Columbia University Press
Publishers Since 1893
New York

First published in the Icon Critical Guides series in 1999 by Icon Books
Ltd.

Library of Congress Cataloging-in-Publication Data

Nathaniel Hawthorne : The scarlet letter / edited by Elmer Kennedy-
Andrews.
    p. cm.—(Columbia critical guides)
    ISBN 0–231–12190–3 (cloth)—ISBN 0–231–12191–1 (paper)
    1. Hawthorne, Nathaniel, 1804–1864. Scarlet letter. 2. Historical
fiction, American—History and criticism. 3. Mothers and daugh
ters in literature. 4. Massachusetts—In literature 5. Puritans in liter
ature. 6. Adultery in literature. 7. Women in literature. I. Kennedy-
Andrews, Elmer, 1948– II. Series.

PS1868 .N38 2000
813'.3—dc21   00–026250

⊖

Casebound editions of Columbia University Press books are printed on
permanent and durable acid-free paper.

Printed in the United States of America

c 10 9 8 7 6 5 4 3 2 1
p 10 9 8 7 6 5 4 3 2 1

Contents

INTRODUCTION

THE SCARLET Letter is generally regarded as the high-point of Nathaniel Hawthorne's literary achievement. For many critics it was more than just a personal success; it was America's declaration of cultural independence, the proof of an emergent distinctively American literary tradition. Henry James expressed the sense of national pride:

■ The publication of *The Scarlet Letter* was in the United States a literary event of the first importance. The book was the finest piece of imaginative writing yet put forth in the country. There was a consciousness of this in the welcome that was given it – a satisfaction in the idea of America having produced a novel that belonged to literature, and to the forefront of it. Something that might at last be sent to Europe as exquisite in quality as anything that had been received, and the best of it was that the thing was absolutely American.[1] □

We know something of the circumstances surrounding the writing of the book from Hawthorne's biographers. Arlin Turner, for example, tells us that Hawthorne had been galvanised into writing *The Scarlet Letter* by the death of his mother on 31 July 1849: 'within a month, Hawthorne was writing nine hours a day, more than twice his normal time at his desk'. During this remarkable outburst of creativity Hawthorne wrote with such demonic energy that his wife 'was almost frightened'.[2] By 3 February, 1850, he had completed *The Scarlet Letter*. Having originally planned it to be a tale, he realised when he had finished writing it that it was too long to include in a volume of tales, but was not quite long enough to stand on its own. His publisher, James T. Fields, who was highly impressed by *The Scarlet Letter*, advised him to publish it, along with a prefatory sketch called 'The Custom-House', as a single volume. Hence, the inclusion of 'The Custom-House'. As it stands, this prefatory sketch is something of a palimpsest: the reader will notice that neither the early reference to the story which follows as 'the most prolix of the tales that make up my volume', or the later reference to an 'article called "Main Street", included in the present volume' was ever edited out.

The least that may be said is that the inclusion of 'The Custom-House' as part of *The Scarlet Letter* challenges our notions of organic unity. In the sketch itself Hawthorne argues for its 'propriety': 'It will be seen, likewise, that this Custom-House sketch has a certain propriety, of a kind always recognized in literature, as explaining how a large portion of the following pages came into my possession, and as offering proofs of the authenticity of a narrative therein contained.' However, we need to be careful not to be fooled, for his 'authenticity' turns out to be a 'fabrication' in more ways than one. Leo Marx, in his introduction to the Signet Classic edition, speaks for those who see no difficulty in detaching 'The Custom-House' from the main narrative:

■ This elegant essay, a charming specimen of its kind, does help some readers cross the bridge into Hawthorne's fictional world. But it is not an integral part of the story, and the impatient reader may begin immediately with the novel and save the other for his leisure.[3] □

In what ways, then, does 'The Custom-House' help the reader into the world of *The Scarlet Letter*? Is it not the differences between the nineteenth-century world of 'The Custom-House' and the seventeenth-century world of the main narrative that strike us first? The sketch has a light, genial, urbanely censorious tone; it presents humorous, satirical caricatures of old men chasing money and comfort; it introduces us to a humdrum, commercial world of nepotism and decay. From this we move to an old world of sombre, allegorical romance, and the intense psychological drama of anguished individuals struggling with sin and conscience. Nevertheless, despite the differences of tone and atmosphere, certain intriguing connections between 'The Custom-House' and the main story are discernible.

First, there is what we might call 'the Puritan theme'. The narrator, in describing his job as Surveyor for the District of Salem, tells us about some ancient Salemites who were his ancestors. He tells us about William Hathorne who arrived in New England in 1630 and was 'a bitter persecutor' of the Quakers, and about John Hathorne who was involved in the notorious Salem witch trials of 1692. We gradually become aware of profound tensions in the narrator/author that inevitably source the main narrative of *The Scarlet Letter*. The troubling conflict between the narrator's/author's conservative, Puritan, masculine side, and his artistic, instinctive, feminine side which values its freedom and creativity may be seen to be projected into the story of Hester and Dimmesdale, and to contribute substantially to the ambiguity and contradictoriness of that story. 'The Custom-House' narrator registers his sense of difference from his oppressive Puritan forefathers, whose profound distrust of art and imagination, he knows, would have led them to regard his writing story-books as 'worthless, if not positively disgraceful'. At the same time he admits that no matter how much he feels their scorn, 'strong traits of their nature have intertwined themselves with mine'.

This tension between the Puritan and the artist in him is palpable in two particularly stressful passages:

■ It will be seen, likewise, that this Custom-House has a certain propriety, of a kind always recognized in literature, as explaining how a large portion of the following pages came into my possession, and as offering proofs of the authenticity of a narrative herein contained. This, in fact – a desire to put myself in my true position as editor, or very little more . . . In accomplishing the main purpose, it has appeared allowable, by a few extra touches, to give a faint representation of a mode of life not heretofore described, together with some of the characters that move in it, among whom the author happened to make one . . .

[. . .]

. . . and it should be borne carefully in mind, that the main facts of that story are authorized and authenticated by the document of Mr. Surveyor Pue. The original papers, together with The Scarlet Letter – a most curious relic – are still in my possession, and shall be freely exhibited to whomsoever, induced by the great interest of the narrative, may desire a sight of them. I must not be understood as affirming, that, in the dressing up of the tale, and imagining the motives and modes of passion that influenced the characters who figure in it, I have invariably confined myself within the limits of the old Surveyor's half a dozen sheets of foolscap. On the contrary, I have allowed myself, as to such points, nearly or altogether as much license as if the facts had been entirely of my own invention. What I contend for is the authenticity of the outline. □

One is struck by the instability of the narrative, its contradictoriness. In the first passage, in the space of a paragraph he moves from 'editor' to 'author', from insisting on 'proofs of the authenticity of a narrative' to claiming an 'allowable' freedom in treating the facts. The second passage contains a similar progression: the narrator wants to reassure his readers and himself that he is writing factual history, but ends up asserting a desire for artistic freedom and imaginative autonomy. The reference to his 'dressing up of the tale' links narrator and Hester. Hester's embroidery (the 'A' she wears stands for 'artist' as well as 'adulterer') has an equivalent in the narrator's storytelling. Both activities involve defiance of Puritan structures and are fraught with guilt. Both are associated with the expression of the feminine side of personality against patriarchal ideology.

The narrator's anxieties may also be seen to find an objective correlative in the characterisation of Dimmesdale as well as that of Hester.

Dimmesdale is a comprehensive incarnation of the narrator's Puritan guilt. Both have secret lives. Just as the narrator has difficulty acknowledging responsibility for the creation of his story, Dimmesdale has difficulty acknowledging what he has paternally engendered in defiance of Puritan constraint, his little daughter Pearl.

Secondly, 'The Custom-House' problematises 'truth' and 'reality', and that problematic is one of the central concerns of the main narrative. In a bold shift from autobiography to fantasy, the narrator of 'The Custom-House' tells us of finding in a forgotten corner the scarlet letter and some papers that had been the property of an 'ancient' Surveyor Pue. With a seamless folding of fiction into fact, he invites us to see the fictional Hester as a real, historical figure ('the reader may smile, but must not doubt my word'), and to take his central fiction of the discovery of the scarlet letter as historical fact. Something of a postmodern Hawthorne emerges here in the way he so coolly and duplicitously plays with the idea of sources, so that we cannot be sure what is real and what is invented. These elisions of fact and fiction perform both a serious 'New Historicist' function of suggesting how treacherously difficult it is to reconstruct the past, and a Deconstructionist joke which deliberately and playfully undermines the authority of history and logic. A similar defiance of authority characterises the main narrative, where Hester and Dimmesdale transgress and manipulate Puritan orthodoxy, the narrator refuses narrative authority, and the text resists determinate meaning. As Raman Selden declares:

■ From a poststructuralist viewpoint Nathaniel Hawthorne's *The Scarlet Letter* is a compelling example. The novel actually seems to be about the devious processes of the signifier . . . Hester's scarlet letter is the novel's central signifier: it weaves its ambiguous and haunting way through the text, scarcely allowing Hester to exist for a moment beyond its insistence. The letter seems to establish Hester's subject position irrevocably. The signifier which Puritanism imposes upon the letter is 'adultery' together with all the connotations of shame and guilt that go with it. However, Hester's identity is not fixed by the signifier – she enters a subject-position which is always unstable despite the appalling power of Puritan ideology.[4] □

And, finally, in 'The Custom-House' Hawthorne tells us about 'romance', which is his preferred generic term to describe *The Scarlet Letter*, as his subtitle for the book – 'A Romance' – would indicate. Having expressed his disillusionment with the 'dreamy brethren' of Brook Farm (a utopian community of high-minded intellectuals devoted to Transcendental ideals of practical brotherhood among whom Hawthorne lived in 1841), and his equally disheartening experience of intellectual and imaginative paralysis in the Custom-House (from which, he says, he was glad to have been ousted on 8 June, 1849), he goes on to describe a space, somewhere between Custom-House materialism and Brook Farm 'dreaminess', that he lays claim to in his fiction – 'a neutral territory, somewhere between the real world and fairy-land, where the Actual and the Imaginary may meet, and each imbue itself with the nature of the other'. In chapter two of this Guide we shall see how, at the time F. R. Leavis in England was describing the 'great tradition' of the English novel, critics such as Richard Chase, Perry Miller, Lionel Trilling and Joel Porte in America were busy elevating romance into the defining term of a distinctive American literary tradition.

If the obvious place to begin a Guide to secondary sources relating to *The Scarlet Letter* is Hawthorne's own guide to the writing of *The Scarlet Letter*, we have also seen that this introductory 'Custom-House' sketch raises as many interpretive problems as it solves, and in this respect, perhaps more than in any other, it serves to prepare the reader for what is to come. In the very first paragraph, the reader-response-minded narrator introduces the question of the relationship between writer and audience:

■ It is scarcely decorous, however, to speak all, even where we speak impersonally. But – as thoughts are frozen and utterance benumbed, unless the speaker stand in some true relation with his audience – it may be pardonable to imagine that a friend . . . is listening to our talk; and then, a native reserve being thawed by this genial consciousness, we may prate of the circumstances that lie around us, and even of ourself, but still keep the inmost Me behind its veil. To this extent and within these limits, an author, methinks, may be autobiographical, without violating either the reader's rights or his own. □

The narrator/author stresses the merits of authorial reserve, indirectness, even of masking – keeping 'the inmost Me behind its veil'. This, we might note, is precisely what both Hester and Dimmesdale do in preserving their guilty secrets and subversive thoughts from the Puritan community. It is also, we might further note, a contradiction of the culminating insight arising out of the story of Hester and Dimmesdale – what is ostensibly the moral of the story trumpeted by the narrator towards the end of the book: 'Be true! Be true! Be true! Show freely to the world, if not your worst, yet some trait whereby the worst may be inferred!' So, while 'The Custom-House' *does* tell us much about the author, the circumstances of his life at the time of writing *The Scarlet Letter*, and the aesthetic theory underlying the writing, it is less an essay in criticism or autobiography than a dramatic, ironic and comic performance. The narrative, far from being a 'showing freely' to the world, is marked by contradiction, concealment and duplicitousness, as in the narrator's pretence to editorship rather than authorship, the central fiction of the discovery of the scarlet letter, and the experiment with 'romance', which, Michael David Bell explains in his essay, 'Arts of Deception: Hawthorne, "Romance", and *The Scarlet Letter*', 'was less a neutral generic label than a revolutionary, or at least antisocial, slogan. To identify oneself as a romancer was to reject far more than "the probable and ordinary course of man's experience"; it was to set oneself in opposition to the most basic norms of society: reason, fact, and "real" business' (see pages 91–3). The central fiction of the discovery of the scarlet letter includes little guidance as to how we should read the various 'signs' that make up the story of Hester Prynne. Surveyor Pue's attempt to tell the story of the letter in his half dozen sheets of foolscap is succeeded by the narrator's more elaborate attempt to tell that story, which, in turn, is succeeded by what has now become a long series of interpretations down through the years since *The Scarlet Letter* was first published.

The purpose of this book is to give an account and a sampling of these varied interpretations, from moral and historical criticism, to New Criticism, to archetypal and myth criticism, to psychoanalytical and feminist criticism, to linguistic and semiotic criticism. What becomes clear is the theoretical multiplicity of the text and its susceptibility to many different methodological approaches, each of which can open it up in new and sometimes unexpected and exciting ways. The introductory sketch's various languages – of Puritan piety and repressed desire; of letters, signs, hieroglyphs, and interpretations; of moonlight, romance, ghosts, and 'neutral territory' – need not limit the approach we employ to discover the 'some deep meaning' which, the narrator is passionately convinced, lies in *The Scarlet Letter*.

CHAPTER ONE

Contemporary Responses and Early Studies

PRIOR TO the publication of *The Scarlet Letter* in March 1850, Hawthorne, apart from his anonymously published novel *Fanshawe* (1828), had for twenty years specialised in tales and sketches, partly because there was a market for these in magazines and 'gift-book' annuals. To a serious, professional writer such as Hawthorne the American literary scene in the 1830s was far from congenial. To have any substantial readership at all he had to resort to periodical publication which brought poor financial rewards and did little to establish an author's reputation since stories were published without attribution. These magazines and annuals were mostly devoted to a popular sentimental kind of literature largely produced and consumed by women. Hawthorne's dark, mysterious tales sat oddly beside such offerings. Hawthorne complained:

■ America is now wholly given over to a damned mob of scribbling women, and I should have no chance of success while the public is occupied with their trash – and should be ashamed of myself if I did succeed.[1] □

The lack of a sustaining tradition or literary environment no doubt exacerbated Hawthorne's famous self-doubt about his role and talent as an artist. J. Donald Crowley observes that 'Hawthorne's failure to present his work in book form led him in his fiction to focus still more sharply on the plight of the artist and his relation to an audience'.[2] Nevertheless, feeling the disapproval of his Puritan ancestors for wasting his time as 'a writer of story-books!', he was determined to achieve something weightier than 'idle stories', a work 'that should evolve some deep lesson, and should possess physical substance enough to stand alone'.[3] While *The Scarlet Letter* may not have won him a large popular readership, it did free him from the need to rely on periodical publication and it earned him widespread critical acclaim. A feeling of failure, however, continued to dog him for the rest of his life. In 1860, in a letter to his publisher, James T. Fields, who had encouraged him to publish *The Scarlet Letter* in book form, he offered this depressed view of his career:

■ My own opinion is, that I am not really a popular writer, and that what popularity I have gained is chiefly accidental, and owing to other causes than my own kind or degree of merit . . . looking at all my productions . . . with a cold or critical eye, I can see that they do not make their appeal to the common mind. It is odd enough, moreover, that my own individual taste is for quite another class of works than those which I am able to write. If I were to meet with such books as mine, by another writer, I don't believe I should be able to get through them.[4] □

The darkness of his vision, he believed, prevented him from ever appealing to a wide readership. His own 'individual taste' was presumably for a less dark and ambiguous class of works than that which, ironically, he was inspired to write. *The Scarlet Letter* he judged to be 'a positively h-ll-fired story, into which I found it almost impossible to throw a cheering light'. At the end of the opening chapter the narrator hopes that the rose-bush growing beside the prison door will 'symbolize some sweet moral blossom, that may be found along the track, or relieve the darkening close of a tale of human frailty and sorrow': but the closing words of the story speak only of 'one ever-glowing point of light gloomier than the shadow . . .'

Hawthorne was determined that his next novel, *The House of the Seven Gables* (1851), would be a more sunshiny book. It was, he said later, 'a more natural and healthy product of mind'.[5] Indeed, he thought 'The Custom-House' section of *The Scarlet Letter*, with its topical and autobiographical interest and its more genial tone, would be more popular than the sombre main story. In his Preface to the Second Edition he defended 'The Custom-House' sketch against its critics:

■ It appears to him [the author] that the only remarkable features of the sketch are its frank and genuine good-humor, and the general accuracy with which he has conveyed his sincere impressions of the characters therein described. As to enmity, or ill-feeling of any kind, personal or political, he utterly disclaims such motives. The sketch might, perhaps, have been wholly omitted, without loss to the public, or detriment to the book; but, having undertaken to write it, he conceives that it could not have been done in a better or kindlier spirit, nor, as far as his abilities availed, with a livelier effect of truth. □

Some of the earliest responses to *The Scarlet Letter* emphasised its darkness. Having read the conclusion of the book to his wife, Hawthorne recalled her reaction:

■ It broke her heart and sent her to bed with a grievous headache – which I look upon as a triumphant success![6] □

It was this 'blackness of darkness' in Hawthorne's work which struck Herman Melville, who, in his 1850 review of Hawthorne's collection of tales and sketches, *Mosses from an Old Manse* (1846), pondered Hawthorne's 'Calvinistic sense of Innate Depravity and Original Sin, from whose visitations . . . no deeply thinking mind is always and wholly free':

■ Still more: this black conceit [of human depravity] pervades him through and through. You may be witched by his sunlight, – transported by the bright gildings in the skies he builds over you; but there is the blackness of darkness beyond; and even his bright gildings but fringe and play upon the edges of thunder-clouds. In one word, the world is mistaken in Nathaniel Hawthorne. He himself must often have smiled at its absurd misconception of him. He is immeasurably deeper than the plummet of the mere critic.[7] □

The first published review of *The Scarlet Letter* was E. A. Duyckinck's. It appeared in the *Literary World* on 30 March 1850. Duyckinck saw two Hawthornes, not just 'the Hawthorne of the present day in the sunshine' who produced 'one of those pleasant personal descriptions which are the most charming of his compositions' ('The Custom-House').

■ There is another Hawthorne less companionable, of sterner Puritan aspect, with the shadow of the past over him, a reviver of witchcrafts and of those dark agencies of evil which lurk in the human soul, and which even now represent the old gloomy historic era in the microcosm and eternity of the individual . . . Romantic in sooth! Such romance as you may read in the intensest sermons of old Puritan divines, or in the mouldy pages of that marrow of Divinity, the ascetic Jeremy Taylor.

The Scarlet Letter is a psychological romance . . . It is a tale of remorse . . . Mr Hawthorne has . . . shown extraordinary knowledge of character in its secret springs and outer manifestations. He blends, too, a delicate fancy with this metaphysical insight . . . Then for the moral. Though severe, it is wholesome, and is a sounder bit of Puritan divinity than we have been of late accustomed to hear from the degenerate successors of Cotton Mather . . . The spirit of his old Puritan ancestors to whom he refers in the preface, lives in Nathaniel Hawthorne.[8] □

George Ripley, a Unitarian minister and Transcendentalist liberal thinker who had been one of the organisers of Brook Farm and founder of *The Dial*, was also full of praise in his review in the *New York Tribune*, 1 April 1850. Ripley emphasised the Gothic elements in *The Scarlet Letter*, remarking that 'the weird and ghostly legends of the Puritanic history present a singularly congenial field for the exercise of Mr Hawthorne's peculiar genius'. Comparing Hawthorne to Poe in his ability to bring before us 'pictures of death-like, but strangely fascinating agony', Ripley proceeds to explain this important difference:

■ Hawthorne's tragedies, however, are always motived with a wonderful insight and skill, to which the intellect of Poe was a stranger. In the most terrific scenes with which he delights to scare the imagination, Hawthorne does not wander into the region of the improbable; you scarcely know that you are in the presence of the supernatural . . . it is the supernatural relieved, softened, made tolerable, and almost attractive, by a strong admixture of the human . . . The elements of terror . . . both in the original conceptions of his characters and the scenes of mystery and dread in which they are made to act, are blended with such sweet gushes of natural feeling, such solemn and tender relations of the deepest secrets of the heart, that the painful impression is greatly mitigated, and the final influence of his most startling creation is a serene sense of refreshment, without the stupor and bewilderment occasioned by a drugged cup of intoxication.[9] □

E. P. Whipple, who, along with Poe and Lowell, was regarded as one of the most influential critics of his day, and one much respected by Hawthorne, also praised Hawthorne's 'beautiful and touching romance'. Whipple noted in particular Hawthorne's intense understanding of 'painful emotions', and though he thought Hawthorne's 'morbid intensity' a possible fault, praised his 'moral purpose':

■ The most abandoned libertine could not read the volume without being thrilled into something like virtuous resolution. . . .
    In his next work we hope to have a romance equal to *The Scarlet Letter* in pathos and power, but more relieved by touches of that beautiful and peculiar humour, so serene and so searching, in which he excels almost all living writers.[10] □

The first English review of the book was Henry F. Chorley's, in the *Athenaeum* on 15 June 1850. Chorley expressed appreciation of the mixture of allegory and realism in *The Scarlet Letter*:

■ There is in his works a mixture of Puritan reserve and wild imagination, of passion and description, of the allegorical and the real. □

Like Whipple, Chorley was struck by the 'more than ordinarily painful' emotions which Hawthorne explores, and admired the way the book stays 'clear of fever and of prurient excitement', avoids making the supernatural 'grossly palpable', and steers clear of sentimentality: Hester's 'slow and painful purification through repentance is crowned by no perfect happiness', while Dimmesdale's 'final confession and expiation are merely a relief, not a reconciliation'. Chorley is unhappy with Hawthorne's subject matter, but nevertheless sees the novel as a fundamentally moral tale:

■ But if Sin and Sorrow in their most fearful forms are to be presented in any work of art, they have rarely been treated with a loftier severity, purity, and sympathy than in Mr Hawthorne's Scarlet Letter.[11] □

Anne W. Abbott, one of that 'damned mob of scribbling women', as Hawthorne called them, in a review of the novel in the *North American Review* in July 1850, declared that 'we like the preface better than the tale'. Writing from a fundamentalist Christian point of view, Abbott shared Chorley's disapproval of Hawthorne's subject matter, but where Chorley admired the way Hawthorne could moderate the excesses of his imagination through the exercise of his moral sense, Abbott believed that Hawthorne had allowed his good judgement to be carried away by 'the magic power of the style'. As far as Abbott was concerned, Hawthorne's characters only continue to hold our interest to the extent that their story exemplifies Christian values.

■ One cannot but wonder . . . that the master of such a wizard power over language as Mr Hawthorne manifests should not choose a less revolting subject than this . . . to which fine writing seems as inappropriate as fine embroidery. The ugliness of pollution and vice is no more relieved by it than the gloom of the prison is by the rose tree at its door. . . .

Thus devils and angels are alike beautiful, when seen through the magic glass; and they stand side by side in heaven, however the former may be supposed to have come here. As for Roger Chillingworth, he seems to have so little in common with man, he is such a gnome-like phantasm, such an unnatural personification of an abstract idea, that we should be puzzled to assign him a place among angels, men, or devils . . . Hester at first strongly excites our pity, for she suffers like an immortal being; and our interest in her continues only while we have hope for her soul, that its baptism of tears will reclaim it from the foul stain which has been cast upon it. We see her humble, meek, self-denying, charitable, and heartwrung with anxiety for the moral welfare of her wayward child. But anon her humility catches a new tint, and we find it pride; and so a vague unreality steals by degrees over all her most humanizing traits – we lose our confidence in all – and finally, like Undine, she disappoints us, and shows the dream-land origin and nature, when we were looking to behold a Christian.

There is rather more power, and better keeping, in the character of Dimmesdale. But here again we are cheated into a false regard and interest . . . We are told repeatedly, that the Christian element yet pervades his character and guides his efforts; but it seems strangely wanting . . . Mere suffering, aimless and without effect of purification or blessing to the soul, we do not find in God's moral world.

But little Pearl – gem of the purest water – what shall we say of her? . . . Let the author throw what light he will upon her, from his magical prism, she retains her perfect and vivid human individuality. When he would have us call her elvish and imp-like, we persist in seeing only a capricious, roguish, untamed child, such as many a mother has looked upon with awe, and feeling a helpless incapacity to rule. Every motion, every feature, every word and tiny shout, every naughty scream and wild laugh, come to us as if our very senses were conscious of them. The child is a true child, the only genuine and consistent mortal in the book . . . We feel at once that the author must have a 'Little Pearl' of his own, whose portrait, consciously or unconsciously, his pen sketches out.[12] □

George Bailey Loring, a physician and political leader, took a more liberal view of *The Scarlet Letter* in his review in the *Massachusetts Quarterly Review*, in September 1850. He called the novel 'extraordinary, as a work of art, and as a vehicle of religion and ethics', and saw Hawthorne's primary interest as an exploration of the tragic conflict between the individual and society. Concentrating on Hawthorne's representation of Puritan oppressiveness, Loring viewed with sympathy Dimmesdale, Hester and the love relationship between them, inviting us to consider society's 'severity' a greater sin than that committed by Hester and Dimmesdale. Contrasting with Abbott's fundamentalism, Loring's historical sense and pragmatic humanism allowed him to view with sympathetic understanding the frailties of Hester and Dimmesdale, and to see their relationship as something positive, the expression of love in a loveless society:

■ We doubt not that, to many minds, this severity constitutes the saving virtue of the book. But it is always with a fearful sacrifice of all the gentler feelings of the breast, of all the most comprehensive humanity, of all the most delicate affections and appreciations, that we thus rudely shut out the wanderer from us; especially when the path of error leads through the land whence come our warmest and tenderest influences. . . .

But is it not most sad and most instructive that Love, the great parent of all power and virtue and wisdom and faith, the guardian of the tree of knowledge of good and evil, the effulgence of all that is rich and generous and luxuriant in nature, should rise up in society to be typified by the strange features of *The Scarlet Letter?*[13] ☐

Orestes Brownson, writing in October 1850 in *Brownson's Quarterly Review* echoed Abbott's complaint that the subject matter was morally unsuitable. Both 'criminals' in the novel, Brownson argues, are motivated by 'pride', not 'remorse' for their act of adultery. Where Loring saw value in the love of Hester and Dimmesdale, Brownson condemns it simply as 'illicit, and highly criminal', and where Loring emphasised society's unchristian 'severity', Brownson believes 'their treatment of the adulteress was far more Christian than his [Hawthorne's] ridicule of it'.[14]

The most critical of all the early reviews was that of Arthur Cleveland Coxe, an Episcopal bishop, whose review in the *Church Review*, January 1851, was reprinted in *Notorious Literary Attacks* (ed. Albert Mordell, 1926). Coxe was outraged by a novel 'in which the whole tendency of the conversation is to suggest a sympathy for their [Hester and Dimmesdale's] sin, and an anxiety that they may be able to accomplish a successful escape beyond the seas, to some country where their shameful commerce may be perpetuated'. Admitting that his interest is more religious than literary, Coxe asks:

■ Should the taste of Mr Hawthorne have preferred as the proper material for romance, the nauseous amour of a Puritan pastor, with a frail creature of his charge, whose mind is represented as far more debauched than her body? Is it, in short, because a running undertide of filth has become as requisite to romance, as death in the fifth act to a tragedy? Is the French era actually begun in our literature?[15] ☐

This collection of opinion represents a highly impressionistic, amateurish criticism, which tends to value literature to the extent that it embodies the correct moral and political values, and thus could contribute positively to the consolidation of the national character – especially at a time of revolutionary upheaval abroad (1848 was 'the year of revolutions') and radical agitation at home (from both abolitionists and the women's movement). Hawthorne's psychological insight and artistic talent are universally acknowledged, but we also find considerable uneasiness with his subject matter and, in some quarters, a residual Puritan suspicion of the power of art and imagination. Following these early reviews, there was relatively little commentary on Hawthorne until the development of literary criticism as a serious subject of study in the universities in the 1930s and 1940s. However, prior to that time there were a few notable studies. The first was Henry James's *Hawthorne* (1879). James was one of the great modern theorists of the novel whose influence is pervasive in the way we view the art of fiction even today. Generally regarded as a precursor of the New Critics and their formalist approach to literary analysis, James's approach is mainly formalist, concentrating on the conscious craft of Hawthorne's fiction. Having despaired of the American writer, in the absence of a usable literary tradition and all the advantages of 'high civilisation', ever attaining world recognition, he nevertheless discovered in *The Scarlet Letter* 'something that might be sent to Europe as exquisite in quality as anything that had been received, and the best of it was that the thing was absolutely American'. However, James was a proponent of realism in the novel, and so there was much in Hawthorne's psychological romance that he found to criticise as well as praise:

■ The work has the tone of the circumstances in which it was produced. If Hawthorne was in a sombre mood, and if his future was painfully vague, *The Scarlet Letter* contains little enough of gaiety or of hopefulness. It is densely dark, with a single spot of vivid color in it; and it will probably long remain the most consistently gloomy of English novels of the first order . . . It is simpler and more complete than his other novels; it achieves more perfectly what it attempts . . . None of his works are so impregnated with that after-sense of the old Puritan consciousness of life . . . And I say this not because the story happens to be of so-called historical cast. . . . The historical coloring is rather weak than otherwise; there is little elaboration of detail, of the modern realism of research; and the author has made no great point of causing his figures to speak the English of their period. Nevertheless, the book is full of the moral presence of the race that invented Hester's penance – diluted and complicated with other things, but still perfectly recognizable. Puritanism, in a word, is there, not only objectively, as Hawthorne tried to place it there, but subjectively as well. Not, I mean, in his judgment of characters, in any harshness of prejudice, or in the obtrusion of a moral lesson; but in the very quality of his own vision, in the tone of the picture, in a certain coldness and exclusiveness of treatment.

The faults of the book are, to my sense, a want of reality and an abuse of the fanciful element – of a certain superficial symbolism. The people strike me not as characters, but as representatives, very picturesquely arranged, of a single state of mind; and the interest of the story lies, not in them, but in the situation, which is insistently kept before us, with little progression, though with a great deal, as I have said, of a certain stable variation; and to which they, out of their reality, contribute little that helps it to live and move.

[. . .]

In *The Scarlet Letter* there is a great deal of symbolism; there is, I think, too much. It is overdone at times, and becomes mechanical; it ceases to be impressive, and grazes triviality. The idea of the mystic A which the young minister finds imprinted upon his breast and eating into his flesh, in sympathy with the embroidered badge that Hester is condemned to wear, appears to me to be a case in point. This suggestion should, I think, have been just made and dropped; to insist upon it and return to it, is to exaggerate the weak side of the subject. Hawthorne returns to it constantly, plays with it, and seems charmed by it; until at last the reader feels tempted to declare that his enjoyment of it is puerile. In the admirable scene, so superbly conceived and beautifully executed, in which Mr. Dimmesdale, in the stillness of the night, in the middle of the sleeping town, feels impelled to go and stand upon the scaffold where his mistress had formerly enacted her dreadful penance, and then, seeing Hester pass along the street, from watching at a sick-bed, with little Pearl at her side, calls them both to come and stand there beside him – in this masterly episode the effect is almost spoiled by the introduction of one of these superficial conceits. What leads up to it is very fine – so fine that I cannot do better than quote it as a specimen of one of the striking pages of the book.

> But before Mr. Dimmesdale had done speaking, a light gleamed far and wide over all the muffled sky. It was doubtless caused by one of those meteors which the nightwatcher may so often observe burning out to waste in the vacant regions of the atmosphere. So powerful was its radiance that it thoroughly illuminated the dense medium of cloud, betwixt the sky and earth. The great vault brightened, like the dome of an immense lamp. It showed the familiar scene of the street with the distinctness of midday, but also with the awfulness that is always imparted to familiar objects by an unaccustomed light. The wooden houses, with their jutting stories and quaint gable-peaks; the doorsteps and thresholds, with the early grass springing up about them; the garden-plots, black with freshly turned earth; the wheel-track, little worn, and, even in the market-place, margined with green on either side; all were visible, but with a singularity of aspect that seemed to give another moral interpretation to the things of this world than they had ever borne

> before. And there stood the minister, with his hand over his heart;
> and Hester Prynne, with the embroidered letter glimmering on her
> bosom; and little Pearl, herself a symbol, and the connecting-link
> between these two. They stood in the noon of that strange and
> solemn splendour, as if it were the light that is to reveal all secrets,
> and the daybreak that shall unite all that belong to one another.

That is imaginative, impressive, poetic; but when, almost immediately
afterwards, the author goes on to say that 'the minister looking
upward to the zenith, beheld there the appearance of an immense letter
– the letter A – marked out in lines of dull red light', we feel that he
goes too far and is in danger of crossing the line that separates the sub-
lime from its intimate neighbour. We are tempted to say that this is not
moral tragedy, but physical comedy. In the same way, too much is
made of the intimation that Hester's badge had a scorching property,
and that if one touched it one would immediately withdraw one's
hand. Hawthorne is perpetually looking for images which shall place
themselves in picturesque correspondence with the spiritual facts
with which he is concerned, and of course the search is of the very
essence of poetry. But in such a process discretion is everything, and
when the image becomes importunate it is in danger of seeming to
stand for nothing more serious than itself. When Hester meets the
minister by appointment in the forest, and sits talking with him while
little Pearl wanders away and plays by the edge of the brook, the child
is represented as at last making her way over to the other side of the
woodland stream, and disporting herself there in a manner which
makes her mother feel herself, 'in some indistinct and tantalising
manner, estranged from Pearl; as if the child, in her lonely ramble
through the forest, had strayed out of the sphere in which she and her
mother dwelt together, and was now vainly seeking to return to it'.
And Hawthorne devotes a chapter to this idea of the child's having, by
putting the brook between Hester and herself, established a kind of
spiritual gulf, on the verge of which her little fantastic person
innocently mocks at her mother's sense of bereavement. This conception belongs, one would say, quite to the lighter order of a
story-teller's devices, and the reader hardly goes with Hawthorne in
the large development he gives to it. He hardly goes with him either, I
think, in his extreme predilection for a small number of vague ideas
which are represented by such terms as 'sphere' and 'sympathies'.
Hawthorne makes too liberal a use of these two substantives; it is the
solitary defect of his style; and it counts as a defect partly because the
words in question are a sort of specialty with certain writers immeasurably inferior to himself.[16] □

The next major book-length study of Hawthorne was George Edward Woodberry's *Hawthorne* (1902), in the American Men of Letters series of literary biographies. Like James, who thought that Hawthorne's story showed 'a want of reality', Woodberry also finds that symbolism takes precedence over strict realism, that characters tend to be reduced to 'types', 'symbolic pictures of states of the soul'. Hawthorne's main concern, according to Woodberry, is with universal themes and issues – conscience, repentance, confession, punishment, absolution. The 'universal experience' of the religious life to which Woodberry particularly alludes is the conflict between secret, unruly, repressed, libidinal energies and the social and religious order which they threaten to subvert. Woodberry, in a manner which anticipates modern psychoanalytical and structuralist theoretical criticism, detects a silence or repression in Hawthorne's narrative at those points where the 'moral scheme' of Hawthorne's 'conscious thought' is unable to accommodate 'the human element' which remains unrepresentable within the given structures of thought and language. Though full of praise for the originality of this 'great and unique romance', Woodberry is uncomfortable with its 'pessimism'.

■ The romance is thus essentially a parable of the soul's life in sin; in its narrower scope it is the work of the moral intellect allegorizing its view of life; and where creative genius enters into it, in the Shakespearean sense of life in its own right, it tends to be a larger and truer story breaking the bonds of its religious scheme. It has its roots in Puritanism, but it is only incidentally a New England tale; its substance is the most universal experience of human nature in religious life, taking its forms only, its local habitation and name, from the Puritan colony in America, and these in a merely allegorical, not historical manner. Certain traits, however, ally it more closely to New England Puritanism. It is a relentless tale; the characters are singularly free from self-pity, and accept their fate as righteous; they never forgive themselves, they show no sign of having forgiven one another; even God's forgiveness is left under a shadow in futurity. They have sinned against the soul, and something implacable in evil remains. The minister's dying words drop a dark curtain over all.

'Hush, Hester, hush!' said he, with tremulous solemnity. 'The law we broke! – the sin here so awfully revealed! – let these alone be in thy thoughts! I fear! I fear! It may be that, when we forgot our God, – when we violated our reverence each for the other's soul, – it was thenceforth vain to hope that we could meet hereafter, in an everlasting and pure reunion.'

Mercy is but a hope. There is also a singular absence of prayer in the book. Evil is presented as a thing without remedy, that cannot change its nature. The child, even, being the fruit of sin, can bring, Hester and Arthur doubt, no good for others or herself. In the scheme of Puritan thought, however, the atonement of Christ is the perpetual miracle whereby salvation comes, not only hereafter but in the holier life led here by grace. There is no Christ in this book. Absolution, so far as it is hinted at, lies in the direction of public confession, the efficacy of which is directly stated, but lamely nevertheless; it restores truth, but it does not heal the past. Leave the dead past to bury its dead, says Hawthorne, and go on to what may remain; but life once ruined is ruined past recall. So Hester, desirous of serving in her place the larger truth she has come to know, is stayed, says Hawthorne, because she 'recognized the impossibility that any mission of divine and mysterious truth should be confided to a woman stained with sin, bowed down with shame, or even burdened with a life-long sorrow.' That was never the Christian gospel nor the Puritan faith. Indeed, Hawthorne here and elsewhere anticipates those ethical views which are the burden of George Eliot's moral genius, and contain scientific pessimism. This stoicism, which was in Hawthorne, is a primary element in his moral nature, in him as well as in his work; it is visited with few touches of tenderness and pity; the pity one feels is not in him, it is in the pitiful thing, which he presents objectively, sternly, unrelentingly. It must be confessed that as an artist he appears un-sympathetic with his characters; he is a moral dissector of their souls, minute, unflinching, thorough, a vivisector here; and he is cold because he has passed sentence on them, condemned them. There is no sympathy with human nature in the book; it is a fallen and ruined thing suffering just pain in its dying struggle. The romance is steeped in gloom. Is it too much to suggest that in ignoring prayer, the atone-ment of Christ, and the work of the Spirit in men's hearts, the better part of Puritanism has been left out, and the whole life of the soul dis-torted? Sin in the soul, the scarlet flower from the dark soil, we see; but, intent on that, has not the eye, and the heart, too, forgotten the large heavens that ensphere all – even this evil flower – and the infi-nite horizons that reach off to the eternal distance from every soul as from their centre? This romance is the record of a prison-cell, unvisited by any ray of light save that earthly one which gives both prisoners to public ignominy; they are seen, but they do not see. These traits of the book, here only suggested, have kinship with the repelling aspects of Puritanism, both as it was and as Hawthorne inherited it in his blood and breeding; so, in its transcendent spirituality, and in that demo-cracy which is the twin-brother of spirituality in all lands and cultures, by virtue of which Hawthorne here humiliates and strips the minister who is the type of the spiritual aristocrat in the community, there is the essence of New England; but, for all that, the romance is a partial story, an imperfect fragment of the old life, distorting, not so much the Puritan ideal – which were a little matter – but the spiritual life itself. Its truth, intense, fascinating, terrible as it is, is a half-truth, and the darker half; it is the shadow of which the other half is light; it is the wrath of which the other half is love. A book from which light and love are absent may hold us by its truth to what is dark in life; but, in the highest sense, it is a false book. It is a chapter in the literature of moral despair, and is perhaps most tolerated as a condemnation of the creed which, through imperfect comprehension, it travesties.[17] □

Appearing more than twenty years after Woodberry's study, D.H. Lawrence's commentary on *The Scarlet Letter*, included in his *Studies in Classic American Literature* (1923), uses Hawthorne's novel to illustrate his own distinctive theories about sex, race and morality. Lawrence's study is an excited polemic emphasising the dark undercurrent of American literature, and of *The Scarlet Letter* in particular: '*The Scarlet Letter* isn't a pleasant, pretty romance. It is a sort of parable, an earthly story with a hellish meaning.'[18] Lawrence sees the novel as expressive of the American elevation of mind and spirit over intuition, instinct, 'blood-knowledge'. Hester and Dimmesdale exemplify a characteristic American denial of the body and the sensual life. Dimmesdale is the pure spirit who falls to the temptations of the flesh, punishes his body for his sin, and loses his 'integrity' and 'manliness'. Hester is the destructive female principle, the devil-woman who delights in making of Dimmesdale a fallen saint ('that was her life work') and who, having had her triumph over the individual man, submits to the 'whole spiritual life of society' and 'blossoms out into a Sister-of-Mercy Saint'. Lawrence thus sees in Hawthorne's narrative a subtext that has little to do with conventional morality or allegory: 'That blue-eyed darling Nathaniel', says Lawrence, 'knew disagreeable things in his inner soul. He was careful to send them out in disguise.' In emphasising the terrible, the diabolic, the uncontrollable and the subversive that lie behind Hawthorne's moralism, Lawrence continues a line of Hawthorne criticism originating in Hawthorne's self-commentary and then carried on by Melville over seventy years earlier, by Woodberry at the turn of the century, and, later, by such influential critics as Leslie A. Fiedler (in *Love and Death in the American Novel*, 1960) and Harry Levin (in *The Power of Blackness*, 1967).

Lawrence is a link with later criticism in yet another important way: his view of American literature as symbolic, mythic, ironic, and concerned with the drama of the self rather than social life prefigures the 'New Criticism' that emerged in the 1940s, and the 'romance reading' of American literature which dominated the critical landscape in the 1950s and early 1960s.

CHAPTER TWO

Formalist and Postformalist Approaches

MUCH HAWTHORNE criticism between the late 1930s and 1950s reflected the formalist emphasis of the New Critical orthodoxy which prevailed in the academy during those years. The New Criticism was a reaction against a kind of journalistic commentary or belle-lettristic impressionism which considered the text as a product of the author's character and personal circumstances, as well as of the larger cultural and historical context. The New Critics insisted on objectivity and detachment. The literary work was to be analysed and understood in isolation from any extrinsic factors, biographical, social or political. The author's intentions were no more relevant to the New Critic than the effects a work might have on the reader. The 'words on the page' were all that counted. A work's meaning is embedded in its form and its content, and the critic's job is to describe these with scientific accuracy. The New Critic relied on close reading, and the analysis of structure, symbol and language to demonstrate the various 'tensions', 'ambiguities' and 'paradoxes' of a text, and the author's success in resolving them in the work's formal unity. *The Scarlet Letter*, with its highly symbolic narrative method, its careful patterning of images and ideas, and its concern with narrative point of view and the relativity of truth, lent itself well to New Critical treatment.

The New Critics were mostly academics, and thus were able not only to institutionalise a particular approach to literary study but also to canonise particular texts of earlier as well as contemporary literature. New Critical formalism reflected a post-World War Two rejection of the social and political, a disillusionment with ideology following the experience of Hitler and Stalin, a suppression or marginalisation of political consciousness. It also reflected a renewed interest in the existential and the psychological, in a universal and basically unchanging human condition. The realistic novel with its social and political concerns, and the naturalistic social protest novel were downgraded in favour of a literature that was more concerned with the ideal than the real, a literature opposed to mimesis and social or historical engagement. The canon of classic American literature was largely constructed by the New Critics of the 1940s and 1950s – F. O. Matthiessen's *American Renaissance* (1941), R. W. B. Lewis's *The American Adam* (1955), Richard Chase's *The American Novel and its Tradition* (1957) and Leslie A. Fiedler's *Love and Death in the American Novel* (1960). These critics saw American literature as symbolic, allegorical, mythic, reflecting notions of the autonomy of the imagination, setting out to construct a world elsewhere. American literature, according to Richard Chase, belonged to the Romance tradition. For the New Critics *The Scarlet Letter* was an exemplary text.

One of the most incisive and influential of the New Critics was Yvor Winters, a traditionalist who sought to counterbalance the Romantic theory of literature as a mainly emotional experience with an 'absolutist' theory of literature which held that 'the work of literature, in so far as it is valuable, approximates a real apprehension and communication of a particular kind of objective truth'. Winters's essay, 'Maule's Curse, or Hawthorne and the Problem of Allegory', written in 1938, appeared in his collection of essays *In Defence of Reason*, first published in 1947. Hawthorne, Winters declares, is 'essentially an allegorist', reflecting a characteristically New England, Puritan allegorical view of life:

■ . . . allegory was realism, the idea was life itself; and his [Hawthorne's] prose, always remarkable for its polish and flexibility, and stripped, for once, of all superfluity, was reduced to the living idea, it intensified pure exposition to a quality comparable in its way to that of great poetry.[1] □

To illustrate the 'compactness and complexity' of Hawthorne's allegorical method, Winters quotes the passage where Hester, waiting to plead with Governor Bellingham to be allowed to keep her daughter, stands with little Pearl before the portraits and suit of armour in the Governor's house. Winters comments as follows:

■ The portraits are obviously intended as an apology for the static portraits in the book, as an illustration of the principle of simplification by distance and by generalization; the new armor, on the other hand, is the new faith which brought the Puritans to New England, and which not only shone with piety – 'especially the helmet and breast-plate', the covering of the head and heart – but supported them in their practical struggles with physical adversaries, and which in addition altered their view of the life about them to dogmatic essentials, so that Hester was obliterated behind the fact of her sin, and Pearl transformed in view of her origin. Governor Bellingham, in his combination of legal training with military prowess, is representative of his fellow colonists, who displayed in a remarkable degree a capacity to act with great strength and with absolutely simple directness upon principles so generalized as scarcely to be applicable to any specific moral problems, which mastered moral difficulties not by understanding them, but by crushing them out.

[. . .]

It is noteworthy that in this passage . . . Hawthorne turns his instrument of allegory, the gift of the Puritans, against the Puritans themselves, in order to indicate the limits of their intelligence. . . . [2] □

Not just specific passages are to be read allegorically, the conception of the whole book is allegorical: 'Hester represents the repentant sinner, Dimmesdale the half-repentant sinner, and Chillingworth the unrepentant sinner.' Winters believes Hawthorne's strength lay in his ability to handle allegorical generalisation rather than novelistic specificity:

■ Hawthorne had small gift for the creation of human beings . . . even the figures in *The Scarlet Letter* are unsatisfactory if one comes to the book expecting to find a novel, for they draw their life not from specific and familiar human characteristics, as do the figures of Henry James, but from the precision and intensity with which they render their respective ideas; the very development of the story is neither narrative nor dramatic, but expository.

[. . .]

In *The Scarlet Letter*, then, Hawthorne composed a great allegory; or, if we look first at the allegorical view of life upon which early Puritan society was based, we might almost say that he composed a great historical novel . . . In turning his back upon the excessively simplified conceptions of his Puritan ancestors, he abandoned the only orderly concepts, whatever their limitations, to which he had access, and in his last work he is restless and dissatisfied. [3] □

F. O. Matthiessen's discussion of the novel in his magisterial work *American Renaissance: Art and Expression in the Age of Emerson and Whitman* (1941) sees *The Scarlet Letter* as part of an extraordinary 'renaissance', when America came to artistic maturity in the half-decade of 1850–55 with the appearance of Emerson's *Representative Men* (1850), Hawthorne's *The Scarlet Letter* (1850) and *The House of the Seven Gables* (1851), Melville's *Moby-Dick* (1851) and *Pierre* (1852), Thoreau's *Walden* (1854) and Whitman's *Leaves of Grass* (1855). Matthiessen's formalist approach was designed to demonstrate the organic 'wholeness' of the novel. In *The Scarlet Letter*, Hawthorne, he says, had 'developed his most coherent plot':

■ Its symmetrical design is built around the three scenes on the scaffold of the pillory. There Hester endures her public shaming in the opening chapter. There, midway through the book, the minister, who has been driven almost crazy by his guilt but has lacked the resolution to confess it, ascends one midnight for self-torture, and is joined by Hester, on her way home from watching at a deathbed, and there they are overseen by Chillingworth. There, also, at the end, just after his own knowledge of suffering has endowed his tongue with eloquence in his great election sermon, the exhausted and death-stricken Dimmesdale totters to confess his sin.[4] □

Matthiessen is also much absorbed by Hawthorne's symbolic method, in particular 'the device of multiple choice', which he relates to the Puritan view of the world as text, in which could be read the mind and will of God.

■ But beyond any interest in ordering of plot or in lucid discrimination between characters, Hawthorne's imaginative energy seems to have been called out to the full . . . by the continual correspondences that his theme allowed him to make between external events and inner significances. Once again his version of the transcendental habit took it straight back to the seventeenth century, and made it something more complex than the harmony between sunrise and a young poet's soul. In the realm of natural phenomena, Hawthorne examined the older world's common belief that great events were foreboded by supernatural omens, and remarked how 'it was, indeed, a majestic idea, that the destiny of nations should be revealed in these awful hieroglyphics, on the cope of heaven.' But when Dimmesdale, in his vigil on the scaffold, beholds an immense dull red letter in the zenith, Hawthorne attributes it solely to his diseased imagination, which sees in everything his own morbid concerns. Hawthorne remarks that the strange light was 'doubtless caused by a meteor "burning out to waste"'; and yet he also allows the sexton to ask the minister the next morning if he had heard of the portent, which had been interpreted to stand for Angel, since Governor Winthrop had died during the night.
   Out of such variety of symbolical reference Hawthorne developed one of his most fertile resources, the device of multiple choice, which James was to carry so much further in his desire to present a sense of the intricacy of any situation for perceptive being. One main source of Hawthorne's method lay in these remarkable providences, which his imagination felt challenged to search for the amount of emblematic truth that might lie hidden among their superstitions. He spoke at one point in this story of how 'individuals of wiser faith' in the colony, while recognizing God's Providence in human affairs, knew that it

'promotes its purposes without aiming at the stage-effect of what is called miraculous interposition.' But he could not resist experimenting with this dramatic value, and his imagination had become so accustomed to the weirdly lighted world of Cotton Mather that even the fanciful possibilities of the growth of the stigma on Dimmesdale did not strike him as grotesque. But when the minister 'unbreasts' his guilt at last, the literal correspondence of that metaphor to a scarlet letter in his flesh, in strict accord with medieval and Spenserian personifications, is apt to strike us as a mechanical delimitation of what would otherwise have freer symbolical range.

For Hawthorne its value consisted in the variety of explanations to which it gave rise. Some affirmed that the minister had begun a course of self-mortification on the very day Hester Prynne had first been compelled to wear her ignominious badge, and had thus inflicted this hideous scar. Others held that Roger Chillingworth, 'being a potent necromancer, had caused it to appear, through the agency of magic and poisonous drugs.' Still others, 'those best able to appreciate the minister's peculiar sensibility, and the wonderful operation of his spirit upon the body,' whispered that 'the awful symbol was the effect of the ever-active tooth of remorse,' gnawing from his inmost heart outward. With that Hawthorne leaves his reader to choose among these theories. He does not literally accept his own allegory, and yet he finds it symbolically valid because of its psychological exactitude. His most telling stroke comes when he adds that certain spectators of the whole scene denied that there was any mark whatever on Dimmesdale's breast. These witnesses were among the most respectable in the community, including his fellow-ministers who were determined to defend his spotless character. These maintained also that his dying confession was to be taken only in its general significance, that he 'had desired by yielding up his breath in the arms of that fallen woman, to express to the world how utterly nugatory is the choicest of man's own righteousness.' But for this interpretation, so revelatory of its influential proponents, Hawthorne leaves not one shred of evidence.[5] □

Three years after Matthiessen's study, another formalist analysis of Hawthorne's work appeared, Leland Schubert's *Hawthorne, the Artist: Fine-Art Devices in Fiction* (1944). For Schubert, *The Scarlet Letter* is a 'perfect' book, fulfilling Schubert's requirement that 'to be good a work of art must be harmonious, rhythmical and balanced. It must have pattern and design'. One of the great strengths of *The Scarlet Letter* is its 'structural plan'. Schubert takes 'The Custom-House' section and the 'Conclusion' as a frame around the story of Hester Prynne, and finds that when we make this separation 'the pattern of the story becomes clear and beautiful'. Like Matthiessen, Schubert sees the scaffold as central:

■ At the beginning, in the middle, and at the end of the story the scaf-fold is the dominating point . . . In chapter two, after the very short first chapter, Hester is taken up on the scaffold. In chapter twelve, the middle chapter (when we omit the concluding chapter), Dimmesdale mounts the scaffold. In chapter twenty-three, the last (omitting the conclusion), Dimmesdale takes Hester and Pearl up there with him. These three incidents are, in every sense, the high points of the novel. The middle chapter, number twelve, tends to divide the story into two parts (or three parts, counting this middle chapter). Thus division is logical when we realize that up to chapter twelve neither the reader nor Chillingworth is certain that Dimmesdale is the father of little Pearl; after chapter twelve, there can be no doubt.

There is more to the pattern than this two-fold division. The scaf-fold, in Boston, stands in the market-place. The setting of the first three and the last three chapters is the market-place. In the first three chapters, Hester's ignominy is established. The last three chapters build up to and include Dimmesdale's victory over Chillingworth. Thus these two groups of chapters are set-off from the remainder of the story by locale as well as by function. The chapters between the first three and the middle one fall nicely into two groups of five and three chapters each. The group of five – chapters four through eight – deal chiefly with Pearl and Hester and describe Hester's struggles in the community. The group of three – chapters nine, ten and eleven – deal with Chillingworth and Dimmesdale and show Chillingworth gain-ing the minister's confidence and digging out his secret. There are also eight chapters between chapter twelve and the last three, and they, too, fall into two groups of three and five chapters each. The group of three – chapters thirteen, fourteen and fifteen – deal with Hester's improved condition both in the community and within herself. The group of five – chapters sixteen through twenty – show the partial reunion of Hester and Dimmesdale and their growing resistance to Chillingworth's power.[6] □

As well as describing the formal arrangement of Hawthorne's plot, Schubert showed how the novel's structural unity and intensity of effect also rely on patterns of 'rhythmic motifs' (tremblings, convulsions, shud-ders), repeated images (the scarlet letter, Dimmesdale's hand upon his heart, images of witchcraft and the supernatural, images of loneliness), repeated sets of words and phrases ('He will be known!', 'I cannot for-give thee!'), use of contrast (young and old, shadow and sunshine), repeated colours (red, black, gold, grey, green), frequent use of spots of light (sunlight, Mr Wilson's lantern, meteor), sound-patterns (thunder and lightning, screams, cackling laughs).

Hyatt Waggoner's study of *The Scarlet Letter* in *Hawthorne: A Critical*

Study (1963), begins by asking why the novel is so 'enigmatic' and 'ambiguous', why there has been 'less agreement about its meaning' than there has been about Hawthorne's other novels. Waggoner answers by referring to Hawthorne's reliance on imagery and symbolism to 'do most of the work for him', images and symbols being always more ambiguous than allegory which operates within a system of one-to-one correspondence between signifier and signified.

■ In the three short paragraphs that make up his opening chapter Hawthorne introduces the three chief symbols that will serve to give structure to the story on the thematic level, hints at the fourth, and starts two of the chief lines of imagery. The opening sentence suggests the darkness ('sad-colored,' 'gray'), the rigidity ('oak,' 'iron') and the aspirtio ('steeple-crowned') of the people 'amongst whom religion and law were almost identical'. Later sentences add 'weatherstains,' 'a yet darker aspect,' and 'gloomy' to the suggestions already begun through color imagery. The closing words of the chapter make the metaphorical use of color explicit: Hawthorne hopes that a wild rose beside the prison door may serve 'to symbolize some sweet moral blossom, that may be found along the track, or relieve the darkening close of a tale of human frailty and sorrow.'

A large part of the opening chapter is allotted to this rose-bush and to some weeds that also grow beside the prison. Having learned to respect the economy with which Hawthorne worked in his tales, we should guess, even if we had not read beyond this first chapter, that these will turn out not to be merely 'realistic' or 'atmospheric' details. We should expect to meet them again, with expanded connotations. Actually, the flower and weed imagery is second in importance only to the color imagery in the novel. The more than thirty occasions on which it is subsequently found are not, like the even more frequent heart images, casual, or partly to be accounted for as stylistic mannerisms, the reflexes as it were of Hawthorne's style, but chief keys to the symbolic structure and intention of this work.

Finally, in addition to the Puritans themselves, the jail before which they stand, and the weeds and the rose, one other object, and only one, is mentioned in this first chapter. In the only generalized comment in a chapter otherwise devoted to objective description, Hawthorne tells us that 'The founders of a new colony, whatever Utopia of human virtue and happiness they might originally project, have invariably recognized it among their earliest practical necessities to allot a portion of the virgin soil as a cemetery, and another portion as the site of a prison.' The three climactic scenes of the novel take place before the scaffold in front of the prison. The cemetery, by contrast, remains in the background. We are not allowed to forget it, we learn that Chillingworth has a special interest in it, but we are not encouraged to make it the center of our attention until the end, when it moves into the foreground as the site of the tombstone with the strange inscription.

The cemetery, the prison, and the rose, with their associated values and the extensions of suggestion given them by the image patterns that intersect them, as the ugliest weeds are later discovered growing out of graves, suggest a symbolic pattern within which nearly everything that is most important in the novel may be placed. The cemetery and the prison are negative values, in some sense evils. The rose is a positive value, beautiful, in some sense a good. But the cemetery and the prison are not negative in the same sense as death, 'the last great enemy,' is a natural evil, resulting as some theologies would have it from moral evil but distinguished by coming to saint and sinner alike; the prison is a reminder of the present actuality of moral evil. Natural and moral evil, then, death and sin, are here suggested. The rose is 'good' in the same sense in which the cemetery is an 'evil': its beauty is neither moral nor immoral but is certainly a positive value. Like the beauty of a healthy child or an animal, it is the product not of choice but of necessity, of the laws of its being, so that it can be admired but not judged. Pearl, later in the story, is similarly immune from judgment. There is no strong suggestion of moral goodness in this first chapter, nor will there be in what is to follow. The cemetery and the weeds contrast with the rose, but only the suggestions of worship in the shape of the hats of the Puritans contrast with the prison, and those steeple-crowned hats are gray, a color which later takes on strongly negative associations.

Among the ideas implicit in the opening chapter, then, are, first, that the novel is to be concerned with the relationships of good and evil; second, that it will distinguish between two types of good and evil; and, third, that moral good will be less strongly felt than moral and natural evil. A symmetrical pattern is theoretically suggested here, and as we shall see, in the rest of the novel. But what is actually felt is an asymmetrical pattern, an imbalance, in which the shapes of moral and natural evil loom so large as to make it difficult to discern, or to 'believe in' once we have discerned, the reality of moral goodness or redemption. The rose, in short, is finally not sufficient to relieve 'the darkening close of a tale of human frailty and sorrow.' The celestial radiance later seen gleaming from the white hair of Mr. Wilson is not sufficient either, nor the snowy innocence said to exist in the bosoms of certain maidens. In writing *The Scarlet Letter* Hawthorne let his genius take its course, and death and sin turned out to be more convincing than life and goodness.

[. . .]

The 'burdock, pigweed, apple-peru, and such unsightly vegetation' growing beside the prison, that 'black flower of civilized society,' where grass should have been, begin the flower and weed imagery, which, in some thirty images and extended analogies, reinforces and extends the implications of the imagery of color and light. Since these implications have already been drawn out, I shall simply call attention briefly to four relationships Hawthorne has set up.

First, and most clearly, the unnatural flowers and unsightly vegetation are aligned with moral evil, and with Chillingworth in particular. He too with his deformity is 'unsightly.' Low, dark, and ugly, he suggests to some people the notion that his step must wither the grass wherever he walks. The sun seems not to fall on him but to create a 'circle of ominous shadow moving along with his deformity.' It is natural enough then to find him explicitly associated with 'deadly nightshade' and other types of 'vegetable wickedness,' to see him displaying a 'dark, flabby leaf' found growing out of a grave, and to hear that prominent among the herbs he has gathered are some 'black weeds' that have 'sprung up out of a buried heart.' When his evil work was done 'he positively withered up, shrivelled away . . . like an uprooted weed that lies wilting in the sun.' Flower and weed imagery unites with light and color imagery to define Chillingworth's position as that of the chief sinner.

But Chillingworth is not the only one so aligned. Less emphatically, the Puritans themselves are associated with weeds and black flowers. The implications of color imagery first set up the association: as their 'Puritanic gloom' increases in the second generation to the 'blackest shade of Puritanism,' we begin to see them as cousins to the 'nightshade' and so are prepared for Pearl's pretence that the weeds she attacks in her solitary games are Puritan children. Accustomed to her apparently infallible instinct for the truth, we see in her game something more than childish imagination.

The second relationship deserving of note also starts in the first chapter. We recall Hawthorne's saying of the wild rose-bush in bloom beside the prison that he hoped it might 'relieve the darkening close' of his tale. No 'sweet moral blossom' plays any significant part in the main story, but the happy fortune of Pearl, related in the concluding chapter, does offer a contrast with the 'frailty and sorrow' of the tale proper. Thus Pearl's final role is foreshadowed in the first chapter. But Hawthorne does not wait until the end to make this apparent. He constantly associates her not only with the scarlet letter on her mother's dress but with the red rose. The rose bears 'delicate gems' and Pearl is the red-clad 'gem' of her mother's bosom. Her flowerlike beauty is frequently underscored. And naturally so, for we are told that she had sprung, 'a lovely and immortal flower,' out of the 'rank luxuriance' of a guilty passion.

The position thus defined is repeatedly emphasized. Pearl cries for a red rose in the governor's garden. She answers the catechetical question who made her by declaring that she had not been made at all but 'had been plucked by her mother off the bush of wild roses that grew by the prison door.' She decorates her hair with flowers, which are said to become her perfectly. She is reflected in the pool in 'all the brilliant picturesqueness of her beauty, in its adornment of flowers.' Her 'flower-girdled and sunny image' has all the glory of a 'bright flower.' Pearl is a difficult child, capricious, unintentionally cruel, unfeeling in her demand for truth, but she has both the 'naturalness' and the beauty of the rose, and like the rose she is a symbol of love and promise.

These are the associations Hawthorne carefully elaborates, but there are two others worth noting briefly. Weeds or 'black flowers' are on several occasions associated with Hester. The most striking instance of this occurs when Pearl pauses in the graveyard to pick 'burrs' and arrange them 'along the lines of the scarlet letter that decorated the maternal bosom, to which the burrs, as their nature was, tenaciously adhered.' The burrs are like Pearl in acting according to nature, and what they suggest in their clinging cannot be wholly false. Hester implicitly acknowledges the truth of what the burrs have revealed when she suggests to Dimmesdale that they let the 'black flower' of their love 'blossom as it may.'

But a more frequent and impressive association is set up between Hester and normal flowers. Even the badge of her shame, the token of her 'guilty' love, is thus associated with natural beauty. The scarlet letter is related to the red rose from the very beginning. As Hester stands before her judges in the opening scenes, the sun shines on just two spots of vivid color in all that massed black, brown, and gray: on the rose and the letter, both red. The embroidery with which she decorates the letter further emphasizes the likeness, so that when Pearl throws flowers at her mother's badge and they hit the mark, we share her sense that this is appropriate. Burrs and flowers seem to have an affinity for Hester's letter. Hawthorne was too much of a Protestant to share the Catholic attitude toward 'natural law': the imagery here suggests that moral law and nature's ways do not perfectly coincide, or run parallel on different levels; they cross, perhaps at something less than a right angle. At the point of their crossing the lovers' fate is determined. No reversal of the implied moral judgement is suggested when nature seems to rejoice at the reaffirmed love of the pair in the forest: 'Such was the sympathy of Nature – that wild, heathen Nature of the forest, never subjugated by human law, nor illumined by higher truth – with the bliss of these two spirits! Love, whether newly born, or aroused from a death-like slumber, must always create a sunshine.'

Hester's emblem, then, points to a love both good and bad. The ambiguity of her gray robes and dark glistening hair, her black eyes and bright complexion, is thus emphasized by the flower and weed imagery. As Chillingworth is associated with weeds, Pearl with flowers, and Dimmesdale with no natural growing thing at all, so Hester walks her ambiguous way between burdock and rose, neither of which is alone sufficient to define her nature and her position.[7] □

As well as identifying significant patterns of imagery in *The Scarlet Letter*, Waggoner is also interested in the way Hawthorne deploys and develops images in his narrative. Hawthorne's images, Waggoner explains, become 'themselves actors in the story that moves through and behind the story'. They are neither static and determined by some abstract scheme nor wholly free and arbitrary, but contextual within a general framework supplied by traditional patterns. Waggoner identifies three kinds of image, 'pure', 'mixed' and 'drained'. On the first page of the novel, the greyness of the hats and the 'weatherstains' of the jail are 'pure' images, sense impressions to be taken literally. 'Mixed' images have more figurative extension than 'pure' images. The jail is 'gloomy' in both physical and emotional senses. When Chillingworth's face 'darkened' we are to understand more than a literal flushing of his face: 'here the symbolic effect of darkness, as that which is feared and evil, is also clear. This is the first reference to the "darkness" of Chillingworth'. With the 'drained' images, there is hardly any literal meaning left. In the description of the prison as the 'black flower' of civilization 'black' is figurative, not literal. The predominance of 'pure' images keeps the 'mixed' and 'drained' variety from losing force by becoming abstractly figurative, and this in turn is one of the reasons why the novel never becomes allegory.

Ambiguity, rather than allegory, is what characterises the novel, as far as Waggoner is concerned. That ambiguity he sees as deriving from the criss-crossing in the narrative of two planes of action and value, one representing 'natural law', the other 'moral law'. From the point of view of 'natural law', what Hester and Dimmesdale have done 'has a consecration of its own', and they enjoy nature's blessing in the form of the flood of sunshine when they meet together in the forest. But from the point of view of Puritan morality, they are sinners. However, the extremes of either 'moral law' (Puritan readiness to 'condemn and punish') or 'natural law' ('unrestrained sexuality') are to be avoided.

Much of the best criticism in, and since, the 1950s represents a blending of New Critical formalism with scholarly interest in the work's historical, biographical and literary contexts. This eclectic approach, which is both textualist and contextualist, is exemplified by Darrel Abel, who for thirty years taught American literature at Purdue University, and who was one of the most prolific and illuminating of Hawthorne's critics in the 1950s. In a series of essays (later collected and published under the title *The Moral Picturesque*, 1988), Abel, while making central use of New Critical analytical strategies, at the same time looked intently at the biographical, social and political data for significant references that could be brought to bear upon the given text. His criticism may be described as 'archetypal', as these opening remarks in *The Moral Picturesque* would indicate:

■ What distinguishes Hawthorne as a writer, besides the seventeenth century elegance of his style, are two characteristics. One is his habitual use of a psychological approach to his subjects. He assumed an absolute of archetypal human experience enacting a providentially directed cosmic drama of which he had uncertain knowledge through sympathy with persons enacting primordial roles. Like his Concord contemporaries, he believed that there was a transcendent Oversoul, but unlike them he did not believe that he could communicate with it directly by what Emerson called the 'tuition' of nature. Instead, he looked for truth in a psychological undersoul.

The second distinctive characteristic of his fiction was his use of the mode he called 'the moral picturesque.' This was a mode of figuration of the archetypal experiences that his psychological preoccupations discovered. . . . Moral did not refer merely to right and wrong behaviour, but to all underlying human reality – vital, spiritual, and psychological. . . . Picturesque meant strikingly graphic and extraordinary . . .[8] □

In separate essays, Abel discusses each of the four main characters in *The Scarlet Letter*. The first essay, on Hester Prynne, '"The Strong Division-Lines of Nature"', is an example of broadly biographical criticism. He begins by exploring Hawthorne's attitude toward Margaret Fuller (1810–50), the feminist theorist and editor of the Transcendentalist journal *The Dial*, arguing that 'it is evident that this actual experience of ambivalent feelings toward a passionate intellectual woman entered into and colored his representations of such women in his romances – notably Hester Prynne, Zenobia, and Miriam Schaefer'.

■ In short, Hawthorne had no liking for the monstrous regiment of women. His ideal of womanhood was 'the sweet, chaste, faithful, and courageous Imogen, the tenderest and womanliest that Shakespeare ever made immortal in the world.' In portraying such an ideal woman, he begins with the idea of an angel-woman who is to be made humanly real by fulfilling a double role to man: the role of Venus, which unites woman to man physically; and the role of mediatrix between the spiritual world and man, which makes man spiritually real by awakening his soul just as man makes woman physically real by arousing her sense. Each gives the other a 'life-giving touch.' . . . There is an obvious difficulty in combining the roles of Venus and angel. The angelic principle may inhibit the venereal principle . . . or the Venus in woman may be developed so early and strongly that a woman's spiritual nature becomes recessive rather than dominant, and persists only as a guilty conscience rather than as an effective monitor, as in such dark ladies as Hester, Zenobia, and Miriam.

The perplexities of these dark ladies are increased by the fact that, having lost their spiritual orientation or 'clue' through carnal license or abuse – that is, having forfeited the birthright of their sex – they attempt to compensate by orienting themselves to mundane realities and directing 'practical' affairs. It is, in Hawthorne's view, the function of women to give life to forms, but of men to give forms to life; so such interferences of women in practical affairs are improper. For all the prominence of women in Hawthorne's fictions, and the fact that they are his warmer and more vivid characters (when they are not his coolest and palest), his plots make them auxiliaries to men.

Such a character as Hester Prynne remained sympathetic and womanly for her author . . . for, although her 'heart had lost its regular and healthy throb,' so that she 'wandered without clew in the dark labyrinth of mind,' obsessed with problems that a woman 'never over-comes' 'by any exercise of thought'; and although she risked the dangers that thereby, 'perhaps, the ethereal essence, wherein she has her truest life, will be found to have evaporated' – nevertheless she never loses the attribute 'essential to keep her a woman,' the capacity of response to 'the magic touch to effect the transfiguration.' Despite her 'studied austerity' and 'the marble coldness of Hester's impres-sion,' when such a life-giving touch was given her, 'her sex, her youth, and the whole richness of her beauty, came back from what men call the irrevocable past' . . . Hawthorne could give pity and sympathy to a 'very woman' who had fallen, but not to a woman who had succeeded in the role of a man.[9] □

Abel goes on to invoke a second historical female figure, Anne Hutchinson, who had been involved in the Antinomian Debate of 1637, and, as a consequence, had been banished from Massachusetts for daring to challenge the right of the theocratic state to determine matters which she declared belonged only to the soul of the individual. Abel notes the two allusions in *The Scarlet Letter* (in Chapter 1 and Chapter 8) which link the historical Anne and the fictional Hester as outcasts whose alienation, instead of making them more amenable to authority, turned them more decidedly away from it. Anne Hutchinson, says Abel, is 'the prototypical Hawthorne heroine'. Drawing on an early sketch of Hawthorne's entitled 'Mrs Hutchinson', Abel shows that Hawthorne did not allow his sympathy with these strong-minded, passionate women victimised by authority to overhaul his recognition of the dangers of their waywardness.

■ The author's feelings toward Anne and Hester are finally and inextricably mixed. The usual either/or presentation of Hester's case is beside the point. Does Hawthorne sympathize with Hester? He does. Does he consider her in error? He does. Does he deplore the severity and inhumanity of the system which tries and punishes her and estranges her from society and inhibits fulfilment of her womanhood? He does. Does he justify the system and its dealings with Hester? He does. Such dark dilemmas of heart and head are, his stories intimate, finally insoluble. Essentially, Hawthorne defines Anne's and Hester's cases as being (so Melville says of Billy Budd's) among those 'involving considerations both practical and moral' in which 'natural justice' must yield to practical 'duty and the law.' . . . Hawthorne the descendent of Puritans may acknowledge the justice of suppression of dissent and rebuke woman's intrusions into a masculine sphere, while his 'other I am' sympathizes deeply with a woman's wrongs and frustrations, and with her impulse toward liberation from the bondage of her sex.[10] □

In another essay, 'Hester: "In the Dark Labyrinth of Mind"', Abel, employing what might be called a history of ideas approach this time, uses Hester to 'exhibit the inadequacy' of the philosophy of 'romantic individualism'.

■ The romantic individualist repudiates the doctrine of a supernatural ethical absolute. He rejects both the authority of God, which sanctions a pietistic ethic, and the authority of society, which sanctions a utilitarian ethic, to affirm the sole authority of nature. Hester, violating piety and decorum, lived a life of nature and attempted to rationalize her romantic self-indulgence; but, although she broke the laws of God and man, she failed to secure even the natural satisfactions she sought.

[. . .]

Although Hawthorne sympathized with Hester's rebellious mood, he did not, as Stuart P. Sherman averred, represent her as 'a free spirit liberated in a moral wilderness,' but as one who 'wandered, without rule or guidance, in a moral wilderness.' 'A woman never overcomes these problems by any exercise of thought,' and Hester's teachers – 'Shame, Despair, Solitude!' – have 'taught her much amiss.' Thus, unfitted by her intense femininity for intellectual speculations, as well as by her isolation from the common experience of mankind, which rectifies aberrant thought, she unwomaned herself and deluded herself with mistaken notions.[11] □

In 'Pearl: The Scarlet Letter Endowed with Life', Abel deals with the characterisation of Pearl, relating it to both 'the romantic child of nature' and 'the Puritan child of nature'. For Abel, the model of the romantic child of nature is Wordsworth's Lucy. She is cut off from human relationships. Her natural character alone is significant. She is totally under the influence of nature. She is an ideal and perfect creature that could not be produced by human upbringing. But, in Abel's opinion, Hawthorne did not share the early Wordsworth's view of the influence of nature on the growing child:

■ Wordsworth conceived of Lucy as a perfect creature fashioned by nature, but Hawthorne supposed that a Child of Nature would lack the most essential human quality, that of moral awareness . . . Pearl, unlike Lucy, is shown to be from the beginning of her development influenced by her human inheritance of traits and by the human relationships she has.

[. . .]

In his conception of the child's inheritance of moral as well as physical traits of resemblance, Hawthorne agreed with Calvinist thought. But he significantly disagreed that she was born with a corrupted nature.

[. . .]

Pearl thus stands as a regenerative possibility, a phenomenal resurgence among the sullied adult members of society of the power of goodness that mankind can obscure but not extinguish in its nature.

Pearl is a reincarnation of the best human possibilities of her progenitors – of potentialities that, imperfectly realized in past generations, are once more offered opportunity for better realization in this 'germ and blossom of womanhood.' Given Hawthorne's conviction that an individual is real and significant only insofar as he or she incarnates a type of humanity, Pearl's role as germ and blossom is more significant than her personal character and fate.

[. . .]

To effect her transformation from a wild infant, however, a critical event was required . . . She needed a 'deep distress' to 'humanize' her soul . . . Her father's dying confession, which announced his resumption of moral truth, supplied her with a connection with the moral order of the world, and simultaneously touched her sympathies deeply, so that an enduring moral impression was made on her.[12] □

Abel notes 'opposed tendencies' of good and bad in Pearl's character, and comments on the 'infinite variety' of her presentation. This compound of Romantic and Calvinist conceptions of childhood, blended with Hawthorne's observations of his daughter, made Pearl, in Abel's opinion, 'the most complex figure in the romance':

■ By burdening her characterization with multiple meaning, the author sacrificed her individuality and with it realism and credibility; but his sacrifice was necessitated by his plot.[13] □

Abel's essay on Chillingworth is subtitled 'The Devil in Boston'. In it, Abel discusses Chillingworth's role as an embodiment of certain Calvinist conceptions of the development of moral personality, and sources these conceptions in various works on Calvinist doctrine, such as Bishop Thomas Fuller's *The Holy State and the Profane State*, which Hawthorne read in 1834, and the writings of the Puritan mystic and intellectual Jonathan Edwards (1703–58). Abel's thesis is that Chillingworth is 'a Miltonic Satan given the meaner, more realistic embodiment appropriate to the villain of an historical romance'.

■ Roger Chillingworth, the diabolized physician in Hawthorne's *The Scarlet Letter*, embodies concepts which more resemble the Calvinist humanism of the seventeenth century in England than the transcendentalist optimism of nineteenth-century New England . . . To Puritan humanists, a good man was a man who had in his earthly career realized his potentialities; whereas to modern humanists (except such 'humanists' as Maritain), a good man is a man who has refined his own nature and erected it above mere naturalism.

[. . .]

Chillingworth was an aborted spirit – not in the sense of the modern humanist, to whom human failure is failure to rise above the brute, but in the sense of the Puritan humanist, to whom human failure is a lapsing from excellence or from the possibility of excellence.

[. . .]

Chillingworth was capable of love, and we sympathize with and approve of his desire for a life cheered by domestic affections . . .

Nevertheless Chillingworth was at fault in marrying a girl a generation younger than himself, who declared moreover that she did not love him . . . In a sense, his malice was less a personal resentment against Dimmesdale than an expression of anger at the scheme of things that had cheated his hopes. Like envious Satan, observing the love of Adam and Eve in the garden, 'Imparadised in one another's arms,' he was 'stirred up with envy and revenge.'

Chillingworth, implacably angry, violent even to frenzy, suffered this diabolical possession. Never very benevolent, he easily converted his injured self-love into hatred of his supplanter. He and Hester agreed that his earlier life had been blameless . . . But Hawthorne emphasizes that the physician's benevolence had never been so innate and habitual that a lapse into malevolence would be implausible. He had been 'kindly, though not of warm affections' . . . and his character had thus always retained the possibility of maleficence . . . Jonathan Edwards taught that true virtue 'has its roots in an emotional rather than intellectual state of mind.' Of this virtue, Chillingworth had never evinced any sign. Therefore, he could say, 'Evil, be thou my good,' and with perfect self-possession bend his energies strenuously toward malign as he had hitherto directed them incidentally toward benign ends. He was too fatally his own master.

That Hawthorne looked upon the power of good and the power of evil as different expressions of identical capacities, rather than as expressions of different capacities in man, is perfectly explicit, especially in the 'Conclusion' to the romance . . . 'It is a curious subject of observation and inquiry, whether hatred and love be not the same thing at bottom . . . Philosophically considered, therefore, the two passions seem essentially the same.'

Chillingworth, then, was not badness incarnate, but goodness perverted . . . In fine, we are to understand Chillingworth's sin as a tragic perversion of a force which sought its right expression in love, and, thwarted in that, turned to hate.[14] □

In his discussion of Dimmesdale in 'Dimmesdale: Fugitive from Wrath', Abel begins by agreeing with those critics such as Henry James and Stuart P. Sherman, who believed that while Hester is a more interesting character to modern readers, Dimmesdale's role is in fact the structural and thematic centre of the romance. Considering that Dimmesdale's 'has been comparatively neglected', Abel undertakes to show that Dimmesdale's is indeed 'the main tragic problem' and that the 'external evolution' and the 'denouement' of the romance depend upon him. Thus, starting with the premise that 'The plot of *The Scarlet Letter* consists of the struggle between God and the devil for the soul of Arthur Dimmesdale', Abel goes on to explicate this plot as 'an illustration of

Puritan conceptions of sinfulness and regeneration'. Following Matthiessen and Schubert, he sees the scaffold as 'the main structural device of the romance', and describes the plot as 'the protracted struggle between the influences seeking to prevent the minister from ascending this emblematic scaffold and assuming this symbolic letter (the scarlet A), and influences seeking to induce him to do so'.

Abel identifies four parts to the main action, in all of which Dimmesdale 'is the character mainly acted upon': the first is that in which organised society is the 'activating agent'; the second is that in which Chillingworth is the 'activating agent': 'for seven years he agitated his victim's tender conscience with continual reminders of his sin; goaded him to the verge of confession and then dissuaded him from it, thereby enfeebling his will and contributing to the inveteracy of his moral inertia'. The third part of the action is that in which Hester is the 'activating agent': 'In this section, Hester's effort to assume control over the minister is brief, intense, and apparently successful.' The fourth and final section of the novel is that in which 'Dimmesdale, apparently doomed to perdition, [is] spectacularly saved by God's grace'.[15]

For Abel, there is no separation between aesthetics and ethics. His criticism reflects an ultimately moral vision of life though he does not, any more than Hawthorne, seek to present specific moral instruction. In revealing the basic patterns of the text he is also discovering not just the mind of the author, but, beyond that, the American mind, and ultimately the human mind and psyche itself. In the Preface to a collection of critical essays in honour of Abel, *Ruined Eden of the Present: Hawthorne, Melville and Poe* (1981), G.R. Thompson and Virgil L. Lokke attempt to summarise a central theme – 'the dialectic of positive and negative' – which they believe informs Abel's criticism and Hawthorne's fiction alike: 'Abel offers through the act of reading and the act of criticism, the only affirmation possible to those of such Hawthorne-like temperament. Eternal verities are refracted in the act of criticism, which is an attempt to recognize an ideal Eden of individual and collective potential in the ruined Eden of the present.'[16]

Roy R. Male, in his *Hawthorne's Tragic Vision* (1957) combines the New Critical strategies of close textual analysis with exploration of Hawthorne's moral and philosophical preoccupations.

■ His [Hawthorne's] real strength will never be revealed by criticism that insists solely upon image-counting or study of fictional techniques. Hawthorne possessed what one of his friends called 'the awful power of insight', and his fiction remains valuable chiefly because of its penetration into the essential truths of the human heart. His one fruitful subject was the problem of moral growth.[17] □

In approaching the novel as a Christian tragedy, Male aims to show that for Hawthorne moral growth comes with sin and suffering. Hawthorne, Male argues, saw in Original Sin – the love of man and woman – the prototype of all tragic action. Hawthorne's theme is 'Fall . . . guilt . . . possible redemption', the 'quest for truth' which is 'an effort to know Pearl'. Dimmesdale 'purifies himself at the terrible human cost of sin, physical decay, and death'. He 'approaches this saintly level' at the end when, divesting himself of his priestly robe, he ascends the scaffold and speaks out his true identity. His Election Sermon sounds like 'a tongue of flame' (which Male takes as the romance's guiding metaphor), expressive of 'the deep ache at the heart of human life itself – a sense of atonement not only for the individual sin but for Original Sin'. In contrast, 'Hester's ascension is limited. She sees the truth, but she will not utter the word', withholding the identity of both her husband and her lover. 'Only in her art does Hester begin to find grace and to grasp the truth; that is, only in her art does she come to know Pearl'. Male thus sees the final mood of Hawthorne's tragedy as being one of 'tempered hopefulness, a realization that out of sin, sorrow, and decay may be born the insights, the "words of flame" uttered by Arthur Dimmesdale in the Election Sermon'.

Other critics in the 1950s, quite explicitly and programmatically, sought to discover 'the American mind', 'the national character', and to construct a theory of cultural identity from the evidence of the national literature. In his book, *The American Adam: Innocence, Tragedy, and Tradition in the Nineteenth Century* (1955), R.W.B. Lewis regarded the essentially tragic vision of life which Male identified in Hawthorne as the sign of a vital culture because tragedy implied the continued existence of an ideal, the persistence of the invigorating dream of Adamic innocence:

■ The vision of innocence stimulated a positive and original sense of tragedy . . . And without the vision, we are left, not with a mature tragic spirit, but merely with a sterile awareness of evil uninvigorated by a sense of loss. For the notion of original sin draws its compelling strength from the prior notion of original innocence. Recent literature has applauded itself for passing beyond the childlike cheerfulness of Emerson and Whitman; but, in doing so, it has lost the profound tragic understanding – paradoxically bred out of cheerfulness – of a Hawthorne or a Melville.[18] □

Lewis, adopting a mythic and symbolic approach, sees American fiction in terms of its archetypes of the isolated self rather than its engagements with society. The characteristic and distinctive theme of the American novel, according to Lewis, was the attempt to recover innocence by fleeing from an oppressive social world.

■ The opening scene of *The Scarlet Letter* is the paradigm dramatic image in American literature. With that scene and that novel, New World fiction arrived at its first fulfillment, and Hawthorne at his. And with that scene, all that was dark and treacherous in the American situation became exposed. Hawthorne said later that the writing of *The Scarlet Letter* had been oddly simple, since all he had to do was to get his 'pitch' and then to let it carry him along. He found his pitch in an opening tableau fairly humming with tension – with coiled and covert relationships that contained a force perfectly calculated to propel the action thereafter in a direct line to its tragic climax.

It was the tableau of the solitary figure set over against the inimical society, in a village which hovers on the edge of the inviting and perilous wilderness; a handsome young woman standing on a raised platform, confronting in silence and pride a hostile crowd whose menace is deepened by its order and dignity; a young woman who has come alone to the New World, where circumstances have divided her from the community now gathered to oppose her; standing alone, but vitally aware of the private enemy and the private lover – one on the far verges of the crowd, one at the place of honor within it, and neither conscious of the other – who must affect her destiny and who will assist at each other's destruction. Here the situation inherent in the American scene was seized entire and without damage to it by an imagination both moral and visual of the highest quality: seized and located, not any longer on the margins of the plot, but at its very center.

The conflict is central because it is total; because Hawthorne makes us respect each element in it. Hawthorne felt, as Brown and Cooper and Bird had felt, that the stuff of narrative (in so far as it was drawn from local experience) consisted in the imaginable brushes between the deracinated and solitary individual and the society or world awaiting him. But Hawthorne had learned the lesson only fitfully apprehended by Cooper. In *The Scarlet Letter* not only do the individual and the world, the conduct and the institutions, measure each other: the measurement and its consequences are precisely and centrally what the novel is about. Hester Prynne has been wounded by an unfriendly world; but the society facing her is invested by Hawthorne with assurance and authority, its opposition is defensible and even valid. Hester's misdeed appears as a disturbance of the moral structure of the universe; and the society continues to insist in its joyless way that certain acts deserve the honor of punishment. But if Hester has sinned, she has done so as an affirmation of life, and her sin is the source of life; she incarnates those rights of personality that society is inclined to trample upon. The action of the novel springs from the enormous but improbable suggestion that the society's estimate of the moral structure of the universe may be tested and found inaccurate.

The Scarlet Letter, like all very great fiction, is the product of a controlled division of sympathies; and we must avoid the temptation to read it heretically. It has always been possible to remark, about Hawthorne, his fondness for the dusky places, his images of the slow movement of sad, shut-in souls in the half-light. But it has also been possible to read *The Scarlet Letter* (not to mention 'The New Adam and Eve' and 'Earth's Holocaust') as an endorsement of hopefulness: to read it as a hopeful critic named Loring read it (writing for Theodore Parker's forward-looking *Massachusetts Quarterly Review*) as a party plea for self-reliance and an attack upon the sterile conventions of institutionalized society. One version of him would align Hawthorne with the secular residue of Jonathan Edwards; the other would bring him closer to Emerson. But Hawthorne was neither Emersonian nor Edwardsean; or rather he was both. The characteristic situation in his fiction is that of the Emersonian figure, the man of hope, who by some frightful mischance has stumbled into the time-burdened world of Jonathan Edwards. And this grim picture is given us by a writer who was skeptically cordial toward Emerson, but for whom the vision of Edwards, filtered through a haze of hope, remained a wonderfully useful metaphor. The situation, in the form which Hawthorne's ambivalence gave it, regularly led in his fiction to a moment of crucial choice: an invitation to the lost Emersonian, the thunder-struck Adam, to make up his mind – whether to accept the world he had fallen into, or whether to flee it, taking his chances in the allegedly free wilderness to the west. It is a decision about ethical reality, and most of Hawthorne's heroes and heroines eventually have to confront it.

That is why we have the frantic shuttling, in novel after novel, between the village and the forest, the city and the country; for these are the symbols between which the choice must be made and the means by which moral inference is converted into dramatic action. Unlike Thoreau or Cooper, Hawthorne never suggested that the choice was an easy one. Even Arthur Mervyn had been made to reflect on 'the contrariety that exists between the city and the country'; in the age of hope the contrariety was taken more or less simply to lie between the restraints of custom and the fresh expansiveness of freedom. Hawthorne perceived greater complexities. He acknowledged the dependence of the individual, for nourishment, upon organized society (the city), and he believed that it was imperative 'to open an intercourse with the world.' But he knew that the city could destroy as well as nourish and was apt to destroy the person most in need of nourishment. And while he was responsive to the attractions of the open air and to the appeal of the forest, he also understood the grounds for the Puritan distrust of the forest. He retained that distrust as a part of the symbol. In the forest, possibility was unbounded; . . . evil inclination was unchecked, and witches could flourish there.

For Hawthorne, the forest was neither the proper home of the admirable Adam, as with Cooper, nor was it the hideout of the malevolent adversary, as with Bird. It was the ambiguous setting of moral choice, the scene of reversal and discovery in his characteristic tragic drama. The forest was the pivot in Hawthorne's grand recurring pattern of escape and return.

It is in the forest, for example, that *The Scarlet Letter* version of the pattern begins to disclose itself: in the forest meeting between Hester and Dimmesdale, their first private meeting in seven years. During those years, Hester has been living 'on the outskirts of the town,' attempting to cling to the community by performing small services for it, though there had been nothing 'in all her intercourse with society . . . that made her feel as if she belonged to it.' And the minister has been contemplating the death of his innocence in a house fronting the village graveyard. The two meet now to join in an exertion of the will and the passion for freedom. They very nearly persuade themselves that they can escape along the forest track, which, though in one direction it goes 'backward to the settlement,' in another goes onward – 'deeper it goes, and deeper into the wilderness, until . . . the yellow leaves will show no vestiges of the white man's tread.' But the energy aroused by their encounter drives them back instead, at the end, to the heart of the society, to the penitential platform which is also the heart of the book's structure.[19] □

Richard Chase in his highly influential *The American Novel and its Tradition* (1957), champions what has been called the 'romance reading' of American literature – 'the greatest American fiction has tended toward the romance more often than the greatest European fiction'. In saying this, Chase was echoing the opinion of another highly influential critic, Lionel Trilling who, in 1947, in an essay entitled 'Manners, Morals, and the Novel', declared that the novel 'has never really established itself in America',[20] and noted that Hawthorne 'insisted that he did not write novels but romances', thereby expressing 'his awareness of the lack of social texture in his work'. (Hawthorne subtitled both *The Scarlet Letter* and *The Marble Faun* a 'Romance', included the word in the title of his 1852 novel *The Blithedale Romance*, and used the preface to *The House of the Seven Gables* to define the romance and clarify the differences between it and the novel.) Trilling and Chase were arguing for a distinctive American literary tradition, a tradition of romance, in an age of realism, when romance tended to be regarded as an antiquated and outmoded form. Nevertheless, during the 1950s and 1960s, the romance hypothesis became something of an academic orthodoxy, even though there was no clear agreement as to what romance actually was. Trilling defined the romance in terms of its lack of 'social texture'; while for Perry Miller it was concerned with Nature, the wilderness, the irrational. Chase describes it as follows:

■ Doubtless the main difference between the novel and the romance is in the way in which they view reality. The novel renders reality closely and in comprehensive detail. It takes a group of people and sets them going about the business of life. We come to see these people in their real complexity of temperament and motive. They are in explicable relation to nature, to each other, to their social class, to their own past. Character is more important than action and plot, and probably the tragic or comic actions of the narrative will have the primary purpose of enhancing our knowledge of and feeling for an important character, a group of characters, or a way of life. The events that occur will usually be plausible, given the circumstances, and if the novelist includes a violent or sensational occurrence in his plot, he will introduce it only into such scenes as have been (in the words of Percy Lubbock) 'already prepared to vouch for it.' Historically, as it has often been said, the novel has served the interests and aspirations of an insurgent middle class.

By contrast the romance, following distantly the medieval example, feels free to render reality in less volume and detail. It tends to prefer action to character, and action will be freer in a romance than in a novel, encountering, as it were, less resistance from reality. (This is not always true, as we see in what might be called the static romances of Hawthorne, in which the author uses the allegorical and moral, rather than the dramatic, possibilities of the form.) The romance can flourish without providing much intricacy of relation. The characters, probably rather two-dimensional types, will not be complexly related to each other or to society or to the past. Human beings will on the whole be shown in ideal relation – that is, they will share emotions only after these have become abstract or symbolic. To be sure, characters may become profoundly involved in some way, as in Hawthorne or Melville, but it will be a deep and narrow, an obsessive, involvement. In American romances it will not matter much what class people come from, and where the novelist would arouse our interest in a character by exploring his origin, the romancer will probably do so by enveloping it in mystery. Character itself becomes, then, somewhat abstract and ideal, so much so in some romances that it seems to be merely a function of plot. The plot we may expect to be highly colored. Astonishing events may occur, and these are likely to have a symbolic or ideological, rather than a realistic, plausibility. Being less committed to the immediate rendition of reality than the novel, the romance will more freely veer toward mythic, allegorical, and symbolistic forms.

[. . .]

As Hawthorne sees the problem confronting the American author, it consists in the necessity of finding (in the words of the Introduction to *The Scarlet Letter*) 'a neutral territory, somewhere between the real world and fairy-land, where the Actual and the Imaginary may meet, and each imbue itself with the nature of the other.' Romance is, as we see, a kind of 'border' fiction, whether the field of action is in the neutral territory between civilization and the wilderness, as in the adventure tales of Cooper and Simms, or whether, as in Hawthorne and later romancers, the field of action is conceived not so much as a place as a state of mind – the borderland of the human mind where the actual and the imaginary intermingle. Romance does not plant itself, like the novel, solidly in the midst of the actual. Nor when it is memorable, does it escape into the purely imaginary.

[. . .]

The fact is that the word 'romance' begins to take on its inevitable meaning, for the historically minded American reader, in the writing of Hawthorne. Ever since his use of the word to describe his own fiction, it has appropriately signified the peculiar narrow profundity and rich interplay of lights and darks which one associates with the best American writing. It has also signified, to be sure, the common trait shared by . . . all romances whatsoever – namely, the penchant for the marvellous, the sensational, the legendary, and in general the heightened effect. But the critical question is always: To what purpose have these amiable tricks of romance been used? To falsify reality and the human heart or to bring us round to new, significant and perhaps startling relation to them?[21] □

Chase is concerned to show that *The Scarlet Letter* is an example of a particular kind of romance – the allegorical romance. Here he is less convincing. He offers useful definitions of allegory:

■ Pure allegory (if it can ever be isolated as such) assumes two fixed discourses – a language of static signs and a set of truths to which they refer. In allegory the signs or symbols have little or no existence apart from their paraphrasable meaning. Allegory flourishes best, of course, when everyone agrees on what truth is, when literature is regarded as exposition, not as discovery. A symbolic or symbolistic literature responds to disagreements about the truth. It purports to discover or create truth. Thus a poetic symbol . . . suggests several meanings.[22] □

But when Chase also says:

■ We can say with relative certainty what the scarlet A stands for. It stands for adultery . . . It is thus a relatively simple sign and not, like the white whale (Moby-Dick), a complicated cluster of meanings . . . Being an ordinary symbol, the scarlet A is thus suitable to an allegorical context. The whale is much more complex and thus fits well the proliferating implications of Moby-Dick[23] □

we may find it harder to accept his application of his own theory. Is it really possible to say with relative certainty what the scarlet A stands for? Does it, too, not gather to itself in the course of the narrative 'a complicated cluster of meanings'? Does Hawthorne's story not bear out the narrator's experience in the Custom-House: 'Certainly, there was some deep meaning in it, most worthy of interpretation . . . but evading the analysis of my mind'? As Chase says, allegory was designed for the elucidation of certainty; but surely both Melville *and* Hawthorne used it in the service of search and scepticism. In the process, what began in *The Scarlet Letter* as Puritan allegorism may be seen to be transformed into a symbolic method.

Harry Levin, who had been a student of Matthiessen's at Harvard, based his own readings of Hawthorne, Poe and Melville in *The Power of Blackness* (1967) on two broad assumptions: 'the symbolic character of the greatest American fiction' and 'the dark wisdom' of its greatest practitioners. Levin reminds us that it was the 'power of blackness' in Hawthorne that had absorbed Melville, and that D.H. Lawrence had advised us 'to look through the surfaces of American art, and see the inner diabolism of the symbolic meaning. Otherwise it is all mere childishness'. Levin recognises that his concern with the theme of blackness runs counter to notions of the American Dream:

■ Taking for granted the obvious American thesis, the cheerfully confident trend of a prosperous and practical culture, it is the antithesis that we find in our greatest writers. Visionaries rather than materialists, rather symbolists than realists, the vision they impart is not rose-colored but sombre, and the symbols through which they impart it are charged with significations that profoundly justify the most searching analysis.[24] □

Such analysis, Levin argues, takes us back 'to the very beginning of things, the primal darkness, the void that God shaped by creating light and dividing night from day'. Levin is not interested in analysing patterns of images in the literary work solely to see how they contribute to the work's organic unity, but to see how they express a timeless human awareness, a 'collective unconscious', a primary mythological intuition of the world. Levin's criticism is another example of 'myth' or 'archetypal' criticism.

■ Having first confronted that book as a classic of the schoolroom, we are cushioned against the shock we should properly feel: the realization that, at the mid point of the nineteenth century, the primly subversive chronicler of the Puritans could base his first major work on an all but unmentionable subject. Not that this subject, the breach of the Seventh Commandment, is the theme of the book; rather it is the presupposition, the original sin from which everything follows. If there was any pleasure in it, any joy of the senses, that has been buried in the past, and Hawthorne has no intention of reanimating it. But its presence in the accusing shape of the majuscule, insisted on with every appearance of the heroine, lends the most vivid particularity to Hawthorne's general vision of evil, and motivates that unspecified remorse to which his characters are so habitually prone. A is for adultery – could any lesson be plainer than the stigma imposed by his title, 'the general symbol at which the preacher and moralist might point?' But morality is not to be so arbitrarily spelled out; nor is it calculated, on this occasion, to warrant any confidence in preachers; and, as for symbols, they derive their ultimate meaning from the emotions with which men and women invest them. The letter A, on the bosom of Chaucer's Prioress, had signified the power of sacred rather than profane love: Amor vincit omnia. Hawthorne had even been tempted to ask himself whether another scarlet letter meant 'adulteress' or 'admirable.' By the final phrase of his book, the badge of dishonor has become a heraldic escutcheon: 'ON A FIELD, SABLE, THE LETTER A, GULES.'

The color-scheme is all the more arresting because the spot of flaming red is set off against the usual background of somber blacks and Puritan grays. The initial sentence introduces a chorus of elders clad in 'sadcolored garments,' standing before 'the black flower of civilized society, a prison.' The opening of the prison door is 'like a black shadow emerging into sunshine'; but the sunshine, as Hawthorne retrospectively sighed, is conspicuous by its rarity. The dark-haired Hester Prynne, emerging to mount the pillory, babe in arms, is presented as a virtual madonna, despite the token of self-denunciation which she has embroidered into her attire. When the Reverend Mr. Dimmesdale is invited to expostulate with her, 'as touching the vileness and blackness of your sin,' the irony is precarious; for we are not yet in a position to recognize him as her guilty partner; nor is it until the next chapter that we witness her recognition-scene with her long estranged and elderly husband, who conceals his identity under the name of Chillingworth. The interrelationship between open shame and secret guilt is dramatized by a tense alternation of public tableaux and private interviews. All men are potentially sinners, though they profess themselves saints. Here in old Boston, as in the Salem of 'Young Goodman Brown,' the Black Man does a thriving traffic in witchcraft. If the letter is his mark, as Hester tells her daughter, it must also be accepted as the universal birthmark of mankind. Once, when she tries to fling it away, it is borne back to her upon a stream; thereafter she accepts it as her doom; she learns to live with it.

Therein she becomes innately superior to those fellow citizens who despise her, and whose trespasses are compounded by their hypocrisies. Their social ostracism may turn her into a 'type of . . . moral solitude'; but it endows her with 'a sympathetic knowledge of the hidden sin in other hearts,' which ultimately leads to a kind of redemption, as it does with the virtuous prostitutes of Victor Hugo and Dostoevsky. The letter proves to be a talisman which establishes bonds of sympathy; whereas the proud mantle of Lady Eleanor cut her off from sympathetic involvements. Though Hester lives a life of saintly penance, she does not repent her unhallowed love. On the contrary, she shields her repentant lover, and tells him: 'What we did has a consecration of its own.' Since their lapse was natural, it is pardonable; it has a validity which her marriage with Chillingworth seems to have lacked. What is unnatural is the pharisaical role into which Dimmesdale is consequently forced. He cannot ease his conscience by wearing a black veil, like the minister of Hawthorne's parable; for he is not mourning the hidden sin of others; he is hiding his own, which is palpable enough. The pulpit and the pillory are the contrasting scenes of his triumph and his self-abasement. His internal anguish, projected against the sky in a gigantic A, is finally relieved when he bares his breast to reveal the counterpart of Hester's letter. Hawthorne is purposefully vague in reporting these phenomena and whether they happen by miracle, hallucination, or expressionistic device. His Dostoevskian point is that every happening must be an accusation to the sinner, who must end by testifying against himself.

Hawthorne rejects an alternative he ironically suggests, whereby the supposedly blameless pastor dies in the arms of the fallen woman in order to typify Christian humility. Nor is her rehabilitation achieved at the expense of the cleric's integrity, as it would be for Anatole France's Thais. Nor is he thoroughly corrupted, like an evangelical beachcomber out of Somerset Maugham. Arthur Dimmesdale is an unwilling hypocrite, who purges himself by means of open confession. Among the possible morals, the one that Hawthorne selects is: 'Be true! Be true! Be true! Show freely to the world, if not your worst, yet some trait whereby the worst may be inferred.' Hester is true; and so is Dimmesdale at last; but the third

injunction rings hollow. These two have been a sinful pair, and he –
by Hawthorne's standard – has been more sinful than she. But the
most sinful member of the triangle is, most unnaturally, the injured
party. Dimmesdale atones for his trespass by his death; Hester for hers
by her life; but for Chillingworth, avenging their violation of his existence, there can be no atonement. 'That old man's revenge has been
blacker than my sin,' exclaims Dimmesdale. 'He has violated, in cold
blood, the sanctity of a human heart. Thou and I, Hester, never did so.'
While their trespass has been sensual passion, Chillingworth's is
intellectual pride. In short, it is the unpardonable sin of Ethan Brand,
of Hawthorne's dehumanized experimentalists, and of that spiritualized Paul Pry whose vantage-point comes so uncomfortably close to
the author's. Chillingworth, whose assumed name betrays his frigid
nature, plays the role of the secret sharer, prying into his wife's illicit
affair, spying upon her lover unawares, and pulling the strings of the
psychological romance.

The drama centers less on the colloquies between husband and
wife, or those between wife and lover, than on the relationship of
lover and husband, each concealing something from the other. 'The
misshapen scholar' is a man of science, a doctor who treats the agoniz-
ing Dimmesdale as his patient. One day the latter inquires where he
has gathered such strange herbs.

> 'Even in the graveyard here at hand,' answered the physician, con-
> tinuing his employment. 'They are new to me. I found them
> growing on a grave, which bore no tombstone, nor other memorial
> of the dead man, save these ugly weeds, that have taken upon
> themselves to keep him in remembrance. They grew out of his
> heart, and typify, it may be, some hideous secret that was buried
> with him, and which he had done better to confess during his life-
> time.' 'Perchance,' said Mr. Dimmesdale, 'he earnestly desired it,
> but could not.' 'And wherefore?' rejoined the physician. 'Where-
> fore not; since all powers of nature call so earnestly for the
> confession of sin, that these black weeds have sprung up out of a
> buried heart, to make manifest an unspoken crime?' 'That, good
> sir, is but a fantasy of yours,' replied the minister. 'There can be, if
> I forebode aright, no power, short of the Divine mercy, to disclose,
> whether by uttered words, or by type or emblem, the secrets that
> may be buried with a human heart. The heart, making itself guilty
> of such secrets, must perforce hold them, until the day when all
> hidden things shall be revealed.'

If the minister cannot shrive himself, the physician has a disease he
cannot cure. Yet it is his concentrated malevolence, more than any-

thing else, that implants the idea of confessing in Dimmesdale's mind. Whether Chillingworth may be his double or else a demon, the spokesman for Dimmesdale's conscience or a devil's emissary – these are possibilities which are raised but scarcely probed. He himself concedes that he is performing a fiend-like office, but considers this 'a dark necessity,' the inevitable consequence of Hester's downfall, perhaps of Calvinistic predestination. 'It is our fate,' he warns her. 'Let the black flower blossom as it may!' At the outset, when Esther was released from the jail, it was compared to a black flower; and afterward, because Dimmesdale unburdens himself, black weeds will not grow upon his grave. The color of the lovers is red, which stands for blood, for life instead of death; and their expiated sin is incarnate in the elfin fairness of their innocent child, the black-eyed Pearl, whose name betokens purity and whose radiance brings a few sunny touches into the book. When we read, in its concluding pages, that she grew up an heiress and traveled abroad, we realize that we can pursue her further adventures through the novels of Henry James.[25] □

Three further important examples of this kind of 'myth' or 'archetypal' criticism are William Bysshe Stein's *Hawthorne's Faust: A Study of the Devil Archetype* (1953), Leslie A. Fiedler's *Love and Death in the American Novel* (1960), and Hugo McPherson's *Hawthorne as Myth-Maker* (1969). Stein is interested in showing how Hawthorne's narratives work on two levels, the historical and the natural – the latter encompassing 'the destiny not merely of historical man but of all mankind'. Stein quotes Jung, who claimed that each mythic image '"contains a piece of human psychology and human destiny, a relic of suffering or delight that has happened countless times in our ancestral story"'. In Stein's analysis, Chillingworth, who dabbles in magic and forbidden knowledge, who usurps God's prerogative of revenge and disowns his brotherhood with man and his reverence for God, enters an informal contract with the devil. Stein notes the point in Hawthorne's narrative where direct allusion is made to Chillingworth's Faustian antecedents – the 'rumour' that 'Heaven had wrought an absolute miracle, by transporting an eminent Doctor of Physic, from a German university, bodily through the air, and setting him down at the door of Mr Dimmesdale's study!'. Chillingworth, according to Stein, is not only Faust, but Mephistopheles, the tempter who aims to lure the sinner Dimmesdale away from God. As well as this, 'Hawthorne feminizes the Faust motif in depicting the character of Hester Prynne'. Stein sees Hester as a feminine counterpart of Faust, 'a virtual Puritan Fausta', who ceases to be 'the standard heroine of the typical romance' from the moment she 'commits her soul to the devil'. This she does, Stein argues, by pledging herself to silence regarding her connection with Chillingworth. In doing so, she recognises 'the authority of the evil principle'. Throughout this conspiracy of silence she continues to hope for earthly happiness with Dimmesdale, and allows herself to become an accessory to Chillingworth's scheme of revenge, thereby contributing to the minister's moral and physical deterioration. Ultimately, her Faustian connections manifest themselves in her intellectual curiosity. Like Chillingworth, Hester too changes from Faust to tempter when she uses her powerful sexual attraction to tempt Dimmesdale in the forest. Dimmesdale, according to Stein, is modelled on the character of Ambrosio in M. G. Lewis's *The Monk*, while Pearl fits into the Faustian complex as 'demon offspring', 'imp of evil' 'of the lineage of the Prince of the Air'.

■ On the basis of this analysis of *The Scarlet Letter* it appears that a fluid conception of the Faust myth is the dynamic principle of composition ruling Hawthorne's creative imagination. Motivating most of the action in the novel is a versatile Faustian devil whose repertory of tricks derives from the Faustian drama and the Faustian Gothic romance. As Hawthorne manipulates the controlling idea, he endows each of his main characters with an aim in life that falls into the pattern of universal human experience. His portrayal of Chillingworth as a Puritan Faust who is victimized by a hereditary interest in sin elevates the latter's fate to a plane of numbing pathos and tragedy. In depicting Hester as a Fausta, Hawthorne separates her from the ordinary romantic heroine accidentally entangled in a net of evil. Her desperate efforts as a Faustian tempter are designed to express the eternal philosophy of womanhood: consistent with her maternal instincts, a woman's destiny is linked firmly with her desire to attain happiness for herself, her children, and her mate. In terms of the variant of the Faust myth, assigning to Dimmesdale the character of the lascivious monk, Hawthorne, with poetic justice that betrays his true feelings about the minister, rewards the latter's ignominious spiritual hypocrisy and moral cowardice. And by recourse to another Faustian phenomenon, Hawthorne ennobles Pearl's struggle to achieve identity in the human family.

The dramatic device of archetypal ritual in the Faust myth, the selling of the soul to the devil, provides Hawthorne with an operational symbol that enables him to analyze vividly the spiritual quandaries of his actors. This symbol effectively enlarges the experiences of the characters beyond the historical theatre of Puritan times. Its associations embrace the whole corpus of human desires that have given to man's life a deep significance and purpose. Hawthorne's Satan is not the principle of evil in Calvinistic theology; he is the dark fatality that eternally works in the affairs of humans who have trespassed into ethically uncharted domains of the intellect and the spirit. Only by conquering this evil which is compounded of the only two worlds man can know, the inner world of the soul and the outer of human activity, can the individual confront bravely the tragic discipline of experience. With such implications underlying the structure of *The Scarlet Letter*, the novel assumes a greater importance than has hitherto been assigned to it in the history of American letters.[26] □

In *Love and Death in the American Novel*, a book of massive scholarship and richly suggestive, often controversial opinion, Fiedler sets out to 'emphasize the neglected contexts of American fiction, largely depth-psychological and anthropological, but sociological and formal as well'. He is particularly exercised by 'the power of blackness' in Hawthorne, whom he describes as a 'tragic Humanist', and sees as initiating a contrary line of development in American thought to that represented by the Transcendentalists. Transcendentalism, says Fiedler, assumes that the real world is a world of ideas not apparent to the senses; that nature is beneficent and rational and that man is, therefore, at home in his world; that both man and nature participate in God, who is not finally separate from either; that the fittest church is Nature itself and the truest Bible is the individual heart. Such beliefs, says Fiedler, 'urge upon man as his essential duty the act of saying "Yea!" to everything, of crying out "I accept the universe!"'. Melville and Hawthorne, in contrast, are seen to 'redeem the complex values of Puritanism from religion to art':

■ Among the assumptions of Melville and Hawthorne are the following: that the world of appearance is at once real and a mask through which we can dimly perceive more ultimate forces at work; that Nature is inscrutable, perhaps basically hostile to man, but certainly in some sense alien; that in man and Nature alike, there is a 'diabolical' element, a 'mystery of iniquity'; that it is impossible to know fully either God or ourselves, and that our only protection from destructive self-deceit is the pressure and presence of others; that to be alone is, therefore, to be lost; that evil is real . . . From this it follows that the writer's duty is to say 'Nay!', to deny the easy affirmations by which most men live, and to expose the blackness of life most men try deliberately to ignore. For tragic Humanists, it is the function of art not to console or sustain, much less to entertain, but to disturb by telling a truth which is not always welcome; and they consequently find it easy to view themselves in Faustian terms, to think of their dangerous vocations as a bargain with the Devil.[27] □

The Scarlet Letter, says Fiedler, was the 'greatest of our gothic fictions', 'the first American tragedy'.

■ It is Hawthorne who first opens up in our literature, as Melville himself explained, the tragic way; and the greatest of his gothic fictions, the first American tragedy, is *The Scarlet Letter*. A 'Puritan *Faust*', it has been called, as if there could be in the United States any other sort of *Faust*; but it is important all the same to be aware that it was Hawthorne who set the diabolical pact in a Puritan context and cast upon the beginnings of life in America a gothic gloom that not even Longfellow's middlebrow idylls could relieve.

The Scarlet Letter is finally not essentially a love story at all; and though it is possible to gain some insights into its theme and tone by considering it an American, which is to say, a denatured and defleshed, *Nouvelle Héloise*, it is more valuable to approach it as an American, which is to say, a less violent and hopeless, version of *The Monk*. Like Lewis's horror novel, Hawthorne's book deals with a man of God led by the desire for a woman to betray his religious commitment, and finally almost (Hawthorne repents at the last moment, as Lewis does not) to sell his soul to the Devil. Certainly it makes more sense to compare the figure of Hester with that of the active Matilda, and Dimmesdale with the passive Ambrosio, who is seduced by her, than to try to find analogues for the American pair in Goethe's Gretchen and Faust. If Hawthorne's novella is, indeed, as has often been suggested, an American *Faust*, it is a *Faust* without a traduced maiden. Much less sentimental and Richardsonian than Goethe, Hawthorne is not concerned with the fall of innocence at the seducer's hand or with that seducer's salvation by the prayers of his victim.

The Faustianism of Hawthorne is the melodramatic Faustianism of the gothic romances: of Lewis, whom he read avidly, and of Maturin, from whose *Melmoth the Wanderer* he borrowed the name of a minor character in *Fanshawe*. Not only Lewis and Maturin, but Mrs Radcliffe and Brockden Brown were favourite authors of the young Hawthorne; and from them he learned how to cast on events the lurid lights, the air of equivocal terror which gives *The Scarlet Letter* its 'hell-fired' atmosphere. The very colour scheme of the book, the black-and-whiteness of its world illuminated only by the baleful glow of the scarlet letter, come from the traditional gothic palette; but in Hawthorne's imagination, those colours are endowed with the natural colours of the wintry forest settlement in which the events unfold, but stand, too, for that settlement's rigidly distinguished versions of virtue and vice; while red is the colour of sexuality itself, the fear of which haunts the Puritan world like a bloody spectre. The book opens with a description of 'the black flower of civilized society, a prison' and closes on a gravestone, a 'simple slab of slate', whose escutcheon is 'sombre . . . and relieved only by one everglowing point of light gloomier than a shadow: – ON A FIELD SABLE , THE LETTER A, GULES.'

It is the scarlet letter itself which is finally the chief gothic property of Hawthorne's tale, more significant than the portents and signs, the meteors in the midnight sky, or even 'the noise of witches; those voices, at that period, were often heard . . . as they rode with Satan through the air . . .'. Into that letter are compressed the meanings of all the demonic fires, scarlet blossoms, and red jewels which symbolize passion and anger in his earlier tales. It glows with a heat genital and Satanic at once – burning his fingers even centuries later, Hawthorne tells us in his introduction, like 'red-hot iron'; and its 'lurid gleam', the text declares, is derived 'from the flames of the infernal pit'. Its 'bale-fire', at any rate, lights up the book with a flickering glare representing at once Hester's awareness of guilt and Hawthorne's: his doubts over his plunge into the unconscious, and hers over her fall through passion into the lawless world of Nature.

What Hester inwardly perceives the book makes explicit: that the scarlet letter belongs not to her alone but to the whole community which has sought to exclude her. It is repeated everywhere: in the child she bears, who is the scarlet letter made flesh; in the heavens of secret midnight; on the tombstone which takes up her monitory role after she is dead; and especially in the secret sign on the breast of the minister, whom the community considers its special saint. In his dumb flesh is confessed what his articulate mouth cannot avow, not his transgression alone but that of all men who have cast the first stone. At the heart of the American past, in the parchment scroll which is our history, Hawthorne has discovered not an original innocence but a primal guilt – and he seeks to evoke that past not in nostalgia but terror.

It is on the frontier, the margin where law meets lawlessness, the community nature, that Hawthorne imagines his exemplary drama played out; but his primitive world is much more like Brockden Brown's than Cooper's. To him, the 'dark inscrutable forest' seems rather the allegorical selva oscura of Dante than Natty Bumppo's living bride: the symbol of that moral wilderness into which man wanders along the byways of sin, and in which he loses himself forever. In its darkness, Hawthorne says of Hester at one point, 'the wildness of her nature might assimilate itself with a people alien to the law . . .'. He projects no idyllic dream of finding in the forest the Noble Savage, only a nightmare of confronting the barbaric warrior and the Devil whom he serves; and the occasional Indian who emerges from his wilderness takes up a place not beside the pariah-artist but the black magician.

The virgin sea seems to him as unredeemed as the land, a second realm of gloomy lawlessness. For him sailors are ignoble savages, too: 'the swarthy-cheeked wild men of the ocean, as the Indians were of the land . . . ' Neither Hawthorne's Indians nor seamen, however, play a critical part in the development of the action; they merely stand symbolically by, in their appropriate garb, speaking no word but watching 'with countenance of inflexible gravity, beyond what even the Puritan aspect could attain'. In the two important scenes at the foot of the scaffold, which so symmetrically open and close the book, there are red men in attendance, on the second occasion flanked by their even wilder confreres, the mariners, 'rough-looking desperadoes, with sun-blackened faces, and an immensity of beard'. Yet neither the black desperadoes of the deep nor the swarthy and stolid Indians play the role in *The Scarlet Letter* entrusted to Cooper's Mingoes or the gothic savages of Brockden Brown.

The Magua of Hawthorne's novella is Chillingworth, the white doctor and man of science, so oddly at home in the alien world of the primitive. 'By the Indian's side, and evidently sustaining a companionship with him, stood a white man, clad in a strange disarray of civilized and savage costume'; 'old Roger Chillingworth, the physician, was seen to enter the market-place, in close and familiar talk with the commander of the questionable vessel'. From his Indian captors and friends, Chillingworth has learned a darker 'medicine' to complement his European science; but he has not ceased to be still 'the misshapen scholar . . . eyes dim and bleared by lamplight', whose 'scientific achievements were esteemed hardly less than supernatural'. If on the one hand Chillingworth is portrayed as the heir to the lore of the 'savage priests', on the other he is presented as a student of the black magic of 'Doctor Forman, the famous old conjurer'. To represent the horror of Europe, however, Chillingworth must be white, while to stand for that of America he must be coloured; he is, in fact, a white man who grows black. Even the other protagonists notice his gradual metamorphosis ('his dark complexion seemed to have grown duskier . . .') into the very image of the Black Man, which is to say, Satan himself: 'a striking evidence of man's faculty of transforming himself into a devil . . . if he only will . . . undertake a devil's office.'

In general, one of the major problems involved in reading *The Scarlet Letter* is determining the ontological status of the characters, the sense in which we are being asked to believe in them. Caught between the analytic mode of the sentimental novel and the projective mode of the gothic, Hawthorne ends by rendering two of his five main characters (Hester and Dimmesdale) analytically, two ambiguously (Chillingworth and Pearl), and one projectively (Mistress Hibbins). Hester and Dimmesdale are exploited from time to time as 'emblems' of psychological or moral states; but they remain rooted always in the world of reality. Chillingworth, on the other hand, makes so magical an entrance and exit that we find it hard to believe in him as merely an ageing scholar, who has nearly destroyed himself by attempting to hold together a loveless marriage with a younger woman; while Pearl, though she is presented as the fruit of her mother's sin, seems hardly flesh and blood at all, and Mistress Hibbins is quite inexplicable in naturalistic terms, despite Hawthorne's perfunctory suggestion that she is simply insane.

The latter three are, perhaps, best understood as the 'daemons' or 'shadows' of the more actual protagonists. Chillingworth is clearly enough the shadow of Dimmesdale, a paternal image, the Bad Father who speaks with the voice of Dimmesdale's Calvinist heritage. He is a tormenting alter ego, capable of slipping past the barriers of cowardice and self-pity to touch the hidden truth. When Dimmesdale, hounded to penitence by his shadow, mounts the scaffold to expose his own long-hidden scarlet letter, Hawthorne offers us what seem alternative explanations of its genesis. It may be, he suggests, the result of some hideous self-inflicted torture, the psychosomatic effect of remorse, or the work, scientific or magical, of Chillingworth; but these we can see are only apparent alternatives, which properly translated reduce to a single statement; Dimmesdale and Chillingworth are one, as body and soul are one.

Certainly Chillingworth cannot survive the minister's death, after which 'he positively withered up, shrivelled away, almost vanished from sight'. And when the process is complete, the old physician gone, leaving to the bastard child of his wife enough money to make her 'the richest heiress of her day' – both that child and her mother disappear, too. From their refuge in the Old World Hester returns alone to her place of shame and assumes again the burden of her guilt; for there is no longer any function for the 'demon child' who was her shadow. From the first, Pearl has been projected as 'a forcible type . . . of the moral agony which Hester Prynne had borne'. Redeemed, however, by her father's last penance, and endowed with the wealth of his shadow, she vanishes, too, not out of the world but into it: 'A spell was broken . . . and as her tears fell upon her father's cheek, they were the pledge that she would grow up amid human joy and sorrow, nor forever do battle with the world, but be a woman in it. Towards her mother, too, Pearl's errand . . . was all fulfilled.'

Taken as a character constructed in psychological depth, Pearl is intolerable. Though she is the first child in American fiction whose characterization is based on painstaking observation of a real little girl (an astonishing number of details in her portrayal come from the notes Hawthorne took on his little daughter, Una), she is so distorted in the interests of her symbolic role that she seems by turns incredible and absurd. It is partly a question of the tone in which her actions are described, a tone sometimes sentimental and condescending

(Hawthorne's son, Julian, interpreted the book as essentially a defence of bastards!), sometimes mystifying and heavily gothic. Daemonic Pearl certainly is, in her immunity to man-made law, her babbling in strange tongues, her uncanny insight into her mother's heart. But she is disconcertingly benign – as often compared to a blossom from a rosebush as to a witch! Her name is the clue to her essential nature, as surely as is Chillingworth's icy appellation; for she is 'the gem of her mother's bosom', the Pearl of great price: not only Hester's torment, but also her salvation. 'Thus early had this child saved her from Satan's snare . . . '

Unaware of exactly what he is doing with his shadow characters: incapable of committing himself unreservedly to the gothic modes, but unable either to translate them into terms of psychological inwardness – Hawthorne tempers the daemonic in Chillingworth's case with melodrama, in Pearl's with sentimentality, and in Mistress Hibbins's with a kind of sceptical irony. The wizard Hawthorne can regard with horror, the elf-child with condescension; but to the full-blown witch, he responds with uneasy evasions, unwilling perhaps to grant reality to the nightmare which had aroused the persecuting zeal of his ancestors. Mistress Hibbins is, nonetheless, the third daemon of the book, the shadow of a sixth protagonist that we have not yet named: the Puritan community itself, which Hawthorne portrays as haunted by 'the noise of witches; whose voices at that period, were often heard to pass over the settlements or lonely cottages, as they rode with Satan through the air'.

The name of Mistress Hibbins is mentioned in Hawthorne's text before that of any of the other major characters of the book; and at four critical moments she appears on the scene. On her first appearance, she pleads with Hester to come with her to the forest and sign her name in the Black Man's book; on her second, she peers from her window into the darkness where the minister stands alone on the scaffold and cries out in anguish; on her third, she hails the minister as a fellow-communicant of Satan after he has met Hester in the forest and agreed to run off. The fourth scene is the longest, involving an interchange with Hester in which Mistress Hibbins claims fellowship not only with her and her lover, but impugns the whole community, for whose undermind of filth and fear she speaks: 'Many a church-member saw I, walking behind the music, that has danced in the same measure with me when Somebody was fiddler, and, it might be, an Indian powwow or a Lapland wizard changing hands with us!' Yet despite her critical role in the book, the dour-faced witch lady is rendered more as hallucination than fact. Her first entrance is hedged about with such phrases as: 'it is averred' and 'if we suppose this interview . . . to be authentic and not a parable . . .'; her second ends:

'the old lady . . . vanished. Possibly, she went up among the clouds'; the third introduces the disturbing phrase, 'and his encounter, if it were a real incident . . .'. Only the fourth does not qualify its assertion of what happened with doubt, merely attributes Mistress Hibbins's diatribe to her 'insanity, as we would term it'.

Yet hedged about with doubts and characterized as mad, Magistrate Bellingham's sister is the mouthpiece through which the Faustian theme is introduced into the book. The Faustian theme, however, constitutes the very centre of *The Scarlet Letter*: a profound crisis of the soul, for which Hawthorne was able to find no other image than one appropriate to the crazy dreams of a selfstyled witch, or the blood-curdling story told to a child. Chapters XVI to XX, which make up the centre of Hawthorne's tale, describe the encounter of Dimmesdale and Hester, the evocation of their old love, their momentary illusion of freedom, and the minister's moral collapse; but what begins as romance ends in gothic horror. It is Pearl who gives us the clue, asking her mother to tell the very story that she and her love have been acting out: 'a story about the Black Man. . . . How he haunts this forest, and carries a book with him – a big, heavy book, with iron clasps, and how this ugly Black Man offers his book and an iron pen to everybody that meets him here among the trees; and they are to write their names with their own blood. And then he sets his mark on their bosoms!' This is, indeed, the tale which Hawthorne tells in *The Scarlet Letter*, though for his characters the problem is not, as in the older versions of the story, whether they shall make such a pact, but whether they have made it; for in this new Faustian legend, one may enter into such an agreement unawares.

Over and over the essential question is asked. Pearl herself puts it to her mother just after her request for a gothic story, 'Didst thou ever meet the Black Man, mother?' and Hester answers, 'Once in my life I met the Black Man! . . . This scarlet letter is his mark!' Even earlier, Hester has inquired of Chillingworth, 'Art thou like the Black Man that haunts the forest round about us? Hast thou enticed me into a bond that will prove the ruin of my soul?' But Chillingworth, smiling, has only evaded her query, 'Not thy soul. . . . No, not thine!' It is Dimmesdale whom he implies he has lured into the infernal pact; and it is Dimmesdale who questions himself finally, though impelled by Hester's temptation rather than Chillingworth's torment, 'Am I mad? or am I given over utterly to the fiend? Did I make a contract with him in the forest, and sign it with my blood?' This time it is Hawthorne himself who answers: 'The wretched minister! He had made a bargain very like it! Tempted by a dream of happiness he had yielded himself with deliberate choice, as he had never done before, to what he knew was deadly sin.'

For Hawthorne, the Faustian man is one who, unable to deny the definitions of right and wrong by which his community lives, chooses nonetheless to defy them. He is the individual, who, in pursuit of 'knowledge' or 'experience' or just 'happiness' places himself outside the sanctions and protection of society. His loneliness and alienation are at once his crime and his punishment; for he commits a kind of suicide when he steps outside of society by deciding to live in un-repented sin; and he can only return to haunt the world of ordinary men like a ghost. Every major protagonist of *The Scarlet Letter* is such a spectre. Of Hester, we are told that 'she was as much alone as if she inhabited another sphere', and that 'It was only the darkened house which could contain her. When sunshine came, she was not there.' Dimmesdale asks of himself, 'Then what was he? – substance? – or the dimmest of shadows?'; and Hawthorne tells us of Chillingworth that 'he chose . . . to vanish out of life as completely as if he indeed lay at the bottom of the ocean.' Pearl, born of the original sin which has obliterated the substance of her elders, begins as 'a born outcast of the infantile world. . . . Mother and daughter stood in the same circle of seclusion from human society.'

Neither hate nor love can penetrate the spheres of unreality to which Hester, Dimmesdale, and Chillingworth have consigned them-selves. The old physician proves incapable of believing himself a fiend or the two lovers sinners except in a 'typical illusion', and meet-ing after seven years, the minister and Hester 'questioned one another's actual and bodily existence, and even doubted of their own. . . . Each a ghost, and awe-stricken at the other ghost!' Indeed, Hawthorne has the same trouble believing his characters real that they have themselves. 'But to all these shadowy beings, so long our acquaintances,' he says by way of valedictory, 'we would fain be mer-ciful.' And we realize the sense in which he himself was, like Dimmesdale or Hester, alienated, removed to a sphere from which like some ghostly Paul Pry he peered down on the ghosts of his imagining. We have spoken of Hester and Dimmesdale as more actual than their shadows; but their actuality is a thin and tenuous thing, though the best at the command of a writer who Poe advised, in critical im-patience, to get a bottle of visible ink![28] ☐

Finally in this chapter we shall briefly consider Hugo McPherson's study of Hawthorne's mythologising and symbolising habit of mind. McPherson, like Fiedler, draws on biographical and myth criticism in approaching *The Scarlet Letter*. Underlying Hawthorne's rational concerns – the problems of sin and redemption, the past, democracy, women's rights, the role of the artist, and the methods of art – McPherson identi-fies a 'deeper current of drama and narrative allied to the patterns of fairytale, romance, and myth'. In an echo of Northrop Frye, with whose critical theories McPherson, like Stein, explicitly allies himself, McPherson suggests that the coherence of Hawthorne's work may depend as much on his 'personal mythology' or 'life of allegory' as on any rational scheme of ideas, aesthetic theory, or external social or religious framework. An understanding of this 'personal legend', the 'inner drama or "hidden life"', in McPherson's view, will bring us closer to the spirit of Hawthorne's art than 'interpretations which stress Freudian psychology, Christian theology, or New Critical analysis of image patterns'.

The most striking features of Hawthorne's 'personal legend', says McPherson, are, first, that, though fatherless, he was haunted by an ancestry of austere and even brutal men who had persecuted the Quakers and witches. Second, he knew very early that he was an artist, adopting the nickname of 'Oberon' when he was an eighteen-year-old at Bowdoin College. For twelve years he felt himself cut off from the practical community and 'the rewards of love and the Heart'. Third, he knew that his Puritan forefathers would have had nothing but contempt for his artistic pursuits. He regarded the society in which he lived as philistine and materialistic. Finally, he was able to 'open an intercourse with the world', and to find a place in the human community through marriage to the virginal 'dove', Sophia Peabody:

■ In synopsis, the young artist-hero 'Oberon', menaced by his aged 'fathers', goes on a twelve-year quest in an illusive world of spectres, and finally returns to claim his place and marry a 'princess'.[29] □

This 'personal allegory', McPherson believes, informs Hawthorne's 'central narrative' of a mythic quest:

■ The hero's quest is an exploration of the menacing darkness of his own identity; it involves a long night journey, as with Perseus and Cadmus, or the entry of a labyrinth or forest, as with Theseus and Jason. The hero's victory is the recognition and control of these forces, and the application of his new power to the problems of his community. . . . The goal of the quest is the brotherhood of man, or in social terms the 'final triumph' of the republic; it will be reached not by reformers or builders but by a growth of self-awareness and vision'.[30] □

McPherson recognises an additional quest narrative incorporated into *The Scarlet Letter*, 'a feminine version of the hero's quest, revealed in the tales of Circe, Pandora, and Proserpina'. The protagonist of this narrative is the Dark Lady, the representative of a creative force who is persecuted by a community which fears both carnal knowledge and the mystery of creativity except as confined within narrow limits set by religion and law.

Dimmesdale, like Perseus, says McPherson, finds his true identity by the end, but only at the point of death: 'His triumph is his recognition that the dark experience which his brethren regard as demonic is an integral part of man's full nature'. Dimmesdale's act of self-recognition and self-assertion – the public reunion with Hester – releases Pearl from the 'spell' which had made her seem a demon child. Pearl 'becomes a complete woman instead of a Puritan half-woman – the first representative of a new breed, the first complete American'. As for Hester, the Dark Lady, she has 'learned to accept her unhappy lot and await the bright revelations of such artists as Nathaniel Hawthorne'. Like Dimmesdale, she, too, at the price of great suffering, 'passed beyond the Puritan vision of evil'. And 'the Black man, Chillingworth, with "no more devil's work to do", shrivelled and died'.

As we shall see in the next chapter, later historically-minded critics were to challenge the dematerialisation of American culture which they perceived to have taken place under the sway of New Critics such as Fiedler, Lewis, Chase, Levin, Stein and McPherson. The construction of Hawthorne's novel in terms of 'mysterious remoteness', 'bold and poetic and legendary outline which may belong to opera', 'lack of engagement with society', absence of 'coherent politics', was adjudged symptomatic of an American literary history which, in abstracting archetypal imaginative patterns, denied reference to the political conditions the writers were actually addressing, and promoted interpretations of the culture that were non-contradictory, apologetic, consensual, WASPish and male. The new revisionist literary history set out to show that the denial of actuality was more surely a New Critical strategy than a predominant feature of the literature which the older critics presumed to describe. Thus, a new generation of critics, in demonstrating how a materialist knowledge can be built, has reinterpreted classic works such as *The Scarlet Letter*, restoring to them the political and historical context denied by New Criticism. The canon of American culture, these new cultural critics have sought to explain, has been constructed as fundamentally Puritan in origin in order to legitimise a male, white, Protestant hegemony.

CHAPTER THREE

Historical Approaches

IN CONTRAST to New Critical formalism, 'historicist' criticism is based on the assumption that for a proper understanding of the literary work we need to look beyond the text itself to consider its situation within a network of particular historical, social and political relations. The work of art is no longer thought of as simply the achievement of individual genius, nor is it, as extreme formalists would have it, an autonomous object cut off from reality altogether: 'historicists' see the work of art as referential – it refers to the world outside itself, it influences that world, even as it is referred to by that world and is influenced by it.

Apart from Julian Hawthorne's biography, 'The making of *The Scarlet Letter*' (1931), which contains much interesting information about his father during the time of writing *The Scarlet Letter* (such as the fact that Hawthorne's first child, Una, served as a model for Pearl, and that the death of Hawthorne's mother cast a shadow over the writing of the book), the most important pioneering 'historicist' studies of *The Scarlet Letter* are Charles Ryskamp's 'The New England Sources of *The Scarlet Letter*' (1959), Charles Boewe and Murray G. Murphey's 'Hester Prynne in History' (1960), and Michael Colacurcio's 'Footsteps of Ann Hutchinson: The Context of *The Scarlet Letter*' (1972). Ryskamp, in the standard source study of *The Scarlet Letter*, illustrates Hawthorne's indebtedness to Caleb Snow's *History of Boston*, the definitive history of New England in Hawthorne's day, and points out Hawthorne's departures from historical fact, as in his having Governor Bellingham stand in judgement over Hester when it was really John Winthrop who was governor at the time in June 1642. Boewe and Murphey, in their essay 'Hester Prynne in History' (1960), consider the historical sources of the character of Hester Prynne, noting an entry in the Salem Quarterly Court records of 1688 that Hawthorne may well have read: 'Hester Craford, for fornication with John Wedg, as she confessed, was ordered to be severely whipped and that security be given to save the town from the charge of keeping the child'.[1] Boewe and Murphey further suggest the possibility of Hawthorne having read the story of Goodwife Mendame of Duxbury who was also found guilty of adultery, whipped and made 'to weare a badge with the capital letters AD cut in the cloth upon her left sleeve'. Most important of all the 'sources' for Hester was Anne Hutchinson. Hawthorne explicitly links his fictional Hester with the historical Anne Hutchinson in the very first chapter of his story. Anne Hutchinson was a famous seventeenth-century antinomian who dared to question Puritan orthodoxy in proclaiming that the individual's intuition of God took precedence over any institutionalised forms of observance or dogma. Colacurcio notes that while Hutchinson's offence was theological and Hester's sexual, both women challenge, and are punished by, 'a theocratic and male-dominated society'.[2]

Traditional 'historicist' criticism, as it became increasingly informed by modern critical theory from the 1970s onwards, reflected a growing scepticism about traditional notions of both 'history' and 'literature'. What evolved has become known as the 'New Historicism', which has been largely shaped by Michel Foucault and the poststructuralists, and is distinguished from traditional 'historicist' criticism in a number of important ways. First, the New Historicists recognised the difficulty of recovering the past: the past could only be grasped in terms of 'interpretations' or 'representations' or 'constructions'. There was no such thing as History, only histories. Any version of the past would bear the imprint of the teller's own prejudices and preoccupations, and it was therefore the responsibility of the teller to theorise his or her own position so that its intentions and limitations would be made evident to the reader. Interpretation must be aware of its status as interpretation. Second, since there is no such thing as a reliably objective account of the past, history is seen as a form of narrative, and thus a kind of fiction. At the same time, since fiction has all kinds of political and ideological implications, it is seen as a form of history. The boundaries between literature and fiction are blurred. Literature is no longer a special, transcendent category. Third, since there is no single, pure version of the past but only a series of conflicting versions, the official version is ratified not by its degree of truth but its capacity to express the values and interests of the dominant social group. History, that is, is determined not by truth but by power.

The New Historicist critics' field of inquiry includes not only the period in which the novel is set (May 1642–May 1649) but also the period in which Hawthorne wrote it (the fall of 1849); and it includes the period in which the novel is read and the history of its reception since that too affects the way the novel is read. The aim is not merely to adduce interesting 'background information', but to show how our understanding and appreciation of text can be enhanced by our knowledge of context. The consideration of context raises questions about the reasons for the various elaborations, distortions, suppressions or omissions of historical detail that occur in the fictional process. And there is the added question of the extent to which the intertextuality is deliberate or unconscious. Do the manipulations of history serve ideological, psychological or artistic purposes?

In an essay entitled '"The Woman's Own Choice": Sex, Metaphor, and the Puritan "Sources" of *The Scarlet Letter*', Michael Colacurcio sets out to examine Hawthorne's engagement with the theological politics of John Winthrop's *Journal* (an eyewitness account of the times in which the novel is set), and indeed with 'the entire context of Puritan thought'. His reading insists on the potent reality and the equally powerful metaphor of sexuality in a tale of unruly love in an ideally lawful Puritan 'utopia'.

Winthrop's *Journal* is invoked as 'prime and obvious source' of both Hawthorne's knowledge of the historical background and of the novel's essential themes. What Hawthorne found there was 'an extreme political anxiety at the heart of the Puritan system . . . a world of flux' which is reflected in the disagreements hinted at in the chapters of Hester's exposure and judgement. Colacurcio interprets Hawthorne's famous historical 'mistake' in making Bellingham and not Winthrop governor at the time of Hester's arraignment as a 'keen historical irony', in the light of the fact that at the time Bellingham had been voted out of office, in May 1642, 'for conduct not so different from Hester's own'. 'At the very least', Colacurcio comments, 'the "matter of Bellingham" reminds us just how literally sexual are the historical matters that lie at the "source" of *The Scarlet Letter*'. Colacurcio further notes that the novel begins at 'the one moment when much of colonial New England seemed to have sex on its official and conscious mind' – a reference to 'Bellingham's other sex scandal of 1641–2', when he and the other Puritan fathers, called upon to adjudicate in a case of sexual abuse of children, revealed themselves utterly unfit to deal with the problem: 'The reader of *The Scarlet Letter* is forced to conclude that the men who judge Hester do not appear to know what they are talking about; and that the famous displacement of Winthrop by Bellingham means to call attention to this fact'. Thus, Hester is seen to pose a problem which her particular world does not know how to address, let alone solve. In Colacurcio's reading, the novel appears, not as a moralistic reflection on the consequences of sin or as a psychological analysis of guilt, but rather as 'a speculative probing of the power of sexual figures to structure religious ideology and confuse natural experience'.[3]

One such figure derives from Winthrop, and it is the typology of pauline marriage which he uses to define the relationship between 'liberty' and 'authority'. In Winthrop's idealised Puritan 'City upon a

Hill', law was just like love; liberty only had meaning insofar as it 'is maintained and exercised in a way of subjection to authority'. The distinguishing mark of Winthrop's New World citizen-saint, says Colacurcio, was the ability 'to love the law as the unfallen Eve had once loved the mated partner of her own Edenic soul: or, as the figure takes its final flight, as the liberated soul will always love its saving Christ, that one promiscuous bridegroom-lover of all truly gracious souls'.

■ At issue, all along, has been something beyond the more than Eve-like 'forwardness' of Hester's unruly female sexuality, flaunted however literally in the 'embroidery' of human art. Deeper down, all along, has lurked the problem of her imperfect subjection to the 'easy and sweet authority' of those who teach that, under the terms of New England's special covenant, all valid human willing is but a 'true wife', who 'accounts her subjection her honor and freedom, and would not think her condition safe and free but in her subjection to . . . the authority of Christ, her king and husband.' No wonder the narrator finds Hester's outward 'humility' so dangerously deceptive; no wonder he portentously concludes that her 'scarlet letter had not done its office.' Its failure is clearly a failure of metaphor. For, given her 'own choice', this woman will always choose her own literal lover before any version of Winthrop's figurative husband, even in hell.[4] □

Larry J. Reynolds, in his essay '*The Scarlet Letter* and Revolutions Abroad' (1985) turned his attention not only to the period in which the novel is set, but also to the period in which it was written. Reynolds aims to show that 'a strong reactionary spirit' underlies Hawthorne's novel, which he sees as reflecting Hawthorne's fear that the European revolutionary turmoil of 1848 (the year before the writing of *The Scarlet Letter*) might spread to America.

■ When Hawthorne wrote *The Scarlet Letter* in the fall of 1849, the fact and idea of revolution were much on his mind. In 'The Custom-House' sketch, while forewarning the reader of the darkness in the story to follow, he explains that 'this uncaptivating effect is perhaps due to the period of hardly accomplished revolution and still seething turmoil, in which the story shaped itself.' His explicit reference is to his recent ouster from the Salem Custom House, his 'beheading' as he calls it, but we know that the death of his mother and anxiety about where and how he would support his family added to his sense of upheaval. Lying behind all these referents, however, are additional ones that have gone unnoticed: actual revolutions, past and present, which Hawthorne had been reading about and pondering for almost twenty consecutive months. These provided the political context for

The Scarlet Letter and shaped the structure, characterizations, and themes of the work.

I

ROME YET UNCONQUERED! FRANCE TRANQUIL. LEDRU-ROLLIN NOT TAKEN. THE HUNGARIANS TRIUMPH! GREAT BATTLE NEAR RAAB! THE AUSTRIANS AND RUSSIANS BEATEN. CONFLICTS AT PETERWARDEIN AND JORDANOW. SOUTHERN GERMANY REPUBLICAN. BATTLE WITH THE PRUSSIANS AT MANHEIM. RESULT UNDECIDED. These are the headlines of the *New York Tribune* for 5 July 1849; and because they are typical, they suggest the excitement and interest generated in America by the wave upon wave of revolution that swept across Europe during the years 1848 and 1849. In Naples, Sicily, Paris, Berlin, Vienna, Milan, Venice, Munich, Rome, and nearly all the other cities and states of continental Europe, rulers and their unpopular ministers were overthrown, most notably Louis Philippe and Guizot in France, Ferdinand I and Metternich in Austria, and Pope Pius IX and Rossi in the Papal States. Meanwhile revolutionary leaders such as Lamartine, Kossuth, and Mazzini became heroes in American eyes as they tried to institute representative governments and alleviate the poverty and oppression that precipitated the revolutions. By the fall of 1849, all of the fledgling republics had been crushed by conservative and reactionary forces, and this fact explains in part why the influence of the revolutions upon *The Scarlet Letter* in particular and the American literary renaissance in general has been overlooked. Unlike the American Revolution (whose influence has received thorough study), the revolutions of 1848–49 came to naught, making them appear inconsequential in retrospect. In addition, the excitement generated in America, while intense, was short lived and soon forgotten; national attention soon turned to the turmoil generated by the slavery issue, which obscured Europe's role as the previous focus of this attention. A third explanation for the neglect is that studies of the literature of this period have tended to focus on native themes and materials. Concomitantly, reference works such as James D. Hart's *Oxford Companion to American Literature* and John C. Gerber's *Twentieth Century Interpretations of 'The Scarlet Letter'* have provided chronological indexes that correlate only American history with the lives and works of American authors, despite the fact that the major newspapers of the day devoted three-fourths of their front-page coverage to European events. Although the European revolutions all failed, from the spring of 1848 to the fall of 1849, the American public displayed its interest and sympathy by mass gatherings, parades, fireworks, proclamations, speeches, and constant newspaper coverage, which swelled with the arrival of each steamer. Members of the American literati, Hawthorne's friends among them, also responded with ardor. To celebrate the French Revolution, Lowell wrote two poems, 'Ode to France, 1848,' in which he linked American Freedom with the fires burning in the streets of Paris, and 'To Lamartine, 1848,' in which he sang the praises of the poet-statesman who headed the new provisional government. Evert Duyckinck, Hawthorne's editor at Wiley & Putnam's, declared himself 'en rapport' with the French Revolution; and S.G. Goodrich, Hawthorne's former publisher, who witnessed events in Paris, wrote an enthusiastic account for the *Boston Courier*. Emerson, who visited Paris in May 1848, expressed reservations about the posturings of the mobs in the streets but was impressed by Lamartine and sympathized with the social activists. 'The deep sincerity of the speakers,' he wrote, 'who are agitating social not political questions, and who are studying how to secure a fair share of bread to every man, and to get the God's justice done through the land, is very good to hear.'[5]

Margaret Fuller, who served as one model for Hester, became, as is well known, more intently engaged in the European revolutions than any of her countrymen. As a witness to the rise and fall of the Roman Republic, she wrote impassioned letters to the *New York Tribune* praising the efforts of her friend Mazzini, describing the defense of Rome, and pleading for American support. 'The struggle is now fairly, thoroughly commenced between the principle of democracy and the old powers, no longer legitimate,' she wrote in the spring of 1849. 'Every struggle made by the old tyrannies, all their Jesuitical deceptions, their rapacity, their imprisonments and executions of the most generous men, only sow more dragon's teeth; the crop shoots up daily more and more plenteous.' . . .[6]

Although Margaret Fuller's former devotee Sophia Hawthorne (in her dutifully childlike manner) expressed approval of the republican successes in Europe as they were occurring in 1848, her husband most likely shared neither her optimism nor the enthusiasm of their literary friends, particularly Fuller. In fact, the book that he wrote in the wake of the revolutions in 1849 indicates that they reaffirmed his scepticism about revolution and reform and inspired a strong reactionary spirit which underlies the work.

Revolution had been a fearful thing in Hawthorne's mind for some time, even though he found the ends it wrought at times admirable. Violent reform and the behavior of mobs particularly disturbed him, as the final scene of 'My Kinsman, Major Molineux' makes clear. This story may celebrate the beginnings of a new democratic era, as some have suggested, but it cannot be denied that Molineux is presented as a noble victim of a hellish mob. 'On they went,' Hawthorne wrote, 'like fiends that throng in mockery round some dead potentate, mighty no more, but majestic still in his agony.' Similarly, in 'The Custom-House' sketch, Hawthorne presents himself as the victim of another 'bloodthirsty' mob, the Whigs, who, acting out of a 'fierce and bitter spirit of malice and revenge,' have struck off his head with the political guillotine and ignominiously kicked it about. This presentation, humorous in tone but serious in intent, gives *The Scarlet Letter* its alternate title of 'THE POSTHUMOUS PAPERS OF A DECAPITATED SURVEYOR' and foreshadows the use and treatment of revolutionary imagery in the novel proper.

This imagery, of course, is drawn from the French Revolution of 1789, which was at the forefront of Hawthorne's mind for several reasons. First of all, the spectacular excesses of that revolution provided the language and metaphors used by conservatives to describe events in 1848–49.

[. . .]

Predictably, the American press drew careless comparisons between the European revolutions and the American political scene. When Zachary Taylor began his series of political appointments in the spring and summer of 1849, they were reported in the Democratic papers as revolutionary acts, as symbolic beheadings of Democratic party members. Some seven times in May and June, for example, the *Boston Post* printed, in conjunction with the announcement of a political appointment and removal, a small drawing presumably of General Taylor standing beside a guillotine, puffing a cigar, surrounded by heads (presumably of Democrats) at his feet. One of these drawings appeared on 11 June and on the following day, a letter to the editor appeared objecting to Hawthorne's removal from the Salem Custom House. 'This is one of the most heartless acts of this heartless administration,' the anonymous writer declared. 'The head of the poet and the scholar is stricken off to gratify and reward some greedy partizan! . . . There stands, at the guillotine, beside the headless trunk of a pure minded, faithful and well deserving officer, sacrificed to the worth of party proscription, Gen. Zachary Taylor, now President.' As Arlin Turner has pointed out, this letter was probably a source of Hawthorne's 'beheading' metaphor;[7] however, behind the reference were two years of revolutionary events in Europe, two years of revolutionary rhetoric and imagery.

II

Such rhetoric and imagery appeared not only in the newspapers, of course, but also in contemporary books, some of which dealt with revolution in a serious historical manner. Although *The Scarlet Letter* has often been praised for its fidelity to New England history, the central setting of the novel, the scaffold, is, I believe, an historical inaccuracy intentionally used by Hawthorne to develop the theme of revolution. The Puritans occasionally sentenced a malefactor to stand upon a shoulder-high block or upon the ladder of the gallows (at times with a halter about the neck),[8] but in none of the New England histories Hawthorne used as sources (viz., Felt, Snow, Mather, Hutchinson, and Winthrop) are these structures called scaffolds. In fact, I have been unable to find the word 'scaffold' in them. The common instruments of punishment in the Massachusetts Bay Colony were, as Hawthorne shows in 'Endicott and the Red Cross,' the whipping post, the stocks, and the pillory. (The gallows, located in Boston at the end of town, was used for hangings and serious public humiliations.) Although Hawthorne in his romance identifies the scaffold as part of the pillory, his narrator and his characters refer to it by the former term alone some twenty-six times, calling it the scaffold of the pillory only four times and the pillory only once.

As early as 1557 and then later with increasing frequency during the first French Revolution, the word 'scaffold' served as a synecdoche for a public beheading – by the executioner's axe or the guillotine. And, because of its role in the regicides of overthrown kings, the word acquired powerful political associations, which it still retains. When King Charles I was beheaded with an axe following the successful rebellion led by Cromwell Andrew Marvell in his 'An Horatian Ode' used the word in the tribute to his king . . . One hundred and forty-four years later, when Louis XVI became a liability to the new French republic, he too, of course, mounted what was termed the 'scaffold' and there became one of the victims of the new device being advocated by Dr. Guillotin. The association of a scaffold with revolution and beheading, particularly the beheading of Charles I and Louis XVI, explains, I think, why Hawthorne uses it as his central and dominant setting. It links the narrator of 'The Custom-House' sketch with the two main characters in the romance proper, and it raises their common predicaments above the plane of the personal into the helix of history.

Hawthorne's desire to connect his narrative with historic revolutions abroad is further shown by the time frame he uses. The opening scenes of the novel take place in May l642 and the closing ones in May 1649. These dates coincide almost exactly with those of the English Civil War fought between King Charles I and his Puritan Parliament. Hawthorne was familiar with histories of this subject and had recently (June 1848) checked out of the Salem Atheneum François Guizot's *History of the English Revolution of l640, Commonly Called the Great Rebellion* . . .

Examination of the simultaneity between fictional events in *The Scarlet Letter* and historical events in America and England verifies that the 1642–1649 time frame for events in the romance was carefully chosen to enhance the treatment of revolutionary themes. When Hester Prynne is led from the prison by the beadle who cries, 'Make way, good people, make way, in the King's name,' less than a month has passed since Charles's Puritan Parliament had sent him what amounted to a declaration of war. Five months later, in October, 1642, the first battle between Roundheads and Cavaliers was fought at Edgehill, and word of the open hostilities reached America in December. Then and in the years that followed, the Bay Colony fasted and prayed for victory by Parliament, but these became times of political anxiety and stress in America as well as England . . . By the final scenes of the novel, when Arthur is deciding to die as a martyr, Charles I has just been beheaded (on 30 January 1649); thus, when Chillingworth sarcastically thanks Arthur for his prayers, calling them 'golden recompense' and 'the current gold coin of the New Jerusalem, with the King's own mint-mark on them,' Hawthorne adds to Chillingworth's irony with his own. Furthermore, given the novel's time frame, the tableau of Arthur bowing 'his head forward on the cushions of the pulpit, at the close of his Election Sermon,' while Hester stands waiting beside the scaffold, radiates with ominous import, particularly when one recalls that Arthur is not a graduate of Cambridge, as most of the Puritan ministers of New England were, but rather of Oxford, the center of Laudian and Royalist sympathies and the place of refuge for King Charles during the Revolution.

By thus setting events in an age when 'men of the sword had overthrown nobles and kings,' Hawthorne provides a potent historical backdrop for the revolutionary and counter-revolutionary battles fought, with shifting allegiances, among the four main characters and the Puritan leadership. Furthermore, his battle imagery, such as Governor Bellingham's armor and Pearl's simulated slaying of the Puritan children, draws upon and reflects the actual warfare abroad and thus illuminates the struggles being fought on social, moral, and metaphysical grounds in Boston.

Bearing upon the novel perhaps even more than its connections with the English 'Rebellion' and its attendant regicide are its connections with the first French Revolution and the execution of Louis XVI. In the romance itself, Hawthorne first alludes to one tie when he describes the scaffold in the opening scenes; 'it constituted,' he writes, 'a portion of a penal machine, which . . . was held, in the old time, to be as effectual an agent in the promotion of good citizenship, as ever was the guillotine among the terrorists of France.' This allusion may be derived from the imagery appearing, as discussed above, in the contemporary press; but it is also shaped, in a more profound way, by an overlooked source of *The Scarlet Letter*, Alphonse de Lamartine's *History of the Girondists*, a history of the first French Revolution published in France in 1847, translated into English by H.T. Ryde and published in the United States in three volumes in 1847–48.

. . . Lamartine was not a scholarly historian, and his account of the first French Revolution is an imaginative and dramatic construct that gains much of its power from its sympathetic treatment of Louis XVI and its suspenseful narrative structure, which includes a tableau at the scaffold as its climactic scene. Throughout the first volume and a half of his history, Lamartine, while detailing the political infighting of the National Assembly and their struggle with the king for power, generates sympathy for Louis . . . In Volume II, Lamartine shows the situation of the royal family becoming more desperate and the king acquiring strength and character as his fate unfolds. In terms a decapitated surveyor could appreciate, Lamartine observes that 'all the faults of preceding administrations, all the vices of kings, all the shame of courts, all the griefs of the people, were accumulated on his head and marked his innocent brow for the expiation of many ages'. 'He was the scape-goat of olden time, that bore the sins of all' . . . The rest of Volume II and all of III detail the excesses of the Revolution: the assassination of Marat, the Reign of Terror, the wave upon wave of bloodletting, and so on, all of which become horrifyingly repetitive.

Lamartine's stirring treatment of revolutionary events and political martyrdom and especially his unprecedented use of the scaffold as both a dramatic setting and a unifying structural device lead one to speculate that Hawthorne may have read this work before he wrote *The Scarlet Letter*; however, speculation is unnecessary. He did. The records of the Salem Atheneum reveal that on 13 September 1849, he checked out the first two volumes of Lamartine's *History*. Moreover, Sophia Hawthorne's letters to her sister and mother, combined with Hawthorne's notebook entries, reveal, as no biographer has yet pointed out, that it was about ten days later, most likely between 21 September and 25 September, that Hawthorne began work in earnest on *The Scarlet Letter*. On 27 September he checked out the third volume of Lamartine's *History* . . . This correlation in dates plus Hawthorne's allusions to the terrorists of France suggests that what has become one of the most celebrated settings in American literature, the scaffold of *The Scarlet Letter*, was taken from the Place de la Revolution of eighteenth-century Paris, as described by Lamartine, and transported to the Marketplace of seventeenth-century Boston, where it became the focal point of Hawthorne's narrative. Along with it came, most likely, a reinforced scepticism about violent reform.

III

Recognition that revolutionary struggle stirred at the front of Hawthorne's consciousness as he wrote *The Scarlet Letter* not only accounts for many structural and thematic details in the novel but also explains some of the apparent inconsistencies in his treatment of his characters, especially Hester and Arthur. The issue of the degree and nature of Hawthorne's sympathies in the novel has been debated for years, at times heatedly, and I have no hope of resolving the debate here; however, I think the revolutionary context of events provides a key for sorting out Hawthorne's sympathies, or more accurately those of his narrator (whose biases closely resemble Hawthorne's). The narrator, as a member of a toppled established order, an *ancien regime* so to speak, possesses instincts that are conservative and anti-revolutionary, consistently so, but the individuals he regards undergo considerable change, thus evoking inconsistent attitudes on his part. Specifically, when Hester or Arthur battle to maintain or regain their rightful place in the social or spiritual order, the narrator sympathizes with them; when they become revolutionary instead and attempt to overthrow an established order, he becomes unsympathetic. The scaffold serves to clarify the political and spiritual issues raised by events in the novel, and the decapitated surveyor of the Custom House, not surprisingly, identifies with whoever becomes a martyr upon it.

Hawthorne's use of the scaffold as a structural device has long been recognized; in 1944 Leland Schubert pointed out that the novel 'is built around the scaffold. At the beginning, in the middle and at the end of the story the scaffold is the dominating point.'[9] The way in which the scaffold serves as a touchstone for the narrator's sympathies, however, has not been fully explored, particularly with reference to the matter of revolution.

As every reader notices, at the beginning of the story, Hester is accorded much sympathy. Her beauty, her courage, her pride, all receive emphasis; and the scaffold, meant to degrade her, elevates her, figuratively as well as literally. The narrator presents her as an image of Divine Maternity, and more importantly, as a member of the old order of nobility suffering at the hands of a vulgar mob. Her recollection of her paternal home, 'poverty-stricken,' but 'retaining a half-obliterated shield of arms over the portal' establishes her link to aristocracy. Furthermore, although she has been sentenced by the Puritan magistrates, her worst enemies are the coarse, beefy, pitiless 'gossips' who surround the scaffold and argue that she should be hanged or at least branded on the forehead. The magistrates, whom Hawthorne characterizes as 'good men, just, and sage' have shown clemency in their sentence, and that clemency is unpopular with the chorus of matrons who apparently speak for the people.

Through the first twelve chapters, half of the book, the narrator's sympathies remain with Hester, for she continues to represent, like Charles I, Louis XVI, and Surveyor Hawthorne, a fallen aristocratic order struggling in defense of her rights against an antagonistic populace. The poor, the well-to-do, adults, children, lay-men, clergy, all torment her in various ways; but she, the narrator tells us, 'was patient, – a martyr, indeed.' It is Pearl, of course, who anticipates what Hester will become – a revolutionary – and reveals the combative streak her mother possesses. 'The warfare of Hester's spirit,' Hawthorne writes, 'was perpetuated in Pearl,' and this is shown by Pearl's throwing stones at the Puritan children ('the most intolerant brood that ever lived'), her smiting and uprooting the weeds that represent these children, and her splashing the Governor himself with water. 'She never created a friend, but seemed always to be sowing broadcast the dragon's teeth, whence sprung a harvest of armed enemies, against whom she rushed to battle'. . .

Hester's own martial spirit comes to the fore in the confrontation with Bellingham, but here she fights only to maintain the *status quo* and thus keeps the narrator's sympathies. She visits the Governor not to attack him in any way but to defend her right to raise Pearl. Undaunted by Bellingham's shining armor, which 'was not meant for mere idle show,' Hester triumphs, because she has the natural order upon her side and because Arthur comes to her aid. Drawing Pearl forcibly into her arms, she confronts 'the old Puritan magistrate with almost a fierce expression'; and Arthur, prompted into action by Hester's veiled threats, responds like a valiant Cavalier. His voice, as he speaks on her behalf, is 'sweet, tremulous, but powerful, insomuch that the hall re-echoed, and the hollow armour rang with it.'

In the central chapters of the novel, when the narrator turns his attention toward Arthur and evidences antipathy toward him, it is not only because of the minister's obvious hypocrisy but also because of the intellectual change that he has undergone at Chillingworth's hands. Subtly, Arthur becomes radicalized and anticipates Hester's ventures into the realm of speculative and revolutionary thought. 'There was a fascination for the minister,' Hawthorne writes, 'in the company of the man of science, in whom he recognized an intellectual cultivation of no moderate depth or scope; together with a range and freedom of ideas, that he would have vainly looked for among the members of his own profession.' And if Arthur is the victim of the leech's herbs and poisons, he is also a victim of more deadly intellectual brews as well. The central scene of the novel, Arthur's 'vigil' on the scaffold, is inspired, apparently, by the 'liberal views' he has begun to entertain. 'On one of those ugly nights,' we are told, 'the minister started from his chair. A new thought had struck him.' This thought is to stand on the scaffold in the middle of the night, but by so doing he joins the ranks of Satan's rebellious legions. As he indulges in 'the mockery of penitence' upon the scaffold, his guilt becomes 'heaven-defying' and reprehensible, in the narrator's eyes. Rather than seeking to reestablish his moral force, which has been 'abased into more than childish weakness,' Arthur, in his imagination, mocks the Reverend Wilson, the people of Boston, and God himself. Furthermore, as Henry Nash Smith has pointed out, the 'lurid playfulness' Arthur indulges in upon the scaffold, calls into question 'the very idea of a solid, orderly universe existing independently of consciousness.'[10] The questioning remains Arthur's, however, not the narrator's, and the scene itself, with the scaffold as its setting, serves to reveal the cowardice and licentiousness Arthur has been reduced to. The blazing A in the sky, which Arthur sees 'addressed to himself alone,' marks Governor Winthrop's death, according to the townspeople, and thus further emphasizes (by its reference to Winthrop's famous leadership and integrity) the nadir Arthur has reached by his indulgence in defiant thought and behavior.

The transformation Hester undergoes in the middle of the novel (which only appears to be from sinner to saint) is a stronger version of that which Arthur has undergone at her husband's hands; she too becomes, like the French revolutionaries of 1789 and the Italian revolutionaries of 1849, a radical thinker engaged in a revolutionary struggle against an established political-religious order. And as such, she loses the narrator's sympathies (while gaining those of most readers). The transformation begins with her regaining, over the course of seven years, the goodwill of the public, which 'was inclined to show its former victim a more benign countenance than she cared to be favored with, or, perchance, than she deserved.' The rulers of the community, who 'were longer in acknowledging the influence of Hester's good qualities than the people,' become, as time passes, not her antagonists but rather the objects of her antagonism. We first see her impulse to challenge their authority when Chillingworth tells her that the magistrates have discussed allowing her to remove the scarlet letter from her bosom. 'It lies not in the pleasure of the magistrates to take off this badge,' she tells him. Similarly, when she meets Arthur in the forest several days later, she subversively asks, 'What hast thou to do with all these iron men and their opinions? They have kept thy better part in bondage too long already!'.

The new direction Hester's combativeness has taken is political in nature and flows from her isolation and indulgence in speculation. In a passage often quoted, but seldom viewed as consistent with the rest of the novel, because of its unsympathetic tone, the narrator explains that Hester Prynne 'had wandered, without rule or guidance, in a moral wilderness. . . . Shame, Despair, Solitude! These had been her teachers, – stern and wild ones, – and they had made her strong, but taught her much amiss.' Hester's ventures into new areas of thought link her, significantly, with the overthrow of governments and the overthrow of 'ancient prejudice, wherewith was linked much of ancient principle.' 'She assumed,' the narrator points out, 'a freedom of speculation, then common enough on the other side of the Atlantic, but which our forefathers, had they known of it, would have held to be a deadlier crime than that stigmatized by the scarlet letter.' Referring for the second time to the antinomian Anne Hutchinson, whom Hawthorne in another work had treated with little sympathy, the narrator speculates that if Pearl had not become the object of her mother's devotion, Hester 'might, and not improbably would, have suffered death from the stern tribunals of the period, for attempting to undermine the foundations of the Puritan establishment.'

Although Hester does not lead a political-religious revolt against the Puritan leadership, these speculations are quite relevant to the action which follows, for Hawthorne shows her radicalism finding an outlet in her renewed relationship with Arthur, which assumes revolutionary form. When they hold their colloquy in the forest, during which she reenacts her role as Eve the subversive temptress, we learn that 'the whole seven years of outlaw and ignominy had been little other than a preparation for this very hour.' What Hester accomplishes during this hour (other than raising the reader's hopes) is once again to overthrow Arthur's system and undermine his loyalty to the Puritan community and the Puritan God. She establishes a temporary provisional government within him, so to speak, which fails to sustain itself. Although Hester obviously loves Arthur and seeks only their happiness together, her plan, which most readers heartily endorse, challenges, in the narrator's eyes, the social order of the community and the spiritual order of the universe, and thus earns his explicit disapproval.

When Hester tells Arthur that the magistrates have kept his better part in bondage, the narrator makes it clear that it is Arthur's better part that has actually kept his worse and lawless self imprisoned. For some time the prison has proved sound, but 'the breach which guilt has once made into the human soul is never, in this mortal state, repaired,' the narrator declares. 'It may be watched and guarded; so that the enemy shall not force his way again into the citadel. . . . But there is still the ruined wall.' Thus, as Hawthorne draws upon the popular revolutionary imagery of 1848–49 to present Hester as a goddess of Liberty leading a military assault, she prevails; however, her victory, like that of the first Bastille day, sets loose forces of anarchy and wickedness. Arthur experiences a 'glow of strange enjoyment' after he agrees to flee with her, but to clarify the moral dimensions of this freedom, Hawthorne adds, 'It was the exhilarating effect – upon a prisoner just escaped from the dungeon of his own heart – of breathing the wild, free atmosphere of an unredeemed, unchristianized, lawless region.'

Unlike the earlier struggle that Hester and Arthur had fought together to maintain the *status quo* – the traditional relationship between mother and child – this struggle accomplishes something more pernicious: 'a revolution in the sphere of thought and feeling.' And because it does, it receives unsympathetic treatment. 'In truth,' Hawthorne writes, 'nothing short of a total change of dynasty and moral code, in that interior kingdom, was adequate to account for the impulses now communicated to the unfortunate and startled minister. At every step he was incited to do some strange, wild, wicked thing or other, with a sense that it would be at once involuntary and intentional.'

Donald A. Ringe among others has suggested that this abrupt change in Arthur's system is beneficent, a fortunate fall, in other words, that gives him insight and powers of expression;[11] however, the narrative emphasizes that it is unfortunate and unholy. Arthur's impulses to blaspheme, curse, and lead innocence astray are a stronger version of those seen during his vigil, and they confirm the narrator's assertion that the minister has acquired 'sympathy and fellowship with wicked mortals and the world of perverted spirits.' It is important to notice also that the success of Arthur's sermon, which is so eloquent, so filled with compassion and wisdom, depends ultimately not upon his new revolutionary impulses but upon older counter-revolutionary sources that are spiritually conservative. He draws upon the 'energy – or say, rather, the inspiration which had held him up, until he should have delivered the sacred message that brought its own strength along with it from heaven.'

The final change of heart and spirit that Arthur undergoes and that leads him to his death on the scaffold is foreshadowed by events in the marketplace prior to his sermon. There the exhibition of broadswords upon the scaffold plus Pearl's sense of 'impending revolution' suggests that while the minister's better self has been overthrown, it will reassert itself shortly. The procession in which Arthur appears dramatizes the alternative to the lawless freedom Hester has offered. Here, as Michael Davitt Bell has observed, we have 'the greatest tribute in all of Hawthorne's writing to the nobility of the founders.'[12] The people, we are told, had bestowed their reverence 'on the white hair and venerable brow of age; on long-tried integrity; on solid wisdom and sad-colored experience; on endowments of that grave and weighty order, which gives the idea of permanence, and comes under the general definition of respectability.' These are the qualities that distinguish Bradstreet, Endicott, Dudley, Bellingham, and their compeers. And, although we are not told who the new governor is (it was Endicott), we know that his election represents orderly change, in contrast to the rebellion and regicide that has recently occurred in England. 'Today,' Hester tells Pearl, 'a new man is beginning to rule over them,' and, in harmony with this event, Arthur acts to reestablish his place within the order of the community and within the order of the kingdom of God.

During the sermon Arthur seems to regain some of his spiritual stature and is described as an angel, who, 'in his passage to the skies, had shaken his bright wings over the people for an instant, – at once a shadow and a splendor.' Because Arthur is still a hypocrite, considerable irony exists within this description; however, when the minister walks to and mounts the scaffold, the narrator's irony turns to sincerity. Arthur attempts, before he dies, to regain God's favor, and as he nears the scaffold, where Hester and Chillingworth will both oppose his effort to confess, we are told that 'it was hardly a man with life in him, that tottered on his path so nervelessly, yet tottered, and did not fall!' The exclamation mark indicates the double sense of 'fall' Hawthorne wishes to suggest, and at the end Arthur seems to escape from the provisional control over him that both Chillingworth and Hester have had.

'Is not this better than what we dreamed of in the forest?' he asks Hester, and although she replies 'I know not! I know not!' the revolutionary context of the novel, the bias toward restoration and order, indicate we are supposed to agree that it is. Arthur's final scene upon the scaffold mirrors Hester's first scene there, even though he proceeds from the church whereas she had proceeded from the prison. But, unlike Hester, Arthur through humility and faith seems to achieve peace, whereas she, through 'the combative energy of her character,' had achieved only 'a kind of lurid triumph'. In the final scaffold scene, Pearl acts as an ethical agent once again and emphasizes Hawthorne's themes about peace and battle, order and revolt. At the moment of his death, Arthur kisses Pearl, and the tears she then sheds are 'the pledge that she would grow up amid human joy and sorrow, nor for ever do battle with the world, but be a woman in it.' In what seems to be a reward for her docility, she marries into European nobility (thereby accomplishing a restoration of the ties with aristocracy her maternal relatives once enjoyed); similarly, Hester at last, we are told in a summary, forsakes her radicalism and recognizes that the woman who would lead the reform movements of the future and establish women's rights must be less 'stained with sin,' less 'bowed down with shame' than she. This woman must be 'lofty, pure, and beautiful, and wise, moreover, not through dusky grief, but the ethereal medium of joy.'

More than one reader has correctly surmised that this ending to the novel constitutes a veiled compliment to Hawthorne's little Dove, Sophia, and a veiled criticism of Margaret Fuller, America's foremost advocate of women's rights and, at the time, suffering from a sullied reputation due to gossip about her child and questionable marriage. Hawthorne's long and ambivalent relationship with Fuller and his response to her activities as a radical and revolutionary in 1849 had a decided effect upon the novel. There are several parallels which indicate Fuller served as a model for Hester: both had the problem of facing a Puritan society encumbered by a child of questionable legitimacy; both were concerned with social reform and the role of woman in society; both functioned as counsellor and comforter to women; and both had children entitled to use the armorial seals of a non-English noble family. All of these Francis E. Kearns has pointed out;[13] however, a more important parallel Kearns fails to mention is that for Hawthorne both women were associated with the ideas of temptation and revolution, with the figures of Eve and Liberty. Fuller was not only the most intelligent, articulate, and passionate woman Hawthorne had ever spent so many hours alone with, she was also, as he began *The Scarlet Letter*, an ardent revolutionary supporting the overthrow of the most prominent political-religious leader in the world.

Certainly Hawthorne's knowledge of and interest in the New England past were considerable; however, as Thomas Woodson has pointed out, his interest in his contemporary world was far greater than the critical emphases of recent decades would indicate.[14] In his writing of *The Scarlet Letter* he drew upon the issues and rhetoric he was encountering in the present, especially those relating to himself as a public figure. Moreover, he responded strongly and creatively to accounts of foreign revolutions and revolutionaries that he found in the newspapers, the periodicals, and books new to the libraries. Although to most of his countrymen the overthrow of kings and the triumph of republicanism were exhilarating events, to a man of Hawthorne's temperament, the violence, the bloodshed, the extended chaos that accompanied the revolutions of 1848–49 were deeply disturbing. Associated in his own mind with his personal plight, they, along with his reading in Guizot and Lamartine, shaped *The Scarlet Letter* in Burkean ways the reader of today finds difficult to accept. We value too highly Thomas Paine and the rights of woman.[15] □

Jonathan Arac, in his essay, 'The Politics of *The Scarlet Letter*' (1986), sets out to define a relation between *The Scarlet Letter* and the political response to slavery, slavery being 'the issue that agitated American politics most deeply in Hawthorne's time'. Like Reynolds, Arac discovers in Hawthorne's narrative a deeply conservative subtext, an aesthetics of 'indeterminacy' that reflects a politics characterised by inertia, the drive towards knowledge rather than action, and preoccupation with personalities rather than issues. Arac offers a critical evaluation of that indeterminacy in Hawthorne's time and in the present, for, according to Arac, 'it still remains effective both in literature and in politics'. Drawing on the theories of Marx, Walter Benjamin, Foucault and Fredric Jameson, Arac's historical interpretation runs strongly against any hermeneutics of indeterminacy:

■ In arguing for a specific interpretation of *The Scarlet Letter* that is neither authorial in the 'interpretationist' sense nor mystifying, as I find indeterminism, I begin from several concrete problems in our received understanding of Hawthorne. Arlin Turner's standard biography finds Hawthorne almost unique among major American writers in the degree to which he is 'extensively and significantly involved' in 'the affairs of his time.'[16] The chapters on this involvement, however, do little more than detail Hawthorne's role in allocating patronage for Pierce's presidency. The problem is, what state of American politics allows such patronage brokering to count as 'significant'?

Patronage haunts my next problem as well. Students marvel that the author of 'The Custom-House' was in less than three years to write *The Life of Franklin Pierce* – that in the decade following publication of *Mosses from an Old Manse* (1846) Hawthorne held patronage positions for seven years, interrupted by a three-year career as a romancer. The problem is to determine a relation, perhaps even a common ground, between the writing of *The Scarlet Letter* and that of *The Life of Pierce*.

The next related problems also arise from the classroom. Students judge *The Scarlet Letter* an intransitive 'work of art,' unlike, say, *Uncle Tom's Cabin* which is 'propaganda' rather than 'art,' for it aims to change your life. If recent revaluations have shown that *Uncle Tom's Cabin* is also art, may it not be equally important to show that *The Scarlet Letter* is also propaganda – *not* to change your life? I at once draw back from the extremity of this last suggestion. *The Scarlet Letter* aims to produce an invisible change, an internal deepening like that which transforms the letter even as its form remains identical. Stowe, too, aims at an internal change, but she holds that this change would visibly affect your outer actions as well. Both Hawthorne and Stowe situate their work as cultural – not political or legal – but they differ on the relation of culture to the other activities of life. It was not yet taken for granted that literature must be intransitive, useless as well as harmless.

My final problem is that a standard classroom text of *The Scarlet Letter* includes 'historical background' materials, but they all relate to the seventeenth century, not to the nineteenth. Has Hawthorne's art truly achieved a timeless escape from his age? I would expect that even if *The Scarlet Letter* is an antithesis to the frustrations of contemporary political life, an escape from that life in the custom house, compensation for those frustrations, nonetheless the situation being turned from should leave some traces, through which to read a relation between the fiction of the 1640s and the history of around 1850. Such reading starts from the relation of 'The Custom-House' to '*The Scarlet Letter*'.

There is always some doubt what we mean when we say '*The Scarlet Letter*'. Do we mean the book that includes 'The Custom-House,' or do we mean only the twenty-four chapters that follow 'The Custom-House'? *The Scarlet Letter* names both the whole book and one of its parts – as well as the coloured work of printer's art on the title page of the first edition and a major element within the fiction. 'The Custom-House' holds a supplementary position, occupying a space that in its absence would not be recognized as vacant; it adds something gratuitous that was not required and thus destabilizes what it claims to support. So it offers to prove the 'authenticity' of narrative to follow but does so in terms of 'literary propriety,' an appeal to convention rather than a warrant of authenticity. By taking possession through 'The Custom-House' of the (physical) scarlet letter as his property, the author of 'The Custom-House' personalizes the narrative. The many correspondences between the authorial figure of 'The Custom-House' and the characters of '*The Scarlet Letter*' – for example, the disapproval shown to both Hester and Hawthorne by the Puritan authorities, the dual status Dimmesdale and Hawthorne share of a passionate inner life wholly at odds with the 'official' public position, the work both author and Chillingworth do as analysts of character – allow us to naturalize the presence of 'The Custom-House' and justify its excess. But they also undermine the self-sufficiency of '*The Scarlet Letter*' – making it an allegory of the writer's situation in 1850. We could say that Hester emerges from the Custom-House as much as she issues from prison; we may even argue that 'The Custom-House' – as the prehistory of the scarlet letter (the thing itself) – stands in lieu of narrating the love affair between Hester and Dimmesdale. Either would suffice to explain how Hester came to stand marked on the scaffold. 'The Custom-House' concludes that the public character of the 'decapitated surveyor' – Hawthorne in the newspapers – is only 'figurative' and that Hawthorne's 'real human being' is a 'literary man.' By the same logic, we may conclude that the public life of Hester – in the novel – is also only figurative, and its reality is Hawthorne's literary life.

A recurrent mood of 'The Custom-House,' emphatic near its end, is harried dejection – like that which sends Ishmael off whaling – which leads Hawthorne to welcome his 'execution' in the change of administrations, as if a man planning suicide had 'the good hap to be murdered.' From this mood issues forth *The Scarlet Letter*, only to end where it began, in the mood of the questions the heartsick women of Massachusetts ask Hester: 'why they were so wretched and what the remedy.' From the man alone in 1850 to the women together in the seventeenth century, there is nothing to do to become happy: With luck you'll be decapitated, or else 'the angel and apostle of the coming revelation' will appear. The only remedy is patient trust in the future. *The Scarlet Letter* does, however, propose a specific source for the misery: Hester once did something, which both found her a child and lost its father – a situation like that of Hawthorne's own family as he grew up with his widowed mother. *The Scarlet Letter* ends with the death of Hester, and its writing began with the death of Hawthorne's own mother. The difference is that Mrs. Hawthorne committed no crime in marrying a mariner who then happened to die in Surinam of yellow fever. Hawthorne's novel transforms his life situation by adding accountable guilt. A complex social fact – involving American trade relations in the Caribbean, the inadequacy of mosquito control, the conditions of medical knowledge – is turned into a crime. Something that might require political action – as it did to empower public health undertaking in the nineteenth century – becomes a matter for ethical judgment and psychological reflection.

A comparable personalization is crucial for the politics of *The Scarlet Letter*. The attempt to separate the artwork from pragmatic concerns, the programmatically willed alienation of the artist that Hawthorne achieved, function within a political world that allowed issues no part in the discourse of the two established parties. Hawthorne's criticism of the 'official' life of the Custom House, its distance from any concerns that could be considered real, is accurate.

Consider a major rhetorical motif in 'The Custom-House,' the insistence that *The Scarlet Letter* arises in all its gloom from an act of revolutionary victimization, the decapitation of the headless surveyor, who now writes as a 'politically dead man.' This joke hinges on a common hyperbole, that of likening patronage dismissals to acts of French revolutionary terror. Franklin Pierce, a man of no linguistic originality, used the figure in a speech of 1841 that Hawthorne quotes,[17] and Turner suggests that Hawthorne himself adapted the figure from an article in the news (p.181). The particular wit of the joke is that patronage changes are not 'revolution' but carry out the etymologically related action of 'rotation' in office: Revolutionary principle has become rotatory patronage. Whether one is in office or out, one is as good as politically dead, for the officeholder, Hawthorne argues, 'does not share in the united effort of mankind'. Paradoxically, then, public office is private. In a polity that allows for no significant action, politics can only be the corrupting hunt for spoils.

As politics became merely officeholding and patronage brokering, articulated, speculative, passionate intelligence had withdrawn from the ranks of the Democrats and Whigs. The sketches of 'official' character that occupy Hawthorne in the avowedly antipolitical literary practice of 'The Custom-House' correspond to his occupation during his maximal political involvement. Turner specifies Hawthorne's political prowess as 'manipulation' and 'understanding of the men involved' (p.254). In *The Life of Pierce*, Hawthorne's claim to authority is knowledge of 'the individual,' his capacity to read Pierce's 'character' and judge his 'motives' (p.349). This emphasis on character is not the idiosyncrasy of a 'literary man'; the Whigs ran exactly the same campaign on their side. The 1852 campaign allowed no issue but personality.

We know the 1850s as a turning point in American political history: The Whig Party was about to disappear; the long Democratic majority, to become a sectionalized and ethnicized minority; and the Republicans were about to emerge and rule for three generations. The Union was about to split and be reunited by bloody conquest. And in all this, slavery was crucial. All this, however, was unthinkable to the still dominant established parties, especially between the Compromise of 1850 and the Kansas-Nebraska troubles of 1854, an interlude of paralytic calm that seemed to mark the extinction of abolitionist and free-soil possibilities for transforming the national polity. When Charles Sumner entered the Senate in 1851, old Thomas Hart Benton took him aside and explained that he had 'come up on the stage too late, sir. Not only have our great men passed away, but the great issues have been settled also. The last of these was the National Bank.'

Consensus reigned between the two established parties. *The Life of Pierce* declared that no 'great and radical principles are at present in dispute' between the Democrats and Whigs, but both are 'united in one common purpose' – that of 'preserving our sacred Union' (p.436). The reason for choosing Pierce is that Pierce is younger, a 'new man' (p.436) to lead us into the future. In the politics of the 1850s, character offered a ground for choice when there were no issues at stake, no policy plans. For Pierce did not undertake to do anything if elected.

Hawthorne recognized slavery as potentially divisive, and he did not favor slavery; he only urged that nothing be done about it. Slavery is 'one of those evils which divine Providence does not leave to be remedied by human contrivances, but which, in its own good time, by some means impossible to be anticipated, but of the simplest and easiest operation, when all its uses shall have been fulfilled, it causes to vanish like a dream' (p.417).

Such a fantasy of evanescence recalls not only Chillingworth's extinction after Dimmesdale's confession, but even more the death of Jaffrey Pyncheon in *The House of the Seven Gables*, like a 'defunct nightmare.' The key to redemption in that book is replacing all human action, which is guilt-ridden, with the beneficent process of nature.

[. . .]

This logic of romance Hawthorne envisaged for America in politics as well. As late as 1863, he wrote to Elizabeth Peabody that the Civil War would only achieve 'by a horrible convulsion' what might have come by 'a gradual and peaceful change,' and Mrs. Hawthorne echoes this judgment to a Union general, agreeing with his conviction that 'God's law' would surely have removed slavery 'without this dreadful convulsive action.'[18]

Action is intolerable; character takes its place. We recognize the Romantic reinterpretation of *Hamlet*, and this move in the American politics of the 1850s and in Hawthorne's writing echoes earlier English experience. Wordsworth's disillusion with the French Revolution, the English anti-French consensus politics that marginalized any attempt at change such as the French example had first promised – all these go into his famous lines:

> Action is transitory – a step, a blow,
> The motion of a muscle – this way or that –
>   'Tis done, and in the after-vacancy
> We wonder at ourselves like men betrayed:
>   Suffering is permanent, obscure and dark,
> And shares the nature of infinity.[19]

Contemporary with Goethe's *Wilhelm Meister*, which drew on *Hamlet* to inaugurate the tradition of the *Bildungsroman*, these lines signal a change in the status of literary character. No longer the traditional Aristotelian one who acts, nor, as in many great nineteenth-century novels, one who speaks, a character becomes one who is known. Coming from tale-writing, Hawthorne maintains in his longer works an extremely high proportion of narration to dialogue, while at the same time abandoning most of the traditional materials – that is, actions – of traditional narration. His fiction in certain ways thus technically anticipates that of Flaubert or Henry James in the emphasis it places on its characters, as narrated. Michel Foucault in *Discipline and Punish* has done the most to help us understand the social basis and political implications of such inquisitorial knowledge.

Within *The Scarlet Letter* Chillingworth, the knower of Dimmesdale (we do not penetrate the 'interior' of Dimmesdale's 'heart' until Chillingworth has led us there), represents the processes of social knowing that Foucault argues have come to produce the 'post-Christian' soul. But personalization is again at work: In projecting the methods of the nineteenth century back into the seventeenth century (which in fact imitated some of them), Hawthorne has transformed anonymous impersonality into a pseudonymous personality, whose relation with Dimmesdale rather anticipates psychoanalysis than corresponds to any actual medical practice from the 1640s or 1850s. Thus, in Chillingworth, Hawthorne focuses the full ambivalence of a fantasy of being personally known: the dream of intimacy, the nightmare of violation. Such extremes are no greater than those in 'The Custom-House' between the wish for 'some true relation with his audience' in literature and its demonic counterpart in official life – the stenciled and black-painted name of Hawthorne that circulates the world on 'all kinds of dutiable merchandise' . . . The characters of the name are known and effective, but through no action of Hawthorne's. Yet even as that of a writer, Hawthorne's signature in the Democratic press was valuable to his party, and appearing where it did, converted book reviews into political capital. Hawthorne's name circulated as a sign in a complex system of exchange that made it worth the party's while to provide him a livelihood, and that gave him the character of a Democrat, without requiring action. Wordsworth's lines questioning action are the words of a successful tempter, who turned out to speak for a whole culture. Evert Duyckinck of the *New York Literary World* alluded to these lines in his review of *The Scarlet Letter*, although without touching on the political implications. Hawthorne had been writing this way for some twenty years; his literary mode did not suddenly change in response to politics, but at this point there was a sudden change in his popularity. The official 'end of ideology' in the 1850s took to Hawthorne, just as it did again in the 1950s. Even now in American political life we displace politics into personality when fundamental debate is marginalized. We assess the reliability of character among the candidates competing to control the nuclear holocaust button. To dismantle that monstrous apparatus is still as unthinkable to major parties now as in Hawthorne's time was dismantling slavery or the Union. Might the Freeze movement have the same catalytic power of political realignment that Free Soil had for the Republicans?

A politics of issueless patience causes rhetorical confusion in a party that aims to the future and claims responsibility for the 'destinies, not of America alone, but of mankind at large' as they are 'carried upward and consummated' (*The Life of Pierce*, p.436). *The Life of Pierce* early identifies Hawthorne and Pierce with the 'progressive – or democratic' political stance, as opposed to the 'respectable conservative' (p.357). But on slavery, Hawthorne judges that 'the statesman of practical sagacity – who loves his country as it is, and evolves good from things as they exist . . . will be likely . . . to stand in the attitude of a conservative' (p.416). So the Democrats become progressive conservatives.

Similar blurring marked legislative activity in the period. David Potter argues that the Abolitionists were hated 'because they insisted upon the necessity to choose' and were dangerous because they converted 'resolvable disputes' into 'questions of principle,' giving a polemical 'false celerity and simplicity' to issues better left 'qualified and diffuse.' Potter is not so happy, however, with the results of his recommended politics of indeterminacy when Congress actually followed such a course. Avoiding both clarity and principle, Congress could no longer agree on anything that both sides understood in the same way, but could pass only 'measures ambiguous enough in their meaning or uncertain enough in their operation to gain support from men who hoped for opposite results.'[20]

Such a politics of Freudian compromise-formation has, according to Sacvan Bercovitch persisted in American life since its Puritan origins. The 'paranosic gain' is large. Such 'both-and' rhetoric offers America an ambiguity that denies contradictions, encouraging a 'multiplicity of meanings' while 'precluding contradiction in fact.' This is a 'mythical mode of cultural continuity' that contrasts with, and prevents, any possible 'historical gesture at cultural discontinuity.' Setting aside their contrasting evaluations, Bercovitch shares this understanding of American Democracy with Arthur Schlesinger, Jr., who claimed, 'Democracy . . . suspends in solution logical antinomies which work out more or less harmoniously in practice.'[21]

Given a political rhetoric, and a national identity, that depend on blurring together what are ordinarily taken as contraries, we may find in Hawthorne's style a response to this situation. His prose negotiates the conflicting realities of past and present, the overlays of Puritan, agrarian, commercial, and industrial ways of life that he encountered in New England, as well as the tension between American politics as a continuing revolution and politics as patronage, mere 'rotation.' Hawthorne's derealizing style represents objects so that we doubt their reality, yet while thus questioning what offers itself as our world, he refuses to commit himself to the authenticity of any other world or way of seeing.

Antinomies may be suspended not only in local stylistic practice but also over the course of a narrative. Claude Lévi-Strauss has defined 'myth' as the narrative mode that so negotiates the fundamental antinomies of a culture, and Fredric Jameson has elaborated a model for analyzing such ideological compromise formations in modern literature.[22]

As in Hawthorne's uncertainty between 'progressive' and 'conservative,' the contradictory wish of the Democrats in the early 1850s was to go ahead into the future without losing control of what they had established: Let us call this the tension between motion and regulation. In the *Life of Pierce* this determines the contradiction between the future we wish to gain and the stability we fear to lose. In *The Scarlet Letter* the turn from action to character means that we should find the terms of our contradiction in Hawthorne's analysis of what prevents a character from acting – as when Hester tempts Dimmesdale in the forest. Hester's 'intellect and heart had their home . . . in desert places, where they roamed as freely as the wild Indian.' In contrast, Dimmesdale 'had never gone through an experience calculated to lead him beyond the scope of generally received laws; although in a single instance' he had transgressed one. Hawthorne elaborates: 'but this had been a sin of passion, not of principle, nor even purpose. . . . At the head of the social system . . . he was only the more trammelled by its regulations, its principles and even its prejudices . . . The framework of his order inevitably hemmed him in.' Dimmesdale's emotional wavering is structured like Pierce's political trimming: The tension of regulation versus motion that determined the contradiction between stability and the future in the *Life of Pierce* here determines the contradiction of 'principle' versus 'passion' (emotion).

From the contradictory pair of terms we may logically generate a further pair – the negation of each of the contradictory pair, giving us four-part matrix in terms of which we may align the characters of a work. This scheme offers a way of interpreting characters as projections of ideological possibilities, given a literature that suppresses the overtly ideological plotting of action and prefers investment in character.

Dimmesdale is the character defined by passion and no principle; opposed to him is the 'iron framework' of Puritanism, defined by principle without passion. In the double negative place, possessing neither passion nor principle, is Chillingworth. He 'violated, in cold blood, the sanctity of the human heart' – violation negating principle and cold blood negating passion. At times, however, the text marks Chillingworth with 'dark passion,' thus making him a double of Dimmesdale (and after all, they are identified as the two men with claims upon Hester). Thus 'Chillingworth,' the proper name, covers both these narrative functions. Finally, the double positive, uniting passion and principle, projects the ideal Hester. We all construct this figure in our readings and then must confront Hawthorne's failure to actualize her in his text. Almost the whole history of interpreting Hawthorne may be charted here: praise for his realism; condemnation for the failure of his imaginative energy; understanding the glimmering half-existence of the ideal Hester as proof of Hawthorne's duplicitous negotiation with his external audience or internal self-censor. Just as Chillingworth's passion when present displaces his significance, so in Hester the usual preponderance of ascetic principle and burial of passion make her a double of the Puritan establishment. Only to the extent that the ideal Hester exists can Hawthorne be considered a fundamentally subversive writer; otherwise, we must value the hope he offers in his openness to our interpretive energies but must recognize his own limitations within a 'framework.'

The Life of Pierce does not hesitate to offer Pierce as the imaginary mediating figure who combines the future with stability. The campaign-biography genre of annunciatory historical fiction saves Hawthorne the need actually to specify the works of such a figure. Pierce's Whig opponent, Scott, shares the value of stability, but he has done his work, he does not belong to the future. Slavery negates stability, for it threatens the Union, and because slavery is also providentially doomed, the slave South combines the two negatives – instability and no future. Free Soilers and Abolitionists point toward the future without slavery, but no less than the slavery they oppose, they threaten stability.

Thus the organization of (in)action in both books works through a structure of conflicting values related to the political impasse of the 1850s. In American legal practice and theory at about this time, a characteristic array of dualisms (comparable to those of motion and regulation) came into use to negotiate the separation of a legal area of competence distinct from that of politics. The predominance of legal interpretive problems and methods in the middle nineteenth century suggests that more than theology (which had predominated in the seventeenth century), American legal experience may cast light on the hermeneutics of the scarlet letter itself.

Consider the problems of reading the letter in relation to the fundamental debates in the 1850s over the meaning of such documents of American life as the Declaration of Independence and the Constitution. As America left behind the directly 'political' statements and actions of the Founders, the age of Clay, Webster, and Calhoun made 'constitutional' questions a matter of 'exegesis.' All the fundamental questions of interpretation arose around these no less than around Hester's letter. Recall particularly that 'adulterer' (or 'adultery'?) is nowhere spelled out in Hawthorne's text, just as 'slavery' is nowhere present in the Declaration or the Constitution. The authorial meaning of the Constitution, in particular, was deliberately 'indeterminate' on the question of slavery, yet at a certain moment in American life a decision, and so a violation, was necessary.

In *The Scarlet Letter*, adultery, unnamed, begins as the 'self-evident' meaning of a woman alone with a child exposed to scorn. As the letter leaves its original context, however, it takes on new meanings: 'Many people refused to interpret the scarlet A by its original significance.' Hester plans never to abandon the letter, for while it endures, it will be 'transformed into something that should speak a different purport.' Early in the nineteenth century, Joseph Hopkinson had opposed statutes 'expressed in black and white' and defended common law: 'Consider the dictionary: scarcely a word in the language has a single, fixed, determinate meaning.'[23] Exploiting such indeterminacy, Hester's letter combines without contradiction the celebratory communal hopes of A for Angel in the sky, together with the anguished solitary pain of Dimmesdale's A in his flesh. John Pickering argues that the 'ambiguity of language,' especially in a 'community where every man has an equal right to decide the construction,' requires the 'positive decision of a tribunal' in order to give 'doubtful words a determinate signification.'[24] If law moves toward this desired scene of authoritative judgment, literature moves toward a community of readers. Hawthorne details a judgment's aftermath, and not on 'every man' but also a woman claims the right of construction. The identification of Pearl with the letter further emphasizes that its meaning must be understood historically, through experience, growth, and development, not as a 'declaration' expressed 'in black and white.' Taken back into politics, such a Burkean emphasis would protect the Constitution against Abolitionists: It denies the need for any tampering innovation and denies also the value of any reductive fixation on the original meaning or intention. Chillingworth's quest of this sort is disgusting and damaging; it makes him the book's villain. So much for genealogy as demystification!

The Scarlet Letter does, however, consider an alternative status for the letter, for its embroidery manifests Hester's will and not only that of the public. Perhaps, then, it might be better understood as a contract. The authoritative Commentaries of Chancellor Kent had defined contract law through the intention of the parties, which should prevail over the strict letter of the contract. In this area, the law 'will control even the literal terms of the contract, if they manifestly contravene the purpose.'[25] Hawthorne, however, deprecates such a line of analysis. Hester is described as not true to the letter when she analyzes it contractually as the mark of her meeting with the black man in the woods. Nor did Hawthorne think William Lloyd Garrison was true to the Constitution when the Abolitionist leader proclaimed it 'a covenant with death and an agreement with hell.' More in keeping with Hawthorne's analysis was the new understanding of contract promulgated by Theophilus Parsons in 1855. The 'intent of the parties' becomes subject to powers beyond it, including not only the rule of law, but also 'the rules of language.'[26]

Yet whether on the model of constitutional law or of contract law, the temporal hermeneutics of the Jacksonian Democrats wanted things both ways. The Constitution was a document appropriate to guide our better future, since it did not mention slavery, yet one must also in our bad present recognize the original constitutional 'guarantees' of slavery (*Life of Pierce*, p.433). This double vision allowed them to deny the need for present action, but in refusing to open itself to the new issues of the day, Jacksonian Democracy became a dead letter.

[. . .]

In juxtaposing *The Life of Pierce* and *The Scarlet Letter* I have operated by adjacency, rather than trusting that I could uncover within *The Scarlet Letter* alone all that I needed for its interpretation. Although the two works could be analyzed as narratives together, the *Life* was 'closed' in its unequivocal endorsement of Pierce as representing the ideal combination of future and stability; *The Scarlet Letter*, by contrast, was 'open' in its refusal to make similarly absolute claims for Hester's transcendence of the contradiction between passion and principle, and also in the overall mobility among the ideological positions that its characters were granted. That very openness, however, mystified as the value of 'art,' has encouraged neglect of the ideological limits on the 'positions' themselves. Perhaps only in the last fifty years has the fundamental opposition of motion versus regulation been sufficiently overcome in America's conception of its economy, polity, and society to allow us from the standpoint of our new social and political contradictions a sharp sense of this earlier phase.[27] □

The 'New Historicist' criticism, as well as exploring literary sources and social and political contexts, has also been exercised by questions of literary form and convention. Michael Bell, for example, has challenged Chase's 'romance reading' of American literature, in particular *The Scarlet Letter*, claiming that to Hawthorne and his contemporaries the term 'romance' was 'less a neutral generic label than a revolutionary, or at least antisocial slogan'. Hawthorne's prefaces, Bell insists, even though they have been taken straightforwardly as statements of artistic intention, and have been used to construct general theories of a distinctive American literary tradition, should be seen to share the 'quality of playfully subversive deception' that characterises his fiction. In his essay 'Arts of Deception: Hawthorne, "Romance", and *The Scarlet Letter*' (1985), he sets out to explore the shifting meanings of the term 'romance' as commonly understood by Hawthorne's contemporaries, as (deceptively) defined by Hawthorne himself, and as redefined by modern critics.

Bell begins by quoting Hawthorne's definition of 'romance' in the first paragraph of his preface to *The House of the Seven Gables*:

■ When a writer calls his work a Romance, it need hardly be observed that he wishes to claim a certain latitude, both to its fashion and material, which he would not have felt himself entitled to assume, had he professed to be writing a Novel. The latter form of composition (i.e., the Novel) is presumed to aim at a very minute fidelity, not merely to the possible, but to the probable and ordinary course of man's experience. The former (i.e., the Romance) – while, as a work of art, it must rigidly subject itself to laws, and while it sins unpardonably, so far as it may swerve aside from the truth of the human heart – has fairly a right to present that truth under circumstances, to a great extent, of the writer's own choosing or creation.[28] □

Bell proceeds to note the vagueness of this definition, and suggests that in his preface, Hawthorne is actually concealing, rather than revealing, the true meaning of romance:

■ According to conventional opinion in the first half of the nineteenth century, imaginative fiction, as opposed to literature based on fact, was deeply dangerous, psychologically threatening, and even socially subversive . . . To Hawthorne's contemporaries, what I have called the authority of romance, of imaginative fiction as opposed to factual history, was clear, and it was clearly dangerous. Romance, according to conventional opinion, derived from 'sickly' imagination rather than from 'wholesome' reason or judgment. To indulge in the delusions of romance was to undermine the basis of psychological and social order, to alienate oneself from 'the real business of life.'

The term 'romance' at least implicitly, was thus less a neutral generic label than a revolutionary, or at least antisocial slogan. To identify oneself as a romancer was to reject far more than 'the probable and ordinary course of man's experience'; it was to set oneself in opposition to the most basic norms of society: reason, fact, and 'real' business.[29] □

Though fascinated with the antisocial and abnormal, Hawthorne, according to Bell, never openly identified himself with them, and so was able to keep his reading public. The same sort of deception, says Bell, is at work in 'The Custom-House'. Hawthorne's self-effacing claim of authenticity is a 'joke'. As a mere editor, Hawthorne claims for his story the kind of authority his culture approved, but by making this claim into a joke he is in fact dismissing reason and fact. Bell takes the statement in 'The Custom-House' – 'Dream strange things, and make them look like truth' – as revealing: it undermines the idea of a 'neutral territory', of a reconciliation of Actuality and Imagination in admitting that the romancer tricks the reader into accepting 'strange dreams' by making them *look* like 'truth'. The romancer manages to present unconscious fantasy in the disguise of socially acceptable reality. Bell goes on to show that the behaviour of Hester and Dimmesdale in the main narrative has much in common with the deception that characterises the romancer, as Hawthorne describes and impersonates him in 'The Custom-House'. Hester and Dimmesdale function 'as artists, manipulating appearances . . . in order to mediate between their own subversive impulses and the orthodox expectations of the society in which they live their public lives.' From the beginning Dimmesdale sets out to deceive, his problem being, of course, that the person he succeeds in deceiving above all is himself. Even his final confession is 'sufficiently equivocal', in Bell's reading, to allow it to be interpreted as a general dramatisation of sinfulness (the way Dimmesdale's previous 'confessions' had been interpreted), rather than as a personal confession of a specific sin. Hester, at first, is as confused as Dimmesdale about the relationship between what she seems and what she is. She manages to give expression to her repressed individuality through her needlework, but to the extent that it reveals 'the passion of her life . . . she rejected it as sin.' Nor can she face openly, even in the privacy of her own thoughts, the idea that one of her motives for staying on in Boston may be her enduring love for Dimmesdale. Instead, she chooses to mask her abiding passion, even from herself, in the language of 'guilt', 'earthly punishment', and 'martyrdom'. And despite her public role as community worker, she harbours a thoroughly subversive sense of her 'individuality', assuming 'a freedom of speculation . . . which our forefathers, had they known of it, would have held to be a deadlier crime than that stigmatized by *The Scarlet Letter*.' But, as Bell adds, 'they do not know of it; they are deceived.' However, in the 'Conclusion', Bell discerns a different Hester, a sincere penitent. Bell focuses on the statement that she has now 'resumed, – of her own free will, for not the sternest magistrate of that iron period would have imposed it, – resumed the symbol of which we have related a dark tale', insisting that the crucial term here is 'free will':

■ Paradoxically enough, it is by forsaking open rebellion, by reassuming her part in society, that Hester is at last able to realize her individuality and freedom. And this paradox lies at the heart, not only of Hester's story, but of Hawthorne's conception of the art of fiction . . . Hawthorne, like Hester, rebels rather through indirection, through ironic subversion.[30] □

CHAPTER FOUR

Psychoanalytical Approaches

WITHIN A broadly psychoanalytical approach, various kinds of analysis are possible. Most psychoanalytical criticism has been concerned with probing the relationship between the author's attitudes and state of mind and the special qualities of the work. Traditional criticism often referred to the details of the author's life in order to throw light on the work, but this older kind of biographical criticism worked in a common-sensical and impressionistic way: new psychological theories made possible a much more systematic approach. The critic may start with the biographical evidence (letters, notebooks, biography, etc.) and from this construct a theory of the artist's personality, which is then used to eluci-date the work, or for which confirmation is sought by reference to the work. The danger here, from a literary critical point of view, is that the 'materiality' of the work itself, its specific formal constitution, tends to be overlooked in the concern to explore the inner life of the author. A second approach would be for the critic to start with the work, psycho-analysing the characters, as Freud and Ernest Jones have famously done with Hamlet. The approach treats characters as if they were real people rather than fictional constructs. The work, of course, may be analysed for what it tells about the author, the critic acting as psychoanalyst listen-ing to the author who speaks to him through his work. The limitation of this approach is that it also does not take account of form. The work is a deliberately crafted, conventionalised and ritualised form of public expression involving rather different processes of transformation than those identified by Freud in the production of dreams (the 'dream-work'), and not at all like the spontaneous expression of a patient on the psychoanalyst's couch. A third approach would be a combination of the two above approaches, with the critic working back and forth between the life and the work, using one to illuminate the other. Yet another approach would be to focus on the reader rather than on the author or the text. Finally, there are the recent developments in modern psycho-analytic criticism, largely associated with the French theorist Jacques

Lacan. This criticism concentrates on 'textuality' and what it reveals (or conceals) of repressed desires, buried motives, unconscious processes. Using the language of psychoanalysis, these critics seek to explain the workings of the text rather than the workings of the author's, character's or even reader's mind. To do so they focus on the evasions, ambivalences and points of stress in the narrative, not just to uncover the 'sub-text', but to uncover the processes, the dream-work, by which the text was produced.

We should be clear what the psychological approach, of whatever kind, can and cannot do. It cannot tell us whether the work is good or bad. It does not provide us with aesthetic criteria. But by illuminating the author's nature and purposes, or by uncovering the textual symptoms of unconscious processes, it can show us how the work became what it is, and help us toward a more fully informed aesthetic understanding and appreciation.

Hawthorne's description of the world of romance in 'The Custom-House' section conjures up a kind of fiction that so closely approximates the condition of dream that it would seem to lend itself particularly well to psychoanalytical criticism. The romance, says Hawthorne, is like a moonlit room in which all the details 'so completely seen, are so spiritualized by the unusual light, that they seem to lose their actual substance, and become things of intellect.' The everyday world is 'now invested with a quality of strangeness and remoteness'; the familiar room 'has become a neutral territory somewhere between the real world and fairyland, where the Actual and the Imaginary may meet . . . Ghosts might enter here.' These are the conditions where a man can 'dream strange things, and make them look like truth'. Richard Brodhead remarks that our experience in the world of the novel is akin to Hawthorne's own in the moonlit room, and proceeds to outline the novel's dream-like quality:

■ Ordinary boundaries become fluid, such that things are both seen as things and felt as thoughts. Above all Hawthorne's world is governed by the moonlit room's sense of haunted interconnectedness. It is not enough to describe it as economical or compact; its fluid interrelatedness of parts and its supersaturation with significant patterns give it the quality of overdetermination that Freud ascribes to dreams.

This double sense of distinctness of individual outline and dream-like interconnectedness is exactly the effect produced by the item that reappears most insistently in the book, the scarlet letter itself. Hester's A is almost always before us, and it has a curious power to replicate itself in a series of visual variants. It is reflected in suits of armor, pools, brooks and eyes; it is repeated in Pearl's clothing and in her seaweed creations; it shines forth in the midnight sky; it burns itself onto Dimmesdale's chest. . . . Images combine, separate, and recombine, the action accelerates and slows down, the characters come together and move apart – but while all of this is happening, infusing it and linking its parts to one another and to itself is the scarlet letter.[1] □

An early, influential, specifically Freudian interpretation of *The Scarlet Letter* was offered by Joseph Levi, a clinical psychologist, in his seminal essay 'Hawthorne's *The Scarlet Letter*: A Psychoanalytic Interpretation' (1953). Seeking to identify the reasons for considering *The Scarlet Letter* 'a great book', Levi refers to its 'universal appeal', its concern with fundamental, timeless human issues such as the Oedipal theme, which he traces to Sophocles as well as Freud. Levi's method is clearly of the first kind described above: starting with biographical evidence (Julian Hawthorne's biography of his father, Randall Stewart's 1948 biography, Hawthorne's private notebook, critical biographical studies by Van Doren (1949) and Van Wyck Brooks) he moves to the novel itself to elucidate a passage from the chapter 'The Minister's Vigil' in terms of a Freudian interpretation of Hawthorne's own life experience:

■ None of its critics seem to relate the greatness of this novel to certain events in Hawthorne's life. Relating these events to the period of his writing of the novel gives a clue to the greatness of *The Scarlet Letter* and to the reason for its captivating effect on the people.

When Hawthorne was four years old, his father died at sea. His father was a ship's captain and, even before his death, was but rarely at home. And Hawthorne's sister was born just two weeks before his father left for his last voyage. It is quite significant that his father died at the height of Hawthorne's oedipal complex. And equally significant was the birth of his younger sister in close proximity in time to the death of his father.

Hawthorne's son, in his biography of his father, gives us a penetrating insight into the spirit of the book. Julian Hawthorne says of the writing of *The Scarlet Letter*: '. . . these (difficult economic) conditions were not, it appears, severe enough by themselves for the birth of *The Scarlet Letter*. Midway in its completion, Madam Hawthorne was taken dangerously ill and after a struggle of a few weeks, she died.'[2] It was only after the death of his mother that Hawthorne was able to complete the novel.

He experienced the same emotions on reading the final portion of *The Scarlet Letter* to his wife that he had first felt consciously at the time of his mother's death. Randall Stewart describes this occurrence: 'On the evening of that day, he read the later part of the book to his wife . . . Of his own reactions on that memorable evening, Hawthorne recalled several years later: "My emotions when I read the last scene of *The Scarlet Letter* to my wife just after writing it – tried to read it, rather, for my voice swelled and heaved, as if I were tossed up and down on an ocean, as it subsides after a storm."[3] The emotion attests to the author's sincerity (if attestation were needed), the more so because Hawthorne was not in the habit of breaking down.' In his notebook, Hawthorne describes his reading of the ending of the book to his wife: 'But I was in a very nervous state then, having gone through a good diversity of emotion, while writing it (*The Scarlet Letter*), for many months. I think I have never overcome my adamant in any other instance.'[4]

But another such instance had occurred, just six months before, at the death of his mother. Describing this disturbing event in his note-book, Hawthorne said: 'I did not expect to be much moved at the time – that is to say, not to feel any overpowering emotions struggling, just then – though I knew that I should deeply remember and regret her. . . . Then I found the tears slowly gathering in my eyes. I tried to keep them down, but it would not be. I kept filling up, till, for a few moments, I shook with sobs. For a long time I knelt there, holding her hand, and surely it is the darkest hour I ever lived.'

There are only two instances, the reading of the last part of *The Scarlet Letter* and the death of his mother, during which he ever admit-ted losing control. That there is a connection between these two events is clear.

The inevitable conclusion is that the death of Hawthorne's mother had a great deal to do with the writing of this book. He must have experienced a substantial liberation of energy which allowed him to produce a book of such universal appeal.

Analysis reveals that the plot of *The Scarlet Letter* deals with the oedipal theme. It describes the struggle of two men – one older, one younger – for the love of a woman. Some rather convincing documen-tation for the oedipal facets of *The Scarlet Letter* exists in a recurring dream of Hawthorne's (his only recorded dream, as a matter of fact) quoted by Van Wyck Brooks: 'He seemed to be walking in a crowded street. Three beautiful girls approached him and, seeing him, screamed and fled. An old friend gave him a look of horror. He was promenading in his shroud.'[5] This recurring dream points to a very strong oedipal complex. The three women represent his mother and two sisters, The man walking in his shroud would be the ghost of his father who haunts him and about whom he feels horror.

That there is guilt concerning his father is mentioned by Van Doren who says that Hawthorne was very much impressed with the scene that Boswell describes in which Johnson stood in the market place at Uttoxeter and bared his head among the crowd and spoke of a sin that he once committed against his father. Hawthorne was extremely impressed by this story. And he told it three times – in the biographical 'Story for Children' in 1842, in *The Scarlet Letter* and in

'Our Old Home.' Hawthorne wrote in his private notebook: 'Dr. Johnson's penance in Uttoxeter market. A man who does penance in what might appear to lookers-on the most glorious and triumphal circumstances of his life. Each circumstance of the career of an apparently successful man to be a penance and torture him on account of some fundamental error in early life.' Van Doren concludes 'That man would be Arthur Dimmesdale,'[6] (the adulterous parson and Hawthorne's representation of himself in *The Scarlet Letter*).

The strength of Hawthorne's rivalry with his father is seen in a quotation from a letter to his mother in which he discusses his choice of profession. He finally decides to be an author and this is the reason: 'How proud you would feel to see my work praised by the reviewers as equal to the proudest productions of the Scribbling Sons of John Bull.'[7] Hawthorne always had great regard and respect for England and always spoke of it as the 'Mother Country.' John Bull would, therefore, represent the father.

Actually, in the chapter of *The Scarlet Letter*, 'The Minister's Vigil,' Dimmesdale's perceptions can be very well interpreted as an oedipal dream: in this scene, Mr. Dimmesdale arises in the middle of the night and ascends the scaffold. He imagines that he has shrieked, and then burst into a great peal of laughter. This laughter is responded to 'by a light, airy, childish laugh, in which, with a thrill of the heart . . . he recognised the tones of little Pearl.' With her is Hester who says: 'It is I, and my little Pearl.' 'She silently ascended the steps, and stood on the platform, holding little Pearl by the hand. The minister felt for the child's other hand, and took it. The moment that he did so, there came what seemed a tumultuous rush of new life, other life than his own, pouring like a torrent into his heart, and hurrying through all his veins, as if the mother and the child were communicating their vital warmth to his half-torpid system. The three formed an electric chain . . . a light gleamed far and wide over all the muffled sky. It was doubtless caused by one of those meteors, which the night watcher may so often observe burning out to waste, in the vacant regions of the atmosphere. So powerful was its radiance, that it thoroughly illuminated the dense medium of cloud betwixt the sky and earth. The great vault brightened, like the dome of an immense lamp.' '. . . the minister, looking upward to the zenith, beheld there the appearance of an immense letter – the letter A – marked out in lines of dull red light. . . . All the time that he gazed upward to the zenith, he was, nevertheless, perfectly aware that little Pearl was pointing her finger towards old Roger Chillingworth, who stood at no great distance from the scaffold. . . . Certainly, if the meteor kindled up the sky, and disclosed the earth, with an awfulness that admonished Hester Prynne and the clergyman of the day of judgment, then might Roger Chillingworth have passed with them for the archfiend, standing there with a smile and scowl to claim his own. So vivid was the expression, or so intense the minister's perception of it, that it seemed still to remain painted on the darkness after the meteor had vanished.' The next day, the author says, Mr. Dimmesdale was so confused that he looked upon the events of the past night as visionary.

The interpretation of this scene is clear. Mr. Dimmesdale's desire is for Hester (representing Hawthorne's mother). Little Pearl represents the mother's vagina. The meteor is the phallus. Freud describes the libido as nearly always phallic. The meteor has a tail, which represents the penis. At the height of his excitation comes the fiend, the punishing superego, and disturbs him.[8] □

The second part of Levi's essay is concerned with examining the ways in which aspects of Hawthorne's personality are reflected in the principal characters of *The Scarlet Letter*. Levi takes the novel as a kind of dream story in which Hawthorne, as in a dream, disguises his own wishes and fears through a process which 'may be described as the opposite of condensation' – a dispersal and projection of aspects of his own personality in the principal characters of his novel. Thus, Dimmesdale is 'the weak ego', 'a morbid personality, or an ego that cannot maintain itself and is unable to control the id impulses which strive to come to the surface'; Chillingworth 'represents Hawthorne's tormenting, cruel superego'; 'the elfish, wild, uncivilized Pearl' is 'an aspect of Hawthorne's own instinctive urges'; and Hester is Hawthorne's 'ideal mother'. With regard to the description of Hester and Dimmesdale's grave – 'yet with a space between, as if the dust of the two sleepers had no right to mingle' – Levi concludes: 'It was his (Hawthorne's) aim that finally he and his mother should be completely reunited.'

One of the most sophisticated, detailed and searching Freudian interpretations of Hawthorne's fiction is to be found in Frederick Crews' book, *The Sins of the Fathers: Hawthorne's Psychological Themes* (1966). Crews deliberately writes against 'the religious-didactic Hawthorne' of the formalist critics who 'have credited Hawthorne with the complexity of image-patterns and the steadiness of moral purpose that characterize a great allegorical poet'. These critics, according to Crews, have ignored the 'self-divided, self-tormented' Hawthorne and the 'submerged intensity and passion' of his work. Julian Hawthorne, Crews reminds us, on reading the tales and romances after his father's death, declared that he found himself 'constantly unable to comprehend how a man such as I knew my father to be could have written such books'. For Julian, the man and the writer were two very different people. There was evidently an elusive Hawthorne, intermittently glimpsed in his work, who was not the 'saintly allegorist' or 'dogmatic moralist' of conventional opinion, but the author of 'a hell-fired story' (Hawthorne's description of *The Scarlet Letter*). Following on from readers such as Melville, D. H. Lawrence and Leslie A. Fiedler, who have recognised dangerous knowledge, 'the blackness of darkness' in Hawthorne's work, Crews sets out to probe this darkness by examining the psychological implications of Hawthorne's plots. In doing so, he opposes those critics who search for some overriding, unifying thematic idea which operates as a controlling principle in the work, whether it is the conventional morality of the theological critics, the archetypal patterns of the myth critics or the 'possibility of a literary iconology' that Harry Levin wished to explore. Rather than seeking to 'compose' Hawthorne's narrative into a coherent message or meaning, Crews accepts the text's ambiguities, discontinuities, internal tensions and self-division.

■ Hawthorne's ambiguity – to which every critic pays lip-service before going on to build a tower of allegory – is not a didactic strategy but a sign of a powerful tension between his attraction to and his fear of his deepest themes. For behind his moralism, and often directly contradicting it, lies a sure insight into everything that is terrible, uncontrollable, and therefore demoralizing in human nature. Hawthorne himself, like his admirers, wanted to be spared this insight, but beneath layers of rationalization and euphemism it asserts its right to expression.[9] □

His 'admirers' included Sophia, his wife who, with her neurasthenic headaches, her naive Transcendentalism, her church-going piety, her taste for moral sentiment, and her censoring of her husband's notebooks after his death, 'had much to do with domesticating Hawthorne's interests after 1838'.

Admitting that 'Hawthorne's art appears to turn outward toward moral simplicity rather than inward toward psychological complexity', Crews nevertheless wants to make a claim for Hawthorne as 'a psychologically profound writer'. He does so by insisting that we revise our notions of psychological portraiture so that we do not think of it merely in terms of the uniquely private, but also in terms of the representatively human.

■ I would insist, however, that Henry James was originally right in saying that Hawthorne 'cared for the deeper psychology,' and that his works offer glimpses of 'the whole deep mystery of man's soul and conscience.' The majority view, I feel, rests on both a misapprehension of 'deep psychology' and an inattentive habit of reading Hawthorne. We must, in the first place, question the popular notion that individuality and detail are the key virtues of psychological portraiture.

A richly particular character, such as James's Isabel Archer, may be represented as living almost entirely in the realm of conscious moral choice, while her instinctual nature and her conflicts of feeling are hidden under an abundance of surface strokes. Hawthorne's Hester Prynne, in contrast, is rendered in terms of struggle between feelings that she neither controls nor perfectly understands. Her remorse toward her husband versus her sympathy for her lover, her desire to flee versus her compulsion to remain, her maternal instinct versus her shame at what Pearl represents, her voluptuousness versus her effort to repent and conform – these tensions are the very essence of our idea of Hester. If she is a more schematic figure than Isabel, her motives are deeper and are better known to us. It is precisely because Hawthorne is not afraid to schematize, to stress underlying patterns of compulsion rather than superficial eccentricities, that he is able to explore the depths of our common nature.

The power of Hawthorne's best fiction comes largely from a sense that nothing in human behavior is as free or fortuitous as it appears. Even with characters much less fully observed than Hester, the emphasis falls on buried motives which are absolutely binding because they are unavailable to conscious criticism. Furthermore, even the most wooden heroes bear witness to a psychological pre-occupation. Whatever is subtracted from overt psychology tends to reappear in imagery, even in the physical setting itself. It is as if there were a law of the conservation of psychic energy in Hawthorne's world; as the characters approach sentimental stereotypes, the author's language becomes correspondingly more suggestive of unconscious obsession. And, in fact, one of the abiding themes of Hawthorne's work is the fruitless effort of people to deny the existence of their 'lower' motives. The form of his plots often constitutes a return of the repressed – a vengeance of the denied element against an impossible ideal of purity or spirituality. Thus it is not enough, in order to speak of Hawthorne's power as a psychologist, merely to look at his characters' stated motives. We must take into account the total, always intricate dialogue between statement and implication, observing how Hawthorne – whether or not he consciously means to – invariably measures the displacements and sublimations that have left his characters two-dimensional.[10] □

Crews' analysis of the characterisation of Dimmesdale is an ingenious application of Freud's theory of repression. *The Scarlet Letter*, he believes, maintains to the end an unresolved conflict between the ego which acts to censor, sublimate or control forbidden desire, and unruly libidinal energies which continually threaten to breach or circumvent the ego's defences and find expression after they have been disguised or sublimated.

Crews starts with a quotation from the novel: 'And be the sad truth spoken, that the breach which guilt has once made into the human soul is never, in this mortal state, repaired. It may be watched and guarded; so that the enemy shall not force his way again into the citadel, and might even, in his subsequent assaults, select some other avenue, in preference to that where he had formerly succeeded. But there is still the ruined wall, and, near it, the stealthy tread of the foe that would win over again his unforgotten triumph.' Crews proceeds to gloss Hawthorne's metaphor as follows:

■ Dimmesdale's conscience (the watchful guard) has been delegated to prevent repetition of the temptation's 'unforgotten triumph.' The deterrent weapon of conscience is its capacity to generate feelings of guilt, which are of course painful to the soul. Though the temptation retains all its strength (its demand for gratification), this is counterbalanced by its burden of guilt. To readmit the libidinal impulse through the guarded breach (to gratify it in the original way) would be to admit insupportable quantities of guilt. The soul thus keeps temptation at bay by meeting it with an equal and opposite force of condemnation . . . The 'other avenue' is the means his libido chooses, given the fact of repression, to gratify itself surreptitiously. In psychoanalytic terms this is the avenue of compromise that issues in a neurotic symptom.

Hawthorne's metaphor of the besieged citadel cuts beneath the theological and moral explanations in which Dimmesdale puts his faith, and shows us instead an inner world of unconscious compulsion. Guilt will continue to threaten the timid minister in spite of his resolution to escape it, and indeed (as the fusion of 'temptation' and 'guilt' in the metaphor implies) this resolution will only serve to upset the balance of power and enable guilt to conquer the soul once more. Hawthorne's metaphor demands that we see Dimmesdale not as a free moral agent but as a victim of feelings he can neither understand nor control . . . If, as Chillingworth asserts, the awful course of events has been 'a dark necessity' from the beginning, it is not because Hawthorne believes in Calvinistic predestination or wants to imitate Greek tragedy, but because all three of the central characters have been ruled by motives inaccessible to their conscious will.

[. . .]

Thus Dimmesdale is helpless to reform himself at this stage because the passional side of his nature has found an outlet, albeit a self-destructive one, in his present miserable situation. The original sexual desire has been granted recognition *on the condition of being punished*, and the punishment itself is a form of gratification. Not only the overt masochism of fasts, vigils, and self-scourging (the last of these makes him laugh, by the way), but also Dimmesdale's emaciation and weariness attest to the spending of his energy against himself. It is important to recognize that this is the same energy previously devoted to passion for Hester. We do not exaggerate the facts of the romance in saying that the question of Dimmesdale's fate, for all its religious decoration, amounts essentially to the question of what use is to be made of his libido.

We are now prepared to understand the choice that the poor minister faces when Hester holds out the idea of escape. It is not a choice between a totally unattractive life and a happy one (not even Dimmesdale could feel hesitation in that case), but rather a choice of satisfactions, of avenues into the citadel. The seemingly worthless alternative of continuing to admit the morally condemned impulse by the way of remorse has the advantage, appreciated by all neurotics, of preserving the status quo. Still, the other course naturally seems more attractive. If only repression can be weakened – and this is just the task of Hester's rhetoric about freedom – Dimmesdale can hope to return to the previous 'breach' of adultery.

In reality, however, these alternatives offer no chance for happiness or even survival. The masochistic course leads straight to death, while the other, which Dimmesdale allows Hester to choose for him, is by now so foreign to his withered, guilt-ridden nature that it can never be put into effect. The resolution to sin will, instead, necessarily redouble the opposing force of conscience, which will be stronger in proportion to the overtness of the libidinal threat. As the concluding chapters of *The Scarlet Letter* prove, the only possible result of Dimmesdale's attempt to impose, in Hawthorne's phrase, 'a total change of dynasty and moral code, in that interior kingdom,' will be a counter-revolution so violent that it will slay Dimmesdale himself along with his upstart libido. We thus see that in the forest, while Hester is prating of escape, renewal, and success, Arthur Dimmesdale unknowingly faces a choice of two paths to suicide.

Now, this psychological impasse is sufficient in itself to refute the most 'liberal' critics of *The Scarlet Letter* – those who take Hester's proposal of escape as Hawthorne's own advice. However much we may admire Hester and prefer her boldness to Dimmesdale's self-pity, we cannot agree that she understands human nature very deeply. Her shame, despair, and solitude 'had made her strong,' says Hawthorne, 'but taught her much amiss.' What she principally ignores is the truth embodied in the metaphor of the ruined wall, that men are altered irreparably by their violations of conscience. Hester herself is only an apparent exception to this rule. She handles her guilt more successfully than Dimmesdale because, in the first place, her conscience is less highly developed than his; and secondly because, as he tells her, 'Heaven hath granted thee an open ignominy, that thereby thou mayest work out an open triumph over the evil within thee, and the sorrow without.' Those who believe that Hawthorne is an advocate of free love, that adultery has no ill effects on a 'normal' nature like Hester's, have failed to observe that Hester, too, undergoes self-inflicted punishment. Though permitted to leave, she remains in Boston not simply because she wants to be near Arthur Dimmesdale, but because this has been the scene of her humiliation. 'Her sin, her ignominy, were the roots which she had struck into the soil,' says Hawthorne. 'The chain that bound her here was of iron links, and galling to her inmost soul, but never could be broken.'

We need not dwell on this argument, for the liberal critics of *The Scarlet Letter* have been in retreat for many years. Their place has been taken by subtler readers who say that Hawthorne brings us from sin to redemption, from materialistic error to pure spiritual truth. The moral heart of the novel, in this view, is contained in Dimmesdale's Election Sermon, and Dimmesdale himself is pictured as Christ-like in his holy death. Hester, in comparison, degenerates spiritually after the first few chapters; the fact that her thoughts are still on earthly love while Dimmesdale is looking toward heaven is a serious mark against her. This redemptive scheme, which rests on the uncriticized assumption that Hawthorne's point of view is identical with Dimmesdale's at the end, seems to me to misrepresent the 'felt life' of *The Scarlet Letter* more drastically than the liberal reading. Both take for granted the erroneous belief that the novel consists essentially of the dramatization of a moral idea. The tale of human frailty and sorrow, as Hawthorne calls it in his opening chapter, is treated merely as the fictionalization of an article of faith. Hawthorne himself, we might repeat, did not share this ability of his critics to shrug off the psychological reality of his work. *The Scarlet Letter* is, he said, 'positively a hell fired story, into which I found it almost impossible to throw any cheering light.'

All parties can agree, in any case, that there is a terrible irony in Dimmesdale's exhilaration when he has resolved to flee with Hester. Being, as Hawthorne describes him, 'a true religionist,' to whom it would always remain essential 'to feel the pressure of a faith about him, supporting, while it confined him within its iron framework', he is ill-prepared to savor his new freedom for what it is. His joy is that of his victorious libido, of the 'enemy' which is now presumably sacking the citadel, but this release is acknowledged by consciousness only after a significant bowdlerization:

'Do I feel joy again?' cried he, wondering at himself. 'Methought the germ of it was dead in me! O Hester, thou art my better angel!

I seem to have flung myself – sick, sin-stained, and sorrow-blackened – down upon these forest leaves, and to have risen up all made anew, and with new powers to glorify Him that hath been mercifull. This is already the better life. Why did we not find it sooner?'

Hawthorne's portrayal of self-delusion and his compassion are nowhere so powerfully combined as in this passage. The Christian reference to the putting on of the New Man is grimly comic in the light of what has inspired it, but we feel no more urge to laugh at Dimmesdale than we do at Milton's Adam. If in his previous role he has been only, in Hawthorne's phrase, a 'subtle, but remorseful hypocrite,' here he is striving pathetically to be sincere. His case becomes poignant as we imagine the revenge that his tyrannical conscience must soon take against these new promptings of the flesh. To say merely that Dimmesdale is in a state of theological error is to miss part of the irony; it is precisely his theological loyalty that necessitates his confusion. His sexual nature must be either denied with unconscious sophistry, as in this scene, or rooted out with heroic fanaticism, as in his public confession at the end.

On one point, however, Dimmesdale is not mistaken: he has been blessed with a new energy of body and will. The source of this energy is obviously his libido; he has become physically strong to the degree that he has ceased directing his passion against himself and has attached it to his thoughts of Hester. But as he now returns to town, bent upon renewing his hypocrisy for the four days until the Election Sermon has been given and the ship is to sail, we see that his 'cure' has been very incomplete. 'At every step he was incited to do some strange, wild, wicked thing or other, with a sense that it would be at once involuntary and intentional; in spite of himself, yet growing out of a profounder self than that which opposed the impulse.' The minister can scarcely keep from blaspheming to his young and old parishioners as be passes them in the street; he longs to shock a deacon and an old widow with arguments against Christianity, to poison the innocence of a naive girl who worships him, to teach wicked words to a group of children, and to exchange bawdy jests with a drunken sailor. Here, plainly, is a return of the repressed, and in a form which Freud noted to be typical in severely holy persons. The fact that these impulses have reached the surface of Dimmesdale's mind attests to the weakening of repression in the forest scene, while their perverse and furtive character shows us that repression has not ceased altogether. Hawthorne's own explanation, that Dimmesdale's hidden vices have been awakened because 'he had yielded himself *with deliberate choice*, as he had never done before, to what he *knew* was deadly sin' [my italics], gives conscience its proper role as a causative factor. Having left Hester's immediate influence behind in the forest, and having returned to the society where he is known for his purity, Dimmesdale already finds his 'wicked' intentions constrained into the form of a verbal naughtiness which he cannot even bring himself to express . . .

In short, the Election Sermon is written by the same man who wants to corrupt young girls in the street, and the same newly liberated sexuality 'inspires' him in both cases. If the written form of the Election Sermon is a great Christian document, as we have no reason to doubt, this is attributable not to Dimmesdale's holiness but to his libido, which gives him creative strength and an intimate acquaintance with the reality of sin.

[. . .]

Thus Dimmesdale's sexual energy has temporarily found a new alternative to its battle with repression – namely, sublimation. In sublimation, we are told, the libido is not repressed but redirected to aims that are acceptable to conscience. The writing of the Election Sermon is just such an aim, and readers who are familiar with psychoanalysis will not be puzzled to find that Dimmesdale has passed without hesitation from the greatest blasphemy to fervent religious rhetoric . . . His libido is now free, not to attach itself to Hester, but to be sublimated into the passion of delivering his sermon and then expelled forever.

[. . .]

'It is a curious subject of observation and inquiry,' says Hawthorne at the end, 'whether hatred and love be not the same thing at bottom. Each, in its utmost development, supposes a high degree of intimacy and heart-knowledge; each renders one individual dependent for the food of his affections and spiritual life upon another; each leaves the passionate lover, or the no less passionate hater, forlorn and desolate by the withdrawal of his object.' These penetrating words remind us that the tragedy of *The Scarlet Letter* has chiefly sprung, not from Puritan society's imposition of false social ideals on the three main characters, but from their own inner world of frustrated desires. Hester, Dimmesdale, and Chillingworth have been ruled by feelings only half perceived, much less understood and regulated by consciousness; and these feelings, as Hawthorne's bold equation of love and hatred implies, successfully resist translation into terms of good and evil. Hawthorne does not leave us simply with the Sunday school lesson that we should 'be true,' but with a tale of passion through which we glimpse the ruined wall – the terrible certainty that, as Freud put it, the ego is not master in its own house. It is this intuition that enables Hawthorne to reach a tragic vision worthy of the name: to see to the bottom of his created characters, to understand the inner necessity of everything they do, and thus to pity and forgive them in the very act of laying bare their weaknesses.[11] ☐

Thirty-three years after Levi's pioneering study, Clay Daniel, also adopting a Freudian approach, extended many of Levi's insights in '*The Scarlet Letter*: Hawthorne, Freud, and the Transcendentalists' (1986). Daniel, like Levi, starts with biographical details, noting the apparent connection between the death of Hawthorne's mother on 30 July 1849, and the great burst of creative energy that enabled Hawthorne to complete *The Scarlet Letter*, just over six months later on 3 February 1850. Following Levi, Daniel interprets Hawthorne's intense creativity at this time as an attempt to resolve his Oedipal complex which was reactivated by the death of his mother. However, Daniel goes beyond Levi's analysis in also relating this complex to an earlier period in Hawthorne's life, when Hawthorne joined the Utopian community of Transcendentalists at Brook Farm, where he hoped to build a home and acquire a modest income, which would enable him to marry Sophia Peabody. Though initially receptive to the optimistic philosophy of Transcendentalism, Hawthorne at Brook Farm, 'subject to the natural ravages of an unresolved Oedipal complex', exacerbated by thoughts of his impending marriage, ultimately rejected the Transcendentalists' emphasis on the sanctity of natural urges. To Hawthorne, struggling with the disquieting effects of his unresolved Oedipal instinct, the Transcendentalist belief in man's natural goodness seemed misplaced.

■ Hawthorne's father died in Surinam when Hawthorne was four, an age at which, according to Freud, the male child forms a crucial attachment to his mother, an attachment concomitant with a sexual awakening. During this initial Oedipal phase, the child wants to supplant his father's position with his mother. Normally this desire is resolved by the child's fear of his father's retaliation, a fear known as the castration complex. However, young Hawthorne had nothing to fear since his father was dead. Consequently, he was indeed able to supplant his father in his mother's affections, and in the lonely years following Captain Hawthorne's death (she never remarried), Mrs. Hawthorne may have directed not only her excess affection but also her libidinous energy towards the boy. Hawthorne as a boy probably thrived in this situation. Indeed, he seems to have enjoyed an extraordinarily happy childhood as 'a very handsome boy and a great favorite not only with the members of his family but with the drivers of the Manning stages'[12] who frequented 'a boy's paradise'[13] in Maine. But as he grew older, his attachment to his mother became an impediment to his psychological maturation, especially at Brook Farm, the scene of his first attempt to separate from his mother, and at his mother's deathbed, the scene of his final attempt. At Brook Farm, his resolution of his feelings for his mother apparently was only partially successful, for his Oedipal complex, shunted to the psychic side, forced its way to the brink of consciousness again when Hawthorne's mother died. Subconsciously driven once again to attempt to resolve these emotions at this time, Hawthorne attempted somehow to experience, or perhaps to create, a castration complex. Since his father was dead, however, he was forced to rely on his genius to create a fictional substitute for his father. Hawthorne, then, through the intensity of his fiction, attempted to resolve his Oedipal complex.

The Scarlet Letter is the story of an older man who supposedly died, like Hawthorne's father, while at sea, and who sneaks back into a New England village and wreaks his devilish revenge on a younger man who has formed an illicit relationship with his 'widow.' The woman, Hester (resonant with Hawthorne?), recognizes her husband, Chillingworth, but is forced to keep his identity a secret. Subsequently, Dimmesdale unwittingly lives under the same roof with Chillingworth, the man whom he has cuckolded, who after discovering Dimmesdale's relations with his wife, reduces him to virtual impotence, performing on him a sort of chemical castration. Behind this lurid sequence of events, we can glimpse Hawthorne haunting himself with the possibility that his father, supposedly buried in Surinam, did not die after all, but had returned to Massachusetts, intent on discovering the 'guilty' relations between his wife and his son, a son who could not possibly recognize him after forty years. This scenario, the possible product of a neurotic mind, provides the requisite framework to support the creation of a castration complex that is necessary to resolve, or at least ameliorate, Hawthorne's Oedipal complex.

In The Scarlet Letter Hester is primarily defined not as a lover or a wife, but as a mother. Throughout the story Hawthorne continually defines Hester in terms of motherhood, especially in relation to Pearl (Hester asserts she would gladly join Mistress Hibbins' witch-frolics if Pearl were taken away). And in the very beginning of the narrative, Hawthorne establishes Hester's relation to the Oedipal underpinnings of the story. When Hester first appears in the story, she steps from the prison with a child in her arms and is identified as a 'young woman – the mother of this child.' When she is described as 'the image of Divine Maternity', we are reminded that 'there was the taint of deepest sin in the most sacred quality of human life,' which sacred quality is motherhood. The emphasis of the guilty, sinful connection between the child and its mother underscores the Oedipal theme in the tale, and the portrayal of Hester as 'the image of Divine Maternity' establishes her dominant symbolic value, that of mother.

The only instance in which Hawthorne does not resort to images of motherhood to define Hester is during Hester and Dimmesdale's meeting in the forest in chapters XVIII and XIX, where Hester changes from mother to lover. . . . When Hester changes from mother to lover, Pearl refuses to come to her until Hester retrieves the scarlet letter, places it back on her bosom, and reassumes her status as mother.

The character Chillingworth resembles in several important points Hawthorne's father. Like Hawthorne's father, Chillingworth is 'a wanderer who has met with grievous mishaps by sea and land' and has 'been long held in bonds among the heathen-folk, to the southward.' Captain Hawthorne also met with 'grievous mishaps by sea and land', dying from yellow fever among the natives in Surinam, held by the bonds of the grave among 'the heathen-folk.' The narrative also emphasizes Chillingworth's relations with Hester, which parallel those of the Captain with Mrs. Hawthorne. A townsman informs Chillingworth that because of the great possibility that 'her husband may be at the bottom of the sea, Hester was strongly tempted to her fall.' Mrs. Hawthorne endured circumstances similar to Hester Prynne's. As a young widow, she was strongly tempted to transfer the feelings she had been directing toward her husband to her young son, who was more than willing to accommodate her. *The Scarlet Letter*, as we can see, is certainly a story of 'forbidden love'.

After his arrival, Chillingworth, vowing that Hester's guilty partner 'will be known – he will be known,' quickly assumes the relation of father-figure to Dimmesdale. Chillingworth's attitude toward Dimmesdale is similar to that of a father to a child – 'that he now breathes, and creeps about on earth, is owing all to me!'. Chillingworth soon becomes intimate with Dimmesdale, and they both are lodged under the same roof in the house of 'a pious widow,' where Chillingworth attends to Dimmesdale, the object of the 'motherly care of the good widow,' with a 'paternal and reverential love.' This arrangement provides the necessary scenario for Hawthorne's castration complex to unfold. Dimmesdale lives with a pious widow, as Hawthorne lived with his pious widow mother, and into this environment, unknown to Dimmesdale, comes the man who has been wronged by Dimmesdale's 'forbidden love' for Hester. Chillingworth, the father-figure, discovers Dimmesdale's sexual relations with Hester, the mother-figure, and works on him 'a more intimate revenge than any mortal had ever wreaked upon an enemy.' Chillingworth, Dimmesdale's 'deadliest enemy,' reduces Dimmesdale to physical impotence, 'bodily disease,' as he is 'gnawed and tortured.'

Chillingworth embodies the terrors of the castration complex. Yet, oddly, this 'physician' aids Dimmesdale in his spiritual regeneration, just as the castration complex helps resolve the Oedipal complex. As the story states, 'Providence – using the avenger and his victim for its own purposes' was 'pardoning, where it seemed most to punish.' The more Dimmesdale suffers the torments inflicted by Chillingworth, the more spiritualized he becomes, a spiritualization that symbolizes a release from, or at least an adequate resolution of, the Oedipal complex. In Dimmesdale's death hour, he admits, then repudiates, his guilty love for Hester . . . At this point, seven years after his sexual encounter with Hester, Dimmesdale dies, and the psychological drama concludes, just as seven years after the Oedipal crisis he experienced at Brook Farm, Hawthorne attempts to resolve that crisis in the writing of *The Scarlet Letter*, which serves as Hawthorne's public confession of his guilty love. As we see in the final pages of the story, Hawthorne comes to terms with his Oedipal feelings sufficiently to reject his Oedipal love for his mother to the extent that he forfeits the hope that he and his dead mother could ever meet 'hereafter, in an everlasting and pure reunion.'

A Freudian reading of *The Scarlet Letter* is necessarily reductive, yet it also provides a fixed viewpoint from which we can make specific judgments about the work. From a Freudian perspective, there are certain passages in the story that cannot be interpreted otherwise than as an attack on the Transcendentalism Hawthorne encountered at Brook Farm. I have attempted to suggest the close connection between Hawthorne's experience at Brook Farm and his writing of *The Scarlet Letter*, and indeed the story begins with a nod, perhaps a sneer, in that direction. In the story's second paragraph, Hawthorne writes,

> The founders of a new colony, whatever Utopia of human virtue and happiness they might originally project, have invariably recognized it among their earliest practical necessities to allot a portion of the virgin soil as a cemetery, and another portion as the site of a prison.

Hawthorne begins his narrative with an insistence on the ineradicable nature of 'human frailty and sorrow,' an insistence that echoes the Calvinism that Transcendentalism was reacting against. Whether the primal forces of the Oedipal impulse can be sweepingly condemned as an evil is not a question that needs to be answered here. Throughout Hawthorne's fiction there is a continual emphasis on the reality of evil, and Hawthorne may have translated the language of the unconscious, 'the heart's native language' as he calls it, to fit the existing vocabulary of his fiction. In *The Scarlet Letter*, nature, the mother of

Hawthorne's Oedipal impulses, is repeatedly represented as an evil, in that it is the catalyst that transforms human frailty into human sorrow. It was the natural force of Hawthorne's attraction to his mother that held him in the isolation of 'Castle Dismal,' where, gripped in the vice of an unnatural, natural relationship, Hawthorne vegetated. Not only was Hawthorne's mental health threatened, but so was his art. In 1837, Hawthorne, still living with his mother, informed Elizabeth Peabody that the domestic situation had 'produced a morbid consciousness that paralyzes my powers.'[14] Here was evil indeed.

I have already suggested the nature of the threat that Hawthorne's Oedipal impulses posed to his mental health and how that threat is represented in *The Scarlet Letter*. But the story also chronicles the struggles of Hawthorne the artist to deliver himself from the 'morbid consciousness' that was destroying his creativity, and the incredible burst of creativity that accompanies the resolution of his Oedipal complex provides an informative contrast to the paralysis of powers that bedevilled Hawthorne in 1837 when he was still living with his mother. A close examination of the story will reveal how closely the career of the Reverend Mr. Dimmesdale reflects that of the writer Mr. Hawthorne. As the story begins, Dimmesdale, dim perhaps from Hawthorne's vague recognition of himself, comes from one of the great English universities, bringing all the learning of the age into 'New England, giving earnest of high eminence in his profession.' Similarly, Hawthorne, who early in his career announced his desire to be counted an equal among 'the scribbling sons of John Bull,' had given promise of high eminence in his profession when he entered Brook Farm. At this time in his life, Hawthorne, like Dimmesdale, 'felt himself quite astray and at a loss in the pathway of human existence, and could only be at ease in some seclusion of his own.' Dimmesdale, as he strives to overcome his love for Hester, achieves an ever-growing reputation that results in 'a brilliant popularity in his sacred office,' a popularity that culminates in the delivery of his awe-inspiring Election Sermon, which coincides with his climactic confession and rejection of his love for Hester. Hawthorne also gains a remarkable reputation during the seven years between his marriage to Sophia Peabody and his final attempt to resolve his Oedipal complex, for the promise evident during his sojourn at Brook Farm results in *The Scarlet Letter*, whose delivery coincides with Hawthorne's rejection, or at least adequate resolution, of his Oedipal love for his mother. And just as Dimmesdale's listeners were reluctant to believe either his confession that he had been Hester's lover or the protestations of guilt that he repeated in his sermons, so Hawthorne's readers have been tardy in comprehending his extremely personal confession in *The Scarlet Letter* or, it might be added, in his prior fiction.

Nature's sympathy with the love between Hester and Dimmesdale, which reflects the natural origins of the Oedipal love threatening Hawthorne's mind and art, provides a profoundly bleak comment on nature. When the narrative states of the condemned criminal 'that the deep heart of Nature could pity and be kind to him,' it is not because the criminal is innocent, but because nature is guilty. This identification of nature with the illicit passion of Hester and Dimmesdale, which is continued throughout the story, reaches its climax in chapters XVIII and XIX, which recount Hester's meeting with Dimmesdale in the forest. During this meeting, as the lovers lay their plans for a permanent gratification of their passion, we learn of

> the sympathy of Nature – that wild, heathen Nature of the forest, never subjugated by human law, nor illumined by higher truth – with the bliss of these two spirits !

As is evident from a Freudian interpretation, nature is indeed in need of illumination by some higher truth, a situation the ordinary Transcendentalist would not have readily acknowledged. As Dimmesdale prepares to flee with Hester to regions that will admit a love sanctioned only by nature, he is called a 'lost and desperate man,' and is swept by a flood of evil impulses, which include everything from wanting to disconcert the Christian faithful to a desire to jest with drunken sailors. Dimmesdale, while gaining nature's favor, has risked his soul and at this point has nearly 'been lost forever,' as he acknowledges in his dying breath. As the narrative clearly illustrates, men must learn to overcome nature, not succumb to it.

Hawthorne's world, where people do not so much need to build as to purify themselves, contrasts sharply with the one envisioned by the Transcendentalists, especially the utopian Brook-Farmers, as is evident in the chapter 'The Leech and His Patient.' In this chapter, Chillingworth dissects Dimmesdale's soul as he searches for the minister's weakness, which he is convinced exists because the pastor has 'inherited a strong animal nature from his father or his mother.'

> Then, after long search into the minister's dim interior, and turning over many precious materials, in the shape of high aspirations for the welfare of his race, warm love of souls, pure sentiments, natural piety, strengthened by thought and study, and illuminated by revelation, – all of which invaluable gold was perhaps no better than rubbish to the seeker, – he would turn back, discouraged, and begin his quest towards another point.

This is not to say man's goodness is 'rubbish,' for it is not; it is 'invaluable gold' and rubbish only to a Chillingworth hunting human frailty. Yet goodness exists side by side with the frailty Chillingworth seeks, and eventually finds, in the pious, selfless, Dimmesdale. As we see in *The Scarlet Letter*, human frailty is a vital reality, and a man's urge to have sex with his mother is as real as his desire for universal brotherhood. In fact, the story suggests that universal brotherhood is based on human frailty. Hester, a 'general symbol at which the preacher and moralist might point, and in which they might vivify and embody their image of woman's frailty and sinful passion,' through her experience, gains 'a sympathetic knowledge of the hidden sin in other hearts' because they too are familiar with human weakness and sorrow. Hester speculates that 'if truth were everywhere to be shown, a scarlet letter would blaze forth on many a bosom besides' her own. And indeed it would blaze from every *bosom*, as the Oedipal stage is at some time common to every mother-son relationship.

The common bond of human weakness and misery, of which Hester is acutely aware, operates as the mysterious force that keeps her among her neighbors, though she is 'free to return to her birthplace, or any other European land.' Indeed, after a lengthy sojourn across the waters, Hester comes back to Boston to take up 'her long-forsaken shame,' for the bond of frailty and sorrow, represented in Hester's relations with her New England brethren, provides a kinship many times stronger than anything offered in a fairy-tale existence among the 'armorial seals' of Europe: 'But there was a more real life for Hester Prynne, here, in New England, than in the unknown region where Pearl had found a home.' Counselling and comforting the 'wounded, wasted, and wronged,' Hester spends her last years, I suggest, as 'the destined prophetess' which she thought herself unworthy to be because of her sin, shame, and sorrow. Ironically, it is the very traits that enable her to reveal the truth that will 'establish the whole relation between man and woman on a surer ground of mutual happiness.' This truth, that men and women, like humanity as a whole, are bound more closely by weakness and sorrow than by strength and joy, reflects the nature of Hawthorne's Oedipal relationship with his mother. And, as Freudians might argue, and as Hawthorne's tale seems to indicate, a healthy awareness of Oedipal forces would provide pure ground on which to establish 'the whole relation between man and woman.'

The proper prophet must be humbly aware of his own frailty, sin, and shame, as Hester was of hers. However, Hester failed to realize her vocation because of her delusion, which was shared by Hawthorne's Transcendental neighbors, that the

> angel or apostle of the coming revelation must be . . . lofty, pure, and beautiful; and wise, moreover, not through dusky grief, but the ethereal medium of joy; and showing how sacred love should make us happy, by the truest test of a life successful to such an end!

This happy expectation about a life lofty, pure, and beautiful rings hollow not only in this instance, but throughout Hawthorne's fiction. Chillingworth in his denouncement of 'wise and pious' men like Dimmesdale, whose speech affected his listeners 'like the speech of an angel,' or like St. Ralph the Optimist (Emerson), whose speech was reputed to exert a similar influence on his audience, expresses a major theme in *The Scarlet Letter*, indeed in all of Hawthorne's writing:

> These men deceive themselves. . . . Their love for man, their zeal for God's service, – these holy impulses may or may not coexist in their hearts with the evil inmates of which their guilt has unbarred the door, and which must needs propagate a hellish breed within them. But, if they seek to glorify God, let them not lift heavenward their unclean hands! If they would serve their fellow-men, let them do it by making manifest the power and reality of conscience, in constraining them to penitential self-abasement!

All men, even prophets, are guilty. Those who would serve mankind are instructed to repent, to preach the gospel of frailty and sorrow with public confessions, as Dimmesdale, and Hawthorne, did. Yet I think it would have been difficult for Hawthorne to imagine a penitent Emerson. Emerson was widely perceived as preaching an energetic optimism to a young, expanding nation, whose optimism was compatible with the belief in man's potential for the pure, beautiful, and lofty. This belief, Hawthorne, whose pessimism seems more appropriate to the seventeenth or twentieth centuries, could not accept. His rejection of this belief, incorporated into the Oedipal drama of *The Scarlet Letter*, endures a vision of frailty and sorrow, his and ours.[15] □

Building on Levi's and Daniel's readings of the novel as an expression of its author's Oedipal feelings through the characterisation of Dimmesdale, Joanne Feit Diehl, Pierce Professor of English at Hawthorne's old *alma mater*, Bowdoin College, in an essay entitled 'Re-reading *The Letter*: Hawthorne, the Fetish, and the (Family) Romance' (1991), explores a subtext that links the motives for writing to a search for the lost mother. The relationship between the authorial self and the lost mother Diehl sees as ambivalent, for the mother is an object of desire that must be denied. Rather than follow any single line of interpretation based on character or character relationships in the novel, Diehl prefers to focus on the letter A for it articulates most compellingly the conflict between desire for the mother and the guilt associated with that desire. The scarlet A, Diehl suggests, functions in ways very like Freud's fetishistic object, a fetish being something which both represents desire and its necessary repression. The desire for the mother and the censoring power of custom conjoin in Hawthorne's 'A'. The excerpt from Diehl's essay, reprinted below, discusses the representation of Hester as a distant, unattainable object of desire, and Dimmesdale's attempts, through language, to re-possess the woman he has lost. The excerpt begins with a consideration of Dimmesdale's Election Day sermon:

■ Hawthorne follows this description of oracular power with a vision of Hester immobile, almost lifeless, listening attentively to the muffled strains of Dimmesdale's voice . . . She is transfixed by history (*his story*), objectified by the passion of the past. The sinful minister reaches out to the mute woman through his voice; but by the close of the afternoon, he will have fallen into her arms in an ultimate appeal for disclosure and reunification.

Before observing this climactic moment (of the final scaffold scene), however, the reader should note how Hawthorne's language prepares his audience to imagine this public reunion between Dimmesdale and Hester not simply as the meeting of two formerly clandestine lovers, but as a reunion of mother and son as well. The dynamics of family interaction (specifically, between infant and mother) and the anxiety over language's capacity to carry the self into the presence of what it most desires dominate the descriptions that precede Dimmesdale and Hester's final meeting. Throughout the Election Day scene, Hawthorne employs images that associate Dimmesdale with the rejected, ever-apprehensive son who longs to journey back to the sexually tainted, yet longed-for mother. Within the description of communal activities of Election Day, Hawthorne sketches the drama of the toddler, reaching out to an immobile, statue-like woman who welcomes him only when he collapses, on the verge of death, in her arms. Stasis and movement acquire great poignancy, as the extreme efforts of a dying man evoke his earliest beginnings. Furthermore, Hawthorne partly builds his sustained narrative of filial return on his characterizations of Hester as an image of death. Her face, he writes, resembled 'a mask; or rather . . . the frozen calmness of a dead woman's features; owing this dreary resemblance to the fact that Hester was actually dead, in respect to any claim of sympathy, and had departed out of the world with which she still seemed to mingle.'

This portrayal of Hester as death mask and statue reinforces the prohibition associated with the son's incestuous fantasy and through its very lifelessness serves to protect the perceiver from his own desires. The scarlet letter alone shines out from the grayness of maternal death, at once preserving the sign of desire and barring the possibility of its fulfillment. The simultaneity of the A's function as both signifier and denier of desire opens the letter to ever-recurrent misinterpretation, for just as Dimmesdale depends on the Puritan community's *mis*interpretation of narrative events (the appearance of the lost glove on the scaffold and the revelation of the A shining in the night sky) to protect his guilt and not to expose it, so the narrative establishes a pattern of substitutive identifications that play equally on the community of its readers to *fail* to recognize the sublimated incestuous wishes covered by the text. This tension between disclosure and concealment is the narrative corollary to the fetish's function: to mask desire while naming it. Both depend on the intersubjectivity of author, narrator, and reader – an affiliative community that for the readers of *The Scarlet Letter* provokes a certain anxiety.

Therefore, what Dimmesdale witnesses is a mask of deception and a sign that discloses, for Hester's frozen calmness belies her passionate conviction that she and Dimmesdale should leave Boston and flee to Europe. As instigator of this plot and in a maternal assumption of responsibility, Hester attempts to direct their mutual future as lovers. That Dimmesdale subverts Hester's intentions by succumbing to his own death speaks to the deeply violative cast of her double role as mother and lover – as well as to the son's desperate psychic need to suppress the incestuous wish and to keep his already violated mother intact. But, although the death mask presages the defeat of Hester's 'solution' on one level of the narrative, the A nevertheless holds before Dimmesdale the sign that the worst has already happened; it is the ever-present sign of transgression kept firmly before his and our eyes.

When Dimmesdale, exhausted from having delivered his sermon, moves from the altar and joins the procession of church fathers, he begins his regressive journey back to the maternal, statue-like form: 'He still walked onward,' Hawthorne writes, 'if that movement could be so described, which rather resembled the wavering effort of an infant, with its mother's arms in view, outstretched to tempt him forward.' By rejecting the hand of the 'venerable John Wilson,' Dimmesdale turns away from the powerful fathers and totters toward his greater need, reunion with the long-denied mother. As Dimmesdale finally reaches his literal family and reunites with them, it is with all the weakness of the child in need of support, yet with the moral righteousness of the savior; he is at once the infant Jesus and a sacrificial Christ . . . Hester lends him her physical support as the crowd next beholds 'the minister, leaning on Hester's shoulder and supported by her arm around him, approach the scaffold, and ascend its steps; while still the little hand of the sin-born child was clasped in his.' It is only when Dimmesdale confesses that he achieves true union with the tainted mother; the comfort of the breast, the reunion with the mother/lover, robs Chillingworth, the vengeful father, of life, as Dimmesdale turns his eyes from his adversary toward the source of maternal comfort. 'He withdrew his dying eyes from the old man, and fixed them on the woman and the child' . . . Yet the kiss he gives Pearl, while freeing her to enter the human community, only further ensures his certain death because it reawakens the knowledge that the chain of desire cannot be broken, that the violative incestuous feelings from which he is barred are awakened in the kiss that the father bestows on his daughter. For Dimmesdale, unable to resolve the terrifying involutions of such a Family Romance, death remains the sole escape.

Must a surrender of health, power, and maturity precede the return to the forbidden woman, and must the return lead to death? This question, shadowed as it is by guilt and longing, speaks not solely of Dimmesdale's predicament but, as I have been suggesting, of deep authorial anxieties as well. If the novel takes as one of its concerns the exploration of the extent of language's power, then the recurrent gestures of appeal and failure within the text signal a disturbing and potentially self-defeating judgment on Hawthorne's capacity as author to attain his desires and survive them, a premonitory warning about the nature of fiction writing that may have contributed to his difficulties in completing the novels – and, by the close of his life – his repeated abandonment of them. *The Scarlet Letter* – that most apparently 'complete' of Hawthorne's fictions, challenges language to reach beyond the grave, to test the powers of the word in order to discover whether language can carry the writer over the ground of human loss.

[. . .]

By obscuring the A's origins while intensifying its power, Hawthorne protects the object from scrutiny as he prepares the way for its special status in the text, *its function as a fetishistic object*. Surveyor Hawthorne must uncover in himself the reasons for such an identification/fixation, and this need for self-mastery through understanding becomes the occasion for the story's retelling. Just as Dimmesdale's Election Day sermon affects Hester in the absence of any articulated speech, so the power of the A depends not on linguistic prowess, but on the direct impact of all that cannot be articulated, the power of those unconscious forces that resist our ability either to adumbrate or to censor them.

Consequently, the A acquires power because among its many meanings it represents what cannot be spoken, the inviolate truth of what is most desired and what must be repressed, predominantly, the longing for the mother. Hawthorne's narrative achieves the identification of the mother's power with the A through its treatment of Hester, who demonstrates woman's ability to revise transgression in order to lead a socially constructive, if psychically restricted, life at the same time that she marks, with the wearing of the letter, the barrier against future temptation, or (given her sociocultural milieu) against 'sin.' Hester's identifying A not only lends her freedom by separating her from the community; it also leads her, in the narrator's view, dangerously close to chaos. For all its apparent freedoms, Hester's marginalization subdues her even as it becomes the source of her strength; even as it bestows compassion on others, motherhood blocks Hester's full intellectual development. In Hester, Hawthorne thus combines a vision of motherhood rendered inviolate with a portrait of the dangerous woman deprived of her full capacity to threaten either the community or contemporary standards of femininity. By making Hester Dimmesdale's contemporary, Hawthorne relaxes the oedipal connection, severing the male from the generational drama of separation anxiety that occurs instead between two females (Hester and *her* daughter, Pearl). Furthermore, by imposing both biological and communal constraints on Hester, Hawthorne reveals her power while he maintains authorial control over her actions and over his own suppressed, unresolved affect toward his biological mother. Narrative displacement serves the authorial 'ego' by protecting it from the full force of its unconscious, yet-to-be-resolved conflicts.

[. . .]

As father and as son, how can he (Hawthorne) afford to acknowledge her (Hester's) power without violating his own sense of authority, the masculine aspect of the self? By sympathizing with the enormity of the woman's task of transforming society, the narrator has rendered her beyond speech. Not only does all society act as an obstruction to woman's full expression, but also her public character mitigates against any speculative freedom that might culminate in action. So, to efface the discourse of woman while longing for her presence is to assign her a role that could not be equaled were she admitted to the community of social and verbal intercourse. By stripping her of her capacity to act, Hawthorne thus renders her safe: by converting her into myth, he condemns her to silence.

Placing such severe personal and historical restrictions on Hester – curtailing her power while granting Dimmesdale, in the midst of his duplicity, the freedom of speech – Hawthorne, as author, withstands being submerged by female presence. Among the rhetorical attempts to control female power, the most audacious is the metaphorical process whereby Hester Prynne, lover and mother, herself becomes orphaned, isolated, and homeless. Venturing too far in her speculative ruminations, she is lost, wandering 'without a clew in the dark labyrinth of mind; now turned aside by an insurmountable precipice; now starting back from a deep chasm. There was wild and ghastly scenery all around her, and a home and comfort nowhere.'

Despite the narrative containment of Hester's threatening power, the A will not relinquish its tenacious hold over the narrator's imagination . . . What are the sources of the A's residual power and why will it not fade with the story constructed to release its power? If the A functions as a hieroglyph within the context of the romance, if its meanings accrue through various points of view, then it may be immune (as Hawthorne had stated in the 'Preface') to unraveling and hence to analysis. The clue to its power, Hawthorne reveals, is contact with the wearer and the ability of the A to draw all eyes toward it, to *fix* the viewer's gaze. By escaping the boundaries of story, the A achieves status as a sign that draws us back to the origins of Hawthorne's romance, and, as I have argued, back to the scene of the mother's death. Desire for the lost mother and the censoring power of the Custom-House merge in the scarlet A. And it is to a discussion of the A as fetish that I now turn.

According to Freud, the origins of the fetish can be traced to its function as a 'substitute for the woman's (the mother's) penis that the little boy once believed in and – for reasons familiar to us – does not want to give up.' Freud continues: 'What happened, therefore, was that the boy refused to take cognizance of the fact of his having perceived that a woman does not possess a penis,' and that 'if a woman had been castrated, then his (the boy's) own possession of a penis was in danger'.[16] As a sign of the history of this fear and longing, which Hawthorne can face only in the disguised form of fictive displacement, the A functions in the narrative both to focus and to dispel such authorial tensions. Whether or not the fetish serves as a textual 'symptom' is not really my concern; of interpretive interest here is the way the scarlet letter operates as a narrative means for resolving an otherwise unresolvable conflict within the fiction; in other words, the text functions therapeutically to provide a means for treating material otherwise closed off from literary production.

The A would therefore represent among its meanings the desired Other whose presence in the fiction can only be acknowledged through its absence, the penis displaced by a vagina that becomes a sign of the female genitalia of the mother forever barred from her son. Indeed, the A articulates through its linear geometry the illustration of forbidden desire. Its divergent verticals suggest a schematic drawing of the vagina, viewed at once frontally and from below, and the horizontal bar of the letter signifies the intact hymeneal membrane, the sign that no violation has occurred. Thus the A signifies a double denial: no marriage and no consummation. Scarlet recalls both the blood of the torn hymen (presenting what is in the same symbol denied – that the mother has [not] been violated) and the color of sexual passion. Moreover, in its artful complexity, the embroidered letter converts this potentially threatening vision of blood and pubic hair, the Medusan coils of active sexuality, into a refined and highly elaborated pattern. Constructed by that most domestic of crafts, the female art of needlework, the letter again operates as a fetish by recalling the forbidden sight even as it protects the gazer from the object's symbolic identity.

The relationship between the scarlet letter and its viewers is not, however, restricted to that of a fetishist and his fetish; for there is no *single* character who defines herself or himself solely in these terms. Instead, the scarlet letter becomes a focus that attracts the kinds of sexual ambivalence and tensions that characterize the text in its entirety and that defines itself in relation to each of the primary characters. For Dimmesdale, the A serves as a mirror of the physical torment he suffers – the outward, external elaboration of the stigmatizing desire for the other disguised as a desire for remorse. Consequently, the flagellation he pursues, the simultaneous stimulation and punishment of the self, is a practice that discloses his libidinal energies as it releases them. For Chillingworth, the A functions as the mark of his home; it is what keeps him on the edges of a civilization therefore negatively defined, and what, through his direct and active intervention, reifies his revenge against Dimmesdale, the transgressor, the son. Hester as the mother who is everywhere present but unattainable, who is given a free imagination yet kept from action, who undergoes 'rehabilitation' in terms of society yet must suffer the constant torture of shame, receives the kind of ambivalent treatment from the author that Freud would also ascribe to the fetishist. When Dimmesdale, in his dying moments, abjures any hope for Hester's soul, we may sense the anger behind the rhetorical orthodoxy of his rejection of the possibility that her soul, too, might be saved. And the wearer of the fetish herself participates in ambivalence toward the object when she attempts to cast it off, to deny its historicity and return instead to her lover. Out of this matrix of identities, the A emerges not simply as a mark of the forbidden phallic mother, but also as a sign of the complex interdependencies that are at the center of all human relationships.

Furthermore, it is not without significance that Hester wears the A on her breast and that she should first be seen leaving that dark prison with the infant Pearl at her bosom, for the sign of the forbidden transmuted into art – the craft of embroidery – is, throughout the romance, associated with female fecundity. The power of the mother as nurturing artist, albeit severely restricted by the innately conservative narrator's control, stands clear before the reader. Trapped by societal expectations, Dimmesdale, unlike Hester, wins verbal power but is denied all earthly freedom. Oppressed and outwardly punished as she may be, it is the woman who, by the very fact of becoming an outcast, discovers her more 'modest' freedom on the margins of community.

This radical, transforming power thus depends on Hester's marginalization; what keeps her from a more austere radicalism are the presence of Pearl and the narrator's convictions concerning the inherently passive nature of woman. However, to the extent that Hester, no matter how tentatively, turns the A into a symbol of compassion, she wins the potential for transmuting guilt into strength. Dimmesdale, unable to do so until his dying hour (itself troubling in its sadistic orthodoxy), spends his postlapsarian years apparently enduring a festering wound that becomes a masochistic sign of the destructive, if supremely eloquent, artist. This somatization of guilt has a double origin in Chillingworth and the minister, as one feeds on the other in a relationship that grotesquely caricatures that of the nursing mother and her infant Pearl.

If, in conclusion, we accept the scarlet letter's resemblance to the fetish, then Hester, rather than Dimmesdale, embodies an alternative prevision to Freudian theories of the fetish. By drawing our eyes to the woman's breast and the art inscribed thereon, Hawthorne not only ensures visibility for the letter, but he also reinforces Hester's roles of nurturer and artist as synonymous and mutually dependent functions. Rather than signifying the fetish as a denial of an unwished-for absence (the way the letter functions for Dimmesdale), for Hester the letter serves to transform the double negative association of the absence of male genitalia and thwarted desire into a sign that represents the combined powers of nursing mother and creative woman. That Pearl is such a difficult child, that through her milk Hester transmits turbulence as well as nourishment, only further underscores the difficulties inherent in the relationship between sexuality and art – an ambivalence toward maternal origins which, in Hawthorne's works, neither man nor woman can evade.

Free to bury, dismiss, or redeem his characters, Hawthorne, at the close of the novel, performs all three gestures, but it is the paradoxical triumph of the A's imaginative life that it will not fade with time, but evades closure to shine with all the initial fervor of the burning desire with which the story began. Vivid as the letter within the narrator's imagination, it shines out past the final moments of the text, but with a telling difference: what we see when we read "'ON A FIELD, SABLE, THE LETTER A, GULES'" is a verbal substitution for the engraving that is inscribed on a tombstone. The sign is doubly displaced, first by the descriptive sentence that contains the sign and second by the heraldic device that represents, or stands in for, the words bearing the message that identifies the letter. Thus, the fetishistic object undergoes a further distancing as it is associated directly both with death and with the two lovers resting, albeit with a space between them, side by side. Despite the narrator's claim that the inscription serves as a motto for the story that precedes it, the heraldic device, when translated into words, does not so much explain or 'sum up' the story as it insists upon the A's abiding presence. In this final description's act of double distancing, Hawthorne reiterates the resilience of what the A symbolizes: the desire for contact and reunion with the forbidden, which must be approached through a language that will protect the very distance the author seeks to traverse.

Theorizing on the character of desire and its relation to denial, Leo Bersani has commented that 'a sense both of the forbidden nature of certain desires and of the incompatibility of reality with our desiring imagination makes the negation of desire inevitable. But to deny desire is not to eliminate it; in fact, such denials multiply the appearances of each desire in the self's history. In denying a desire, we condemn ourselves to finding it everywhere.'[17] In narrative terms, this would suggest that the A, rather than diminishing in force, gathers its own momentum, just as writing provides access to the origins of the scene of repression but cannot, of course, restore the scene with the incestuous wish intact. Although in the opening pages of 'The Custom-House,' the narrator had announced his desire to depart Salem and escape the 'press of the familiar,' the romance's close reveals instead a desire to return to the motherland and to speak with a voice that will reach the dead. Like the archives of the unconscious that, as Derrida maintains, 'are always already transcriptions,' so the worn yet still powerfully evocative A-shaped piece of cloth Surveyor Hawthorne discovers already represents the transcription of his author's unconscious transgressive desire for the dead mother. As a sign that bars itself, the A operates for Dimmesdale within *The Scarlet Letter* as does the fetish, both to presence the forbidden desire and to keep that forbidden incestuous wish from being brought to consciousness. That the A, on the other hand, empowers rather than defeats Hester, that the experience of mothering affords her the capacity to transmute the stigma of shame into a badge of commitment and charity, suggests the regenerative power of the woman – a fact that she is nevertheless prohibited from displaying in verbal discourse, forbidden as she is from becoming the prophet of a new and more enlightened age. In my judgment, that she is so deprived speaks to the Hawthornian insistence on silencing the mother and thereby of further identifying the deeply troubled but verbally empowered fetishist with the father and the son.

Shadowing the text and shining beyond it, the scarlet A therefore signifies at once the articulated oedipal anxieties and the covert incestuous desires expressed in the fetishistic silence. Yet the A also signifies a breaking of that silence, for it represents a conflict between the desiring authorial son and the yearnings of the phallic mother, the mother who would free herself from his fetishizing imagination to achieve the authority tested, but finally denied her, in *The Scarlet Letter* – the power of the woman's voice. Imprisoned in her maternal identity while protected by it, Hester cannot escape its stigmatization as Pearl can, because the mother is drawn back to the scene of the 'crime,' as much victimized by the altruism that converts her A into 'Angel' as by the adultery for which it ostensibly stands. Similarly, Dimmesdale, the transgressing son, can acknowledge his paternity only at the moment of his death: punishment for the violation that has always already occurred is the price of adulthood. That maternity and paternity are psychically illicit from the point of view of the child only underscores the significance of the primal scene. Finally, when we, as readers, gaze at the scarlet letter, we might imagine the unconscious text Hawthorne recollects in his narrative, witnessing along with him the scar of primal desire, the bleeding yet inviolate wound, the cultural script, or, as Chillingworth would have it, the 'dark necessity' that implicates us all in the novel's fatal Family Romance.[18] □

CHAPTER FIVE

Feminist Criticism

FEMINIST LITERARY criticism is a product of the women's movement that emerged in the late 1960s. Early feminist criticism examined the classics, for the most part the work of males, usually to discover in them negative and even destructive attitudes to women. Hawthorne was, of course, among the writers who were studied, but, according to Nina Baym, one of the leading feminist commentators on Hawthorne's work, he presented problems for the feminist critic who wished simply 'to define him as an orthodox espouser of patriarchal attitudes'. Despite Baym's claim that 'feminists abandoned him for other writers more suited to their aims', *The Scarlet Letter*, with its strong, independent, central female character struggling to define herself in an oppressive Puritan and patriarchal world, has produced some extremely interesting and challenging criticism from a feminist perspective.

A feminist critique can not only open up the text in new ways, but allow us to see the limitations of other critical approaches. Baym, in 'Thwarted Nature: Nathaniel Hawthorne as Feminist' (1982), has shown how prefeminist criticism analysed Hawthorne's women within one of three larger interpretive frameworks. First, there were the moralist critics who treated Hester as a symbol or type within Hawthorne's religious or moral allegory. In some of these analyses she was the 'dark woman' who represented sin and temptation; in others, especially those influenced by the New Criticism, she was seen as a more complex and ambiguous figure, representing passional and liberalising tendencies as well as, say, pride, secularism and subversiveness. Second, there were the psychological critics who viewed Hester as a projection of Hawthorne's sexual psychology, specifically as a mother-figure through whom he sought to work out his own troublesome Oedipal feelings. And there were the historicist critics who treated Hester as an aspect of what was usually taken to be Hawthorne's deeply conservative social commentary, expressive of a traditional view of the role of women in society and a critical attitude to contemporary reform movements. Baym faults all of these approaches for seeing women as functions controlled by a larger design, whether ideological, psychological, or social. Such criticism she condemns as fundamentally reductive: 'The analysis, describing Hawthorne as a conservative in his ideas about women's place, patronizing in his estimate of their capacities, while all the while secretly fearful of their sexual power, identifies precisely the sort of patriarchal mind-set that feminists expect to find in writings by men.' Baym advertises her own criticism as an antidote to this picture of Hawthorne as antifeminist, reactionary and patriarchal, taking the 'unpopular line' that his writing does indeed possess 'feminist tendencies'. She summarises her view of Hawthorne's women as follows:

■ They represent desirable and valuable qualities lacking in the male protagonist. They offer him the opportunity to attain these qualities through erotic alliance or marriage. The man's invariable failure to take the opportunity is harshly judged by the narrator in fiction after fiction. During the first phase of Hawthorne's career (to 1849), he created male protagonists who suffer from isolation and self-absorption: women offer sociality, self-forgetfulness, connection . . . Later in his career, Hawthorne created males who were oversocialized and women signifying interior strength, passion, and individuality.

[. . .]

The psychological critics are right in claiming that the rejection of women is a major, even obsessive, motif in Hawthorne's fiction. What the psychological critics have not grasped is the fullness of Hawthorne's awareness of this obsession, as well as the nature of the repressed feelings about it. Unlike machismo authors who join their heroes in boasting about cruelty to women; unlike patriarchal authors who present gestures of contempt or dislike toward women disguised as affection, Hawthorne knows exactly what this sort of behavior means and depicts it as stupid, ugly, and evil. Far from affirming the rightness of traditional patriarchal politics, he sees them as deeply warped.

Ultimately, he holds men and the society that men have created responsible for mistaking neurosis for truth and elevating error into law, custom and morality. While condemning these obsessions, however, Hawthorne must represent them, and thus the question of his own motivation as an artist enters his discourse. He must hold himself responsible along with other men for injuries done to women; he inflicts injuries on imaginary women through the stories he creates, in which women are injured. To some degree he has a higher degree of responsibility than other men, because he has an awareness that others lack, and because therefore he knows how his moralizing art provides a license to depict what he condemns. His guilt and duplicity as a writer can be richly related to his full apprehension of the suspect ethical status of his achievement as the creator of compelling tales about mistreated women.

It is no wonder that critics have found it well nigh impossible to make the opposing tendencies in his work – the valorization of women, the abuse of women – cohere. . . . The task of a sophisticated feminist criticism would be to achieve in its discourse the coherence that so improbably exists in Hawthorne's work. Such a criticism would be based on the presumption that the question of women is *the* determining motive in Hawthorne's works, driving them as it drives Hawthorne's male characters. The question of woman is determining because these men are obsessed by their fantasies of women, controlled by them (and, as controllers of women, they engulf women in their fantasies as well).[1] □

Baym sees *The Scarlet Letter* as the pinnacle of Hawthorne's achievement because in it he experienced a 'freedom and excitement' through his unique deployment of a strong woman as his protagonist: '"Hester" gave Hawthorne the fullest command of his artistic powers that he had yet known. And, as events proved, the fullest command he was ever to know.'

■ Although criticism of *The Scarlet Letter* for a long time took Dimmesdale as the central character, it has more recently re-acknowledged what was well understood in Hawthorne's own time, that Hester is protagonist and center. The narrator allies himself with her and, despite occasional adverse judgments, devotes himself to her cause. His cause as narrator is to obliterate her obliteration, to force the reader to accept Hester's reading of her letter as a badge of honor instead of a mark of negation. The narrator forces us, just as Hester forces her Puritan townsmates, to see her as a good woman on her own terms. In contrast to the two distorted male personalities who counterpoise her – the one obsessed with revenge, the other with his own purity – Hester appears almost a miracle of wholeness and sanity. While these men struggle with their own egos and fantasies, she has real battles – to maintain her self-respect in a community that scorns her, to stay sane in solitude, to support herself and her child, to raise that child to normal adulthood despite so many obstacles. Curiously, though she has been cast out of society, Hester remains very much in the world, whereas Chillingworth and Dimmesdale at the very center of society are totally immured in their self-absorption. In her inner integrity and her outer responsiveness, Hester is a model and a counter-statement.

Cautiously, Hawthorne advances the notion that if society is to be changed for the better, such change will be initiated by women. But because society has condemned Hester as a sinner, the good that she can do is greatly circumscribed. Her achievements in a social sense come about as by-products of her personal struggle to win a place in the society; and the fact that she wins her place at last indicates that society has been changed by her.[2] □

While criticising reductive feminist critics in 'Thwarted Nature: Nathaniel Hawthorne as Feminist', for seeing only patriarchal conformism in Hawthorne, in a slightly earlier essay, 'The Significance of Plot in Hawthorne's Romances' (1981), she takes issue with a male critic, the influential Darrel Abel (see pages 35–41), who, despite his insistence on the limitations of New Criticism, undertakes an essentially New Critical reading of *The Scarlet Letter* which, in Baym's view, ignores the plot in order to play down the centrality of Hester's role in the novel, and both the romantic and 'radical' aspects of Hawthorne's moral vision. Abel, she says, seeks to 'diminish the significance of Hester' and, like many other critics of the 1950s, treats Dimmesdale not Hester as the true centre of the story. From a structural point of view, Baym argues, this is untenable.

■ Of the romance's twenty-four chapters, thirteen are 'about' Hester, three are 'about' Hester and Dimmesdale both, and eight are 'about' Dimmesdale. In 'The Custom-House' the scarlet letter is associated entirely with Hester, and Surveyor Pue charges the author to tell Hester Prynne's story. 'The Custom-House' says not a word about Arthur Dimmesdale.[3] □

In considering the reasons why so many critics of the 1950s refused to give Hester her proper place as protagonist of the novel, Baym believes part of the answer lies in the overt social ideology of New Criticism:

■ Within important constraints, Hester and her behavior are associated with the ideals of passion, self-expression, freedom, and individualism against ideals of order, authority, and restraint. If she were in fact the heroine, then Hawthorne would have to be understood as a kind of romantic: exactly what the New Critics were trying to disprove. Hence, she had to be relegated to a subordinate role and seen as the object of Hawthorne's disapproval.

Beyond this, however, I have come to the regretful conclusion that some of the unwillingness, perhaps much of it, to recognize Hester as the protagonist came from a more covert aspect of the New Critical social ideology, its strong sense of appropriate male/female roles and its consequent conviction that it would be improper for a woman character to be the protagonist in what might well be the greatest American book. It is for this reason, I believe, that so many of the arguments 'against' Hester's importance in the book focus on the assertion that during the course of the romance she steps out of her proper woman's place, defeminizes herself, and ceases to be a woman in some conventional sociobiological definition of the term.[4] □

Thus, in the major, book-length statement of her ideas – *The Shape of Hawthorne's Career* (1976) – Baym considers the novel as the presentation of the conflict between ideals of passion, self-expression, freedom and individualism on one hand, and on the other hand, ideals of order, authority, and restraint. Hester is identified as a representative of 'the human passionate and creative forces', while Dimmesdale is the 'guilt-prone male, torn between rebellious and conforming impulses' (p. 124). Hester is a figure of the artist who, through her fantastic embroidery of the scarlet letter, escapes the authority of the Puritan fathers and re-creates her donated identity: 'By making the letter beautiful, Hester is denying its literal meaning and thereby subverting the intention of the magistrates who condemn her to wear it' (p. 132). At the heart of Baym's argument is the idea that Hawthorne's identification with Hester, especially with her subversive and transforming activity, is the fundamental inspiration of his own creativity. A connection is suggested between femininity, embroidery, storytelling ('imagination'), and defiance of patriarchal structures.

■ 'The Custom-House' . . . essay tells the story of a conversion to the idea of literature as self-expression, in defiance of external and introjected social demands. It suggests that the psychological survival of the 'I' depended upon that conversion.

[. . .]

Hawthorne represents his romance, *The Scarlet Letter*, as originating in the attempts of his imagination to make itself felt and keep itself alive in the deadly atmosphere of the Custom House. His withdrawal from the tedium of the first-floor routine into the cluttered chambers of the upper story signifies Hawthorne's withdrawal into his own mind, his escape into fantasy. But in these circumstances, fantasy is an escape to freedom rather than a retreat from life. It is an affirmative rather than a denying gesture.

[. . .]

Because in *The Scarlet Letter* the A signifies a social crime, Hawthorne suggests that the writing of his romance is in some sense an analogously guilty act. My analysis of *The Scarlet Letter*, stressing the self-expressive and passionate nature of Hester's and Dimmesdale's act, indicates why there is an analogy. For Hawthorne, the romance originated as expression of his own feelings of social defiance and discontent, as a reaction to the stifling position of surveyor in the Custom House at Salem. The decision to write the romance, or to try to write it, involves a transference of Hawthorne's allegiance from his Puritan conscience to his imagination, personified in 'The Custom-House' by Surveyor Pue. Adopting this figure as his 'official ancestor,' Hawthorne accepts the former surveyor's charge that he publicize Hester's story.[5] □

A slightly earlier feminist text than Baym's, Judith Fryer's *The Faces of Eve: Women in the Nineteenth-Century American Novel* (1976), emphasises a greater degree of 'ambivalence' in Hawthorne's treatment of Hester than Baym admits. Fryer's traditional close reading of the text combines biographical criticism with myth criticism. As her title indicates, Fryer revisits the traditional trope of the New World Garden of Eden which goes back through R. W. B. Lewis (see pages 42–5) to the early explorers' and settlers' narratives.

■ Hester Prynne is warm, alive, human – so much so that it is difficult to determine just where Hawthorne's sympathies lie. In making her the best – the most 'human' – character in the book he is at his most ambiguous in his valuation of both community mores and individual deviance, with Hester's life-giving but threatening sexuality once again standing for the hazard which individuality poses to the very survival of the community. I do not use the word 'ambiguous' lightly here; I believe that Hawthorne was not finally able to resolve his own dilemma. He, as his own marriage to the 'safe' Sophia demonstrates, needed the security of community; but as alienated artist he felt estranged from that community which defined 'masculinity' in terms of success in the commercial world. His profound sense of alienation led him in 1825 to seclude himself in his 'owl's nest' from a world in which he perceived no way to acknowledge the 'femininity' of his own artistic nature. In an attempt to reestablish contact with the human community, he wrote to Longfellow on June 4, 1837: 'By some witchcraft or other – for I really cannot assign any reasonable why and wherefore – I have been carried apart from the main current of life, and find it impossible to get back again. Since we last met . . . I have secluded myself from society; and yet I never meant any such thing, nor dreamed what sort of life I was going to lead. I have made a captive of myself and put me into a dungeon; and now I cannot find the key to let myself out – and if the door were open, I should be almost afraid to come out. . . . For the last ten years I have not lived, but only dreamed about living.' His few attempts to find his 'place' in the world were futile. He sees himself, in 'The Custom-House' preface to *The Scarlet Letter*, as an 'idler,' an oddity to have sprung from 'the old trunk of the family tree, with so much venerable moss upon it,' and never regards his sojourn there as anything other than 'a transitory life' because in the quest for 'Uncle Sam's gold' all 'imaginative delight . . . passed away out of my mind.' His sojourn at Brook Farm proved no more successful. As he wrote to Sophia in the fall of 1841, 'A man's soul may be buried and perish under a dung-heap or in the furrow of a field, just as well as under a pile of money.' His salvation was his marriage to Sophia; she provided him with both a link to society and protective solitude – the combination necessary for his creativity. 'Thou only hast revealed me to myself,' he wrote to her in 1840, 'for without thy aid, my best knowledge of myself would have been merely to know my own shadow – to watch it flickering on the wall, and mistake its fantasies for my own real actions. Indeed, we are but shadows – we are not endowed with real life, and all that seems most real about us is but the thinnest substance of a dream – till the heart is touched. That touch creates us – then we begin to be – . . . '

But Sophia was no richly vital, fully sexual Hester Prynne. She is, in the same letter, his 'Dove': 'I begin to understand why I was imprisoned so many years in this lonely chamber, and why I could never break through the viewless bolts and bars; for if I had sooner made my escape into the world, I should have grown hard and rough, and been covered with earthly dust, and my heart would have become callous by rude encounters with the multitude; so that I should have been all unfit to shelter a heavenly Dove in my arms.'

Hawthorne, then, places great value on belonging to the society *through* Sophia, his dove, the preserver of society's standards; yet at the same time, as an artist he is at odds with that very society. Whoever touches Uncle Sam's gold, he warns in 'The Custom-House,' 'should look well to himself, or he may find the bargain to go hard against him, involving, if not his soul, yet many of its better attributes; its sturdy force, its courage and constancy, its truth, its self-reliance, and all that gives emphasis to manly character.' His use of the word 'manly' here is different from his perception of society's definition of that term elsewhere in 'The Custom-House.' It suggests the difficulty he has accepting what he feels to be the 'unmanly' qualities of his artistic self, and is therefore a clue to his own sexual insecurity. Those 'manly' attributes are also the very qualities which both make Hester Prynne attractive and condemn her: 'sturdy force,' 'courage and constancy,' 'truth,' 'self-reliance,' – attributes diametrically opposed to those of Sophia, qualities which in a woman cannot preserve the community, but would destroy it.

Hawthorne's ambiguity about Hester, then, is an attempt to work out his ambiguity toward himself, as artist, as man, as member of the human community. When he places her scarlet letter on his own breast in 'The Custom-House,' he experiences 'a sensation not altogether physical, yet almost so, as of burning heat; and as if the letter were not of red cloth, but red-hot iron.' The 'A' of the alienated artist is the subject of most of Hawthorne's tales. This warning from 'Wakefield,' for example (later echoed by Zenobia in *The Blithedale Romance*), is a warning for Hawthorne the artist and Hester the woman alike: 'Amid the seeming confusion of our mysterious world, individuals are so nicely adjusted to a system, and systems to one another and to a whole, that, by stepping aside for a moment a man exposes himself to a fearful risk of losing his place forever.'

The importance of 'place' must not be discounted by twentieth-century readers who would see Hester Prynne as 'androgynous' and Hawthorne as a writer with 'feminist' sympathies. If Hawthorne the artist was not sure which values – those of Uncle Sam or those of 'truth' and 'self reliance' – were manly, how much less did Hester Prynne lack a context for her androgynous qualities. Hawthorne himself would deny women such a context. He wrote, for example, in his biography of 'Mrs. Hutchinson':

Woman's intellect should never give the tone to that of man; and even her morality is not exactly the material for masculine virtue. [It is] a false liberality, which mistakes the strong division-lines of Nature for arbitrary distinctions. . . . As yet, the great body of American women are a domestic race; but when a continuance of ill-judged incitements shall have turned their hearts away from the fireside, there are obvious circumstances which will render female pens more numerous and more prolific than those of men . . . and the ink-stained Amazons will expel their rivals by actual pressure, and petticoats wave triumphantly over all the field. Fame does not increase the peculiar respect which men pay to female excellence, and there is a delicacy . . . that perceives, or fancies, a sort of impropriety in the display of woman's natal mind to the gaze of the world. . . . In fine, criticism should examine with a stricter, instead of a more indulgent eye, the merits of females at its bar, because they are to justify themselves for an irregularity which men do not commit in appearing there; and woman, when she feels the impulse of genius like a command of Heaven within her, should be aware that she is relinquishing a part of the loveliness of her sex, and obey the inward voice with sorrowing reluctance, like the Arabian maid who bewailed the gift of prophecy.

I have quoted this long passage on Anne Hutchinson because it is necessary to understand Hawthorne's attitude toward strong women in
any attempt to decide upon his sympathies for Hester Prynne, and
because *The Scarlet Letter* is set in Anne Hutchinson's Boston. There are
two deliberate references linking Anne Hutchinson to Hester Prynne.
In the initial chapter a wild rose-bush blooms by the prison door from
which Hester emerges; it is said to have 'sprung up under the footsteps
of the sainted Anne Hutchinson.' And in the chapter called 'Another
View of Hester' we are told that had little Pearl not come to her from
the spiritual world, then 'she might have come down to us in history,
hand in hand with Anne Hutchinson as the foundress of a religious
sect. She might . . . have been a prophetess. She might, and not
improbably would, have suffered death from the stern tribunals of the
period, for attempting to undermine the foundations of the Puritan
establishment.' This is a clue to the whole questions of Hester and of
Hawthorne's ambiguity in posing her against a group of grim, intolerant and even unChristian Puritans, who do, nevertheless, comprise a
community. Hester's deviance from its norms represents not an alternative community, not the Garden, but the wildness of the forest.

   The Scarlet Letter is a novel about a failed community. Like *The
Blithedale Romance*, the novel specifically about Hawthorne's involvement in a (failed) utopian community, the earlier *Scarlet Letter* is
contemporaneous with that experience. As he saw the attempt to re-
create Eden at Brook Farm as a doomed attempt in Blithedale, so he
perceived the vision of the founders of the Massachusetts Bay Colony
as doomed from the beginning. He believed the roots of evil to exist in
the individual, not in social institutions; he was more interested in
psychology than in social change. One is prepared by the remark in
the preface that 'Neither the front nor the back entrance of the Custom-
House opens on the road to Paradise' for the opening of *The Scarlet
Letter*: 'The founders of a new colony, whatever Utopia of human virtue
and happiness they might originally project, have invariably recognized
it among their earliest practical necessities to allot a portion of the virgin soil as a cemetery, and another portion as the site of a prison.'
There is not only death in this New World Garden of Eden; there are
deviants who are so obnoxious or dangerous to the community that
they must be locked up. Such malefactors might be Antinomians,
Quakers or other 'heterodox religionists,' Indians, or witches, among
them Anne Hutchinson and Hester Prynne – the one represented by
the wild rose-bush, and the other, in contrast to the 'sad-colored garments' of the Puritans, by the 'fantastic flourishes of gold thread' of the
letter A, embroidered with 'much fertility and gorgeous luxuriance of
fancy.' The community is grim, but it is lawful; the rose-bush is beautiful, but it is wild; and the fantastically embroidered scarlet letter has

the effect of taking Hester 'out of the ordinary relations with humanity, and enclosing her in a sphere by herself.'

Hester's prideful stance upon the scaffold as she faces her judges, then, is deliberately modeled upon Anne Hutchinson's; they pose the same threat to the community. 'In the midst, and in the centre of all eyes, we see the woman,' Hawthorne wrote in his portrait of Anne Hutchinson. 'She stands loftily before her judges with a determined brow; and unknown to herself, there is a flash of carnal pride half hidden in her eye.' The members of this 'community,' in the words of John Winthrop's 'A Modell of Christian Charity' of 1629, the written compact for the Massachusetts Bay Colony, entered into a 'covenant' with God to do His will, literally to found 'a city upon a hill,' a New World Garden of Eden. Winthrop himself, in this document, is the Moses who will lead his people to the promised land. As Erikson points out in *Wayward Puritans*, . . . 'every community has its own set of boundaries, and its boundaries are determined by the behavior of its members.' The boundaries of the Massachusetts Bay Colony were clear; Winthrop defined them in his 'Little Speech on Liberty,' where 'civil' or 'federal' liberty is a covenant between God and man, represented politically by the subjection of citizens to those in authority as God's representatives. It is this same kind of 'liberty' which makes a wife, after she has chosen her husband through her own free will, subject to him: 'a true wife accounts her subjection her honor and freedom.' Ostensibly punished for her Antinomian (literally, against the law) beliefs, Anne Hutchinson was a woman who did not keep 'in the place God had set her.' Witch or feminist, depending on one's point of view – her skills as nurse and midwife indicating her knowledge of the secrets of birth and healing outside the realm of men, and her theological discussion groups our first women's consciousness-raising sessions – she opposed the church fathers, among them the same John Wilson who takes part in condemning and punishing Hester.

Hester, too, has perpetrated a crime against church and state: she has committed adultery and borne an illegitimate child. But her refusal as a woman to keep to her appointed place would have placed her outside the boundaries of the self-righteous community had her conduct been otherwise irreproachable. And Hester is a real, not an imagined threat to the community, as her 'natural dignity and force of character' – unusual in a person just emerging from a long prison confinement to face a public humiliation – make clear. Had no stigma attached itself to her, she would have attempted nothing less than revolution. Hester often broods upon the 'dark question' of 'the whole race of womanhood,' and her conclusions – that the 'system of society is to be torn down and built up anew' – are bothersome to Hawthorne because it would mean a modification of 'the very nature of the opposite sex' necessary to women's being 'allowed to assume what seems a fair and suitable position.' There can be no reforms, he says, until woman shall have undergone a mighty change 'in which, perhaps, the ethereal essence, wherein she has her truest life, will be found to have evaporated.' A man who himself married a pale maiden can only be at best ambivalent in his admiration for Hester. He calls the 'ethereal essence' her 'truest life.' And he cannot help adding, 'A woman never overcomes these problems by any exercise of thought. They are not to be solved, or only in one way. If her heart chance to come uppermost, they vanish.'

In Hawthorne's later books the 'ethereal essence' of the dark lady will have evaporated; it will belong to the pale maiden, the blonde or brown-haired New England girl. Because Hester is not split into schizophrenic segments, she comes across as a whole person, one who elicits the reader's admiration. She is his most perfect Eve, combining sensuality with an 'ethereal essence.' Like Eve's, Hester's crime was not really in tempting Adam, but in disobeying God the Father. Her exotic beauty, then, is an emblem of her spiritual deviance. She is tall, 'with a figure of perfect elegance.' Her dark and abundant hair is 'so glossy that it threw off the sunshine with a gleam,' and her face, 'besides being beautiful from regularity of feature and richness of complexion, had the impressiveness belonging to a marked brow and deep black eyes.' Her physical appearance 'seemed to express the attitude of her spirit, the desperate recklessness of her mood, by its wild and picturesque peculiarity.' Most significant, of course, is the fantastically embroidered scarlet letter, an emblem of Hester's extravagant beauty, deviance and alienation.

What makes Hester so interesting is that she has chosen both her act of illicit love and her feminist philosophy. She is a woman who acts, not a woman who is acted upon. Hester's emergence from prison into the open air 'as if by her own free will' is an act of self-reliance both literally and symbolically. 'Shame, Despair, Solitude,' will make a weak person – like Dimmesdale – weaker, but they have only served to harden Hester's strength. Although the shame of the scarlet letter burns, 'the tendency of her fate and fortunes had been to set her free. The scarlet letter was her passport into regions where other women dared not tread.'[6] □

Where Fryer saw the 'ambiguity' in Hawthorne's presentation of Hester as contributing to a pleasing roundedness and complexity of characterisation (though emanating from a personal 'dilemma'), Mary Suzanne Schriber, in *Gender and the Writer's Imagination* (1987), argues that, rather than an aesthetically satisfying effect, Hawthorne's 'celebrated ambiguity' is really an authorial confusion arising from an unfortunate contradiction between the words of the narrator and the deeds of Hester Prynne. Schriber sees Hester as a radically imaginative characterisation which challenged the culture's ideology, but once the challenge of her character had been issued, Hawthorne 'seemingly suffers a failure of nerve, investing his narrator with a series of speculations that serve to undermine the meaning of Hester's character and the unity of the romance'.

■ The opening scene of *The Scarlet Letter* depends heavily on implicit preconceptions of woman's nature to engage both the authorial audience assumed by the text and the narrative audience gathered at the scaffold. The situation is intrinsically interesting and would draw onlookers, no matter who mounted the scaffold. The implied author increases attention to the situation, however, by exploiting Hester's status as a woman as well as an accused sinner. He shows her to be a transgressor of woman's nature and of the law, a woman who apparently feels proper shame but also an improper defiance, manifested by her proud self-presentation. The town beadle first comes through the doorway, stretches forth his staff in his left hand, and lays 'his right upon the shoulder of a young woman, whom he thus drew forward; until, on the threshold of the prison-door, she repelled him, by an action marked with natural dignity and force of character, and stepped into the open air, as if by her own free will.' This is clearly a woman who refuses to be restricted and guided; in repelling a representative of the law, she acts out her rejection of the law itself. This woman next resists the natural and motherly impulse to clutch the child she carries in her arms. Restraining herself, 'wisely judging that one token of her shame would but poorly serve to hide another,' she makes a mental calculation and gives priority to herself rather than to her child. Looking first not to protecting the child but to coping with her own humiliation, she took the baby on her arm, and, with a burning blush, and yet a haughty smile, and a glance that would not be abashed, looked around at her townspeople and neighbours.' Assertive, rather than submissive, Hester's ambivalent behavior, her defiant yet conventional nature is paralleled in the scarlet letter itself, which uses the womanly craft of 'elaborate embroidery and fantastic flourishes of gold thread to draw attention to her shame.' Although her handiwork may indicate a less than solemn attitude toward the community's instrument of torture, it may signify as well her acquiescence in the community's conviction that sin and retribution should be made public matters.

Just how perplexing Hester is intended to be, to narrative and authorial audiences alike, is registered in the narrator's description of the crowd around the scaffold and by his own reactions to Hester. He reports that some people were aware of a strange phenomenon in connection with her: 'Those who had before known her, and had expected to behold her dimmed and obscured by a disastrous cloud, were astonished, and even startled, to perceive how her beauty shone out, and made a halo of the misfortune and ignominy in which she was enveloped.' It is almost as though adversity becomes Hester. She captivates the narrator with her dark and abundant hair: ' . . . a face which . . . had the impressiveness belonging to a marked brow and deep black eyes. She was lady-like, too, after the manner of the feminine gentility of those days; characterized by a certain state and dignity.' While drawn to her more conventional gentility, the narrator is also taken with her strength and her energy and her spirit.

In short, Hawthorne imagined in Hester Prynne a complexity that defies the conventional understandings of woman in his time. The implied author gets the attention of his audiences by displaying Hester against the backdrop of societal norms; he holds their attention by evoking Hester's conventional, womanly dimension as proof that her adultery was not merely a venal act but was an expression of womanly love. Thus he attempts to soften and to intercept simple, hasty judgments of the adulterous woman who exceeds ordinary expectations, bringing the thematic implications of Hester's characterization into line with other revolutionary tendencies of his work. From start to finish, *The Scarlet Letter* seeks to puncture the complacency and self-righteousness of its narrative and authorial audiences alike, complicating their vision and forestalling absolute judgments by encouraging simultaneous perception of good and evil. Whether Hester's characterization successfully contributes to the work's overall intent depends on the ability of the implied author to sustain that complexity of character established in the opening scene. To 'resolve' the problem that is Hester, it is essential to the unity and the intended meanings of the text that the implied author prevent Hester's character from being overwhelmed by either her defiant or her conventional dimension. A capitulation to either pole would simplify and deny the psychological complexity toward which the other elements of the text tend.

The conventional dimension of Hester's character, which eventually brings the community, one portion of the text's narrative audience, to side with her despite the blemish of her sin, is emphasized by the implied author in Hester's deeds and demeanor. Having isolated Hester, treated her child as a pariah, threatened to take her child from her, forced her to live without the comfort of friends, and even reviled her in her charitable acts, the community eventually comes around, attributing to Hester's A the meaning of 'Angel' and 'Able' rather than adulteress. What accounts for this change of heart on the part of the community is Hester's faithfully playing the part of the repentant woman restored to virtue. She has cared for her little Pearl, tended the sick and dying, and comported herself in a humble manner. She 'submitted uncomplainingly' to the 'worst usage' of the public and 'made no claim upon it' until finally 'the blameless purity of her life . . . was reckoned largely in her favor.' Meeting people in the street, she 'never raised her head to receive their greeting . . . she laid her finger on the scarlet letter, and passed on.' Adopting the demeanor of repentance, Hester finally wins the respect of her jurors, but this is the public Hester.

To sustain the unconventional dimension of her character, the plot is complicated by a secret meeting between Hester and her cuckolded husband, Chillingworth, and by a rendezvous in the forest between Hester and her lover, Dimmesdale. The community, ignorant of these acts, would have been shocked by them (and perhaps provoked to revise its softened judgment of Hester in the light of them). The authorial audience, witnesses to these events, knows that Hester, separated from her legal spouse, proposes to Dimmesdale that they run off together; it knows that Hester remains more defiant and less conventional than the community within the novel suspects. The authorial audience overhears Hester's radical speech to Dimmesdale in the forest when she declares that 'what we did had a consecration of its own. We felt it so! We said so to each other!' Hester never does admit that in her deed she sinned with Dimmesdale, as the community would have her admit. Instead, she holds that she sinned against Dimmesdale by concealing Chillingworth's identity. She is not a repentant sinner but, rather, a repentant lover.

Further, the authorial audience is instructed in the ambiguity of Hester's behavior, in her complexity, by an editorializing narrator who offers at least two interpretations of Hester's deeds: one substantiates her conformity to the standards of the community and another details her rebellion against them. While reporting that Hester eventually appears to the community as an exemplary figure, humble and acquiescent in her fate, the narrator explains that her behavior 'might be pride, but was so like humility, that it produced all the softening influence of the latter quality on the public mind . . . society was inclined to show its former victim a more benign countenance than she cared to be favored with, or, perchance, than she deserved.' This apparently humble woman, the narrator insightfully notes, may not be humble or repentant at all. Rather, she may be remarkably proud and unworthy of the gentle treatment she eventually evokes so self-deprecatingly from the community. The narrator also observes that Hester dresses with a '*studied* austerity' [my italics] and shows a careful 'lack of demonstration in her manners.' This is a woman, the narrator implies, who very possibly is posing and playing at repentance, the same woman who will later meet her lover in the forest and insist on the consecration of an adulterous act.

Successfully sustaining Hester's complexity before his authorial audience, the implied author faces another challenge: eliciting audience sympathy for Hester despite her defiance of conventional norms, particularly as they apply to the woman taken in adultery. The implied author must manipulate Hester's characterization in a way that will prevent his audience from dismissing her out of hand and reverting, in the process, to the same simplistic judgments that her complex character is designed to forestall. He achieves this by referring Hester's motives to her 'womanly' nature.

In depicting Hester with Chillingworth, for example, the narrator draws a 'womanly' Hester. The narrator reports that Hester was absolutely frank with Chillingworth when she married him. Chillingworth knew it was not a love match and, in fact, asserts that he committed the first wrong when he married a younger woman. Nonetheless and quite admirably, if notions of woman's nature are normative, Hester insists to Chillingworth, 'I have greatly wronged thee.' Although unfaithful to Chillingworth, Hester is shown to believe in the ideal of fidelity and in woman's responsibility to honor it. Hester's act of adultery transgressed against the system, but Hester does not challenge the values on which the system stands. She does not reject the system itself. In her meeting with Chillingworth, Hester agrees to Chillingworth's request that she conceal his identity as restitution for her failure to keep her vows. Her promise unwittingly facilitates his torture of Dimmesdale. Having discovered the evil that her promise unleashed, Hester reacts in ways that elicit sympathy for her. Rather than simply accusing Chillingworth of heinous deeds, she again takes responsibility and blame upon herself. When Chillingworth asks who made him a fiend, Hester cries out, shuddering, 'It was myself . . . It was I, not less than he. Why hast thou not avenged thyself on me?' By conceding Chillingworth's right to some sort of revenge, Hester's statement expresses her willingness to protect Dimmesdale and shoulder his burden, and casts Hester in the role of a woman who loves as the culture's horizon of expectations would have it – absolutely and self-sacrificially. Surely the authorial audience will be unable to condemn peremptorily a woman who acts consistently out of love rather than revenge.

In the forest meeting with Dimmesdale, those aspects of Hester's character are reinforced that make it unlikely that the authorial audience will simply dismiss her. In this scene, Hester finally reveals Chillingworth's identity to her lover, the minister. Aware of the 'deep injury for which she was responsible to this unhappy man,' Hester cries out, 'O Arthur, . . . forgive me! In all things else, I have striven to be true!'. Ironically, all these years Hester has held herself to a standard to which she has not held Dimmesdale, the man who has, after all, hidden his truth, his sin, for seven years, leaving Hester to suffer alone. She now invokes this standard against herself, and she does not invoke it against Dimmesdale. Her love conquers any conceivably base motives, even in the face of Dimmesdale's rather despicable (from a twentieth century perspective) response to her plea for forgiveness: 'Woman, woman, thou art accountable for this! I cannot forgive thee!' Despite his office of minister, and despite his failure to be true to Hester and to share her lot publicly, Dimmesdale presumes that he can withhold forgiveness. Worse, he refuses to forgive the human being who has born the brunt of the community's scorn while he has cowered in his study and his pulpit. Nonetheless, compassionate and guilt-ridden and in love, Hester collapses before Dimmesdale and passionately reveals her commitment to him despite his abandonment of her. '"Thou shalt forgive me!" cried Hester, flinging herself on the fallen leaves beside him. "Let God punish! Thou shalt forgive!".' Finally Dimmesdale condescends to say, 'I do forgive you, Hester, . . . I freely forgive you now'. Having appeared on the scene a weak and defeated man, Dimmesdale is temporarily restored by Hester's courage, love, and persistence. While the authorial audience can see, of course, that the very fact of this rendezvous transgresses the moral law as understood in Hester's community, the scene shows that Hester's motives uphold the spirit of the law of woman's nature. Hester supports the man she loves, as a woman should. A sinner, she nonetheless behaves as a woman can be expected to behave, accepting guilt, humbling herself, and sacrificing her pride for her beloved. The implied author would encourage his audience to believe that because Hester has loved much, much is to be forgiven her. Thus the private, unconventional acts of Hester, serving to develop the defiant and potentially alienating side of Hester's character, are justified by the narrator's implicit appeal to acceptable, 'womanly' motives for Hester's behavior. The implied author forces the authorial audience to see and to sustain a complex view of Hester.

Yet, having done all this, the implied author seems to lose his courage. He allows the same construct of woman's nature to which he has appealed in Hester's behalf to intervene in the text against her. Much to our astonishment, the narrator who could see that Hester's humility was perhaps pride and that her manner was perhaps calculated is suddenly made to turn away from his own perceptions and to deny his own insightfulness. He imposes on Hester an idea of woman's nature that deprives her character of that manipulative dimension that has appeared since the first chapter of the romance. He converts her 'studied' austerity of dress into a change in her attractive-ness, as if unaware of the implications of his own word 'studied.' He claims that 'all the light and graceful foliage of her character had been withered up' by the scarlet letter and that the fact that Hester cut her hair or hid it 'by a cap' signifies that Hester's womanhood is being snuffed out: 'There seemed to be no longer any thing in Hester's face for Love to dwell upon. . . . Some attribute had departed from her, the permanence of which had been essential to keep her a woman.'

Ignoring the gains in the public's estimate of her that he himself claims Hester has achieved, the narrator goes on to attribute the change in Hester to matters that pertain to the culture's assumptions about woman's nature and role: 'Such is frequently the fate, and such the stern development, of the feminine character and person, when the woman has encountered, and lived through, an experience of peculiar severity. If she be all tenderness, she will die. If she survive, the tender-ness will either be crushed out of her, or – and the outward semblance is the same – crushed so deeply into her heart that it can never show itself more. . . . She who has once been woman, and ceased to be so, might at any moment become a woman again, if there were only the magic touch to effect the transfiguration.' Apparently being a 'woman' has nothing to do with anatomy but is, rather, a state of mind and emotion. In any case, the narrator here is most baffling. He has, after all, just reported Hester's many errands of mercy that, although per-haps calculated to ease her lot, nevertheless also indicate a certain kindness on her part. Moreover, Hester's attachment to Pearl is far from hard and unaffectionate. Because Hester's deeds, as recorded by the narrator, do not correspond with the narrator's analysis of Hester's state of heart and soul, he must base his analysis on something other than the evidence Hester's deeds provide.

The narrator goes on to lay Hester's condition at the doorstep of intellect: 'Much of the marble coldness of Hester's impression was to be attributed to the circumstance that her life had turned, in great mea-sure, from passion and feeling, to thought. . . . She assumed a freedom of speculation, then common enough on the other side of the Atlantic, but which our forefathers, had they known of it, would have held to be a deadlier crime than that stigmatized by the scarlet letter. In her lonesome cottage, by the sea-shore, thoughts visited her, such as dared to enter no other dwelling in New England.' The narrator would have his audience believe that not only has Hester ceased to be 'a woman' but that this has happened because she turned from passion and feel-ing to thought and freedom of speculation. This is a most perplexing position for the narrator to assume and a most odd direction for the meanings of the text to take. After all, Hester has withstood the onslaught of her accusers. She has manipulated their expectations in a way that allows her to wrest as much freedom as she can from severely constricting circumstances. Surely, it must be that her intelligence, her ability to think and to speculate that the narrator finds 'unwomanly,' has permitted Hester to direct and control the minimally satisfactory life she has. Her intelligence has enabled her to abstract from her own experience certain countercultural convictions about the nature of sin and guilt. Because Hester has arrived at her own norms of conduct and definitions of sin and guilt, she can respond to Dimmesdale in the forest in the 'womanly' way she does. Hester's ability to think prevents her from absorbing the strictures of her community and this, in turn, enables her to remain admirably, self-effacingly, and self-sacrificially faithful to Dimmesdale. Were Hester Prynne all passion and feeling as the narrator wishes, she would have been crushed long since.

Moreover, the narrator is incorrect when he claims that Hester is no longer capable of feeling, a distorted vision that comes from the culture's horizon of expectations with its multifarious assumptions about woman. Contrary to the narrator's statement, Hester is moved to considerable compassion for Arthur Dimmesdale when she encounters him at midnight on the scaffold, as he attempts in a convoluted way to purge himself of his sin. She goes to him in this night vigil and joins her hand with his. Further, Hester is brought to ask herself if she has failed Dimmesdale and if she should correct that failure despite society's disapproval. Her feeling here is prompted by her assessment of fact, an intellectual process. The narrator creates a dichotomy between thought and feeling that the text does not substantiate but that the gender distinctions of the culture, with their assignment of different traits to men and women, encourage. Having described Hester as 'unwomaned' because especially thoughtful, the narrator himself says that she was 'strengthened by years of hard and solemn trial. . . . She had climbed her way . . . to a higher point.' Surely the 'unwomanly' speculation that her isolation and her rebellious nature encouraged contributed to Hester's ascent.

Textual evidence forces the conclusion, then, that the implied author here brings to the narrator's analysis of Hester an idea of woman and her relationship to thought that exists outside *The Scarlet Letter* and is wheeled in to be imposed on Hester's fictional life, although unsupported by her actions and circumstances. That this is in fact the case becomes abundantly clear in the chapter entitled 'Another View of Hester,' in a passage which is particularly problematic because it is difficult to determine to whose mind the content is to be attributed – the narrator's or Hester's. The frame sentences of the paragraph suggest that the narrator is reporting Hester's thoughts through indirect discourse. Unfortunately, the matter is not this simple because the narrator seems to render his own mind as well as Hester's. For example, the narrator says, 'A tendency to speculation, though it may keep woman quiet, as it does man, yet makes her sad.' To whom does this generalization belong? Eschewing the more usual practice of putting a 'she thought that' or a 'in her case' before 'a tendency to speculation,' a strategy that would tie the tendency unambiguously to a specific mind, the narrator launches directly into the thought without identifying the subject who performs the speculation, allowing the reader to ascribe it to Hester or to the narrator or to both. Then he says, 'She discerns, it may be, such a hopeless task before her.' Who is 'she'? Woman? Hester? Both? And what are we to make of 'it may be'? Does Hester speculate that women who think about woman's lot may discern a hopeless task before them? Or does Hester see the task as hopeless? And why does the narrator equivocate in any case? Or is it the narrator who imagines what a woman in Hester's situation would imagine? This last is the most likely possibility. The narrator straightforwardly tells us what 'it may be' that Hester thought. He tells us his imagination of her thoughts rather than telling us her thoughts.

Whether the reader concludes that the narrator's imagination and Hester's thoughts are the same depends on whether the reader finds that the thoughts here ascribed to Hester (or is it to the narrator?) square with her character and with the dramatic action of the novel. I find that sometimes they do and that, at other times, they clearly do not. When they do not, they coincide most handily with cultural presuppositions about women. The problematic paragraph is this:

> Indeed, the same dark question often rose into her mind, with reference to the whole race of womanhood. Was existence worth accepting, even to the happiest among them? As concerned her own individual existence, she had long ago decided in the negative, and dismissed the point as settled. A tendency to speculation, though it may keep woman quiet, as it does man, yet makes her sad. She discerns, it may be, such a hopeless task before her. As a first step, the whole system of society is to be torn down, and built up anew. Then, the very nature of the opposite sex, or its long hereditary habit, which has become like nature, is to be essentially modified, before woman can be allowed to assume what seems a fair and suitable position. Finally, all other difficulties being obviated, woman cannot take advantage of these preliminary forms, until she herself shall have undergone a still mightier change; in which, perhaps, the ethereal essence, wherein she has her truest life, will be found to have evaporated. A woman never overcomes these problems by any exercise of thought. They are not to be solved, or only in one way. If her heart chance to come uppermost, they vanish.

Thus, Hester Prynne, whose heart had lost its regular and healthy throb, wandered without a clew in the dark labyrinth of mind.

In the opening sentence, the narrator begins to talk about Hester. But then, as if so overwhelmed by her gender that he forgets her individuality, he slips from Hester's mind into that perceived universal, 'woman's' mind. From that point forward, the narrator assumes, apparently, that Hester is 'woman' and that he can therefore generalize from his male point of view about woman as a class and simultaneously explain Hester's thoughts. When he does so, he gives us his own mind, the frame sentences notwithstanding. Speculation, for which woman is, strictly speaking, unsuited in the first place will lead to sadness (as if Hester didn't have sufficient cause for sadness, never mind speculation about larger issues). The sadness is caused by the immensity of reforms that, even if possible to achieve, may destroy woman's 'ethereal essence.' Apparently the narrator and the authorial audience know so well what 'ethereal essence' means that it need never be defined. Whatever it is, it can evaporate. In any case, 'a woman,' and therefore Hester, presumably, cannot resolve these problems because they are pseudoproblems; when a woman's heart is touched, they vanish, we are told. This must be the thought of the narrator rather than of Hester Prynne; in the chapter preceding this, 'The Minister's Vigil,' the degree to which Hester's heart was and is touched by Dimmesdale has been abundantly demonstrated during the midnight meeting on the scaffold. This thought, belonging to the narrator alone, is of course among the most patronizing possible. It dismisses what women perceive to be problematic as non-problems that dissolve when woman assumes her proper place – when she gets her priorities in order – according to the Divine design of woman's nature. In the concluding frame sentence, the narrator says that Hester is confused because her heart has lost its 'healthy throb.' Yet as we have seen, Hester's heart throbs quite soundly, even as her head devises strategies to cope with her situation.

Conflating Hester Prynne with 'woman,' the implied author of *The Scarlet Letter* allows the words of his narrator to contradict the deeds of Hester Prynne. He creates a work in which the editorializing of the narrator and the norms he articulates are at odds with the implications of dramatic action, as if he finally must pull Hester back into line with the ideology of woman or make her seem less 'womanly' for transgressing its boundaries. Thus norms are obscured and the intended meanings of the work lead to irreconcilable oppositions, calling on the authorial audience to take up, on the one hand, a sympathetic attitude toward Hester because her deeds stem from her conformity to woman's nature and yet, on the other hand, to understand that Hester is 'unwomaned' by the very speculation that makes her able to sustain her 'womanly' fidelity and love.

The sexual poetics that emerge from the text when it is referred to the culture's horizon of expectations explain this disjunction. The narrator exercises the privileges of omniscience, taking up a position that demands both interpretation and value judgment. The narrator is an instance of that neutral omniscience that expresses universal wisdom, establishes norms, and forecloses the possibility of an intellectual and moral distance between the implied author and the narrator. The narrator is, then, a spokesperson for the implied author, and Hawthorne stands behind both. Hawthorne's ambiguity has become celebrated, and we know that Hawthorne chose to write romances rather than novels in order, as he declares in his prefaces, to claim the latitude the romance tradition offers. We know as well that Hawthorne, like Cooper, deploys all the devices of the romance tradition in order to suggest an ambiguous world that by its very nature escapes our rational explanations and categories. Hawthorne uses shadowy family backgrounds, coincidences, suspense, and all the other tools of the romancer to set a mood and to create a sense of the mystery of life. Ambiguities introduced in the interests of a complex world view, however, must not be confused with an artist's ambivalence with respect to norms. Reliable authorial intrusions into fiction have a particular purpose and must follow certain laws in order to fulfill their purpose. As Wayne Booth points out, narrative intrusions define for us 'the precise ordering of values on which our judgment should depend . . . in fiction the concept of writing well must include the successful ordering of your reader's view of a fiction . . . an author has an obligation to be as clear about his moral position as he possibly can be.'[7] Hawthorne fails us in this regard in *The Scarlet Letter*. His implied author admirably complicates the romance heroine type, but he falls into a confusing ambivalence in his evaluation of her conduct because of his very success in rounding her character. He suggests that we apply to Hester norms of judgment that are at variance with the facts of Hester's fictional life.

Hawthorne hangs *The Scarlet Letter* on the same romance frame that Cooper used, but he imagines more powerfully than Cooper when he creates Hester Prynne. Her character pushes against the boundaries of romance and of the culture's ideology as well. But the implied author could not break away from the horizon of expectations to which Hawthorne's assumptions finally held him. Hawthorne's artistic achievement in *The Scarlet Letter* is foiled by the restrictions that *a priori* ideas of woman lead him to place on Hester. Given the splendor of Hester Prynne that emerges even amidst the narrator's ambivalences, imagine what she might have been had Hawthorne been more bold.[8] □

Leland S. Person, in *Aesthetic Headaches: Women and a Masculine Poetics in Poe, Melville, and Hawthorne* (1988), agrees with Baym that 'Hawthorne embodied his deepest creative impulses in his strongest female characters', but also emphasises the 'tension between identification with women whose creative energy resists any easy formalization and the containment of such women in artistic forms that subject creative energy to the artist's control – often to the detriment of the work as a whole'. Like Baym, Person is concerned to rescue Hawthorne, along with other nineteenth-century male writers, from a typological critique that assigns discrete and limited meanings to female characterisations. He refers particularly to Leslie A. Fiedler (*Love and Death in the American Novel*), for whom the 'Dark Lady' is 'a surrogate for all the Otherness against which an Anglo-Saxon world attempts to define itself'; Paul John Eakin (*The New England Girl: Cultural Ideas in Hawthorne, Stowe, Howells and James*, 1976), whose characterisation of the 'New England girl' is 'an all-purpose symbol of the ideals of the culture'; and Judith Fryer's categories of Temptresses, Princesses, Great Mothers and New Women. Such typological criticism of female characters, Person complains, 'is rooted in a reductive, oppositional, essentially phallocentric concept of male writing, which emphasizes male authority and dominance over female characters and, through them, female readers'. Such a view of male writing, in Person's opinion, ignores the 'potential complexity' of a masculine poetics. Hawthorne, says Person, was a writer who did not take 'an exclusively phallic view of male identity or creativity', but who was able to create female characters who could 'respond to men out of their "otherness", offering a new vision – a reflection of themselves – that men may imitate'. Hawthorne's fiction, Person insists, exhibits 'considerable unease' with prevailing assumptions about gender differences, and a concern to expose the destructive as well as self-destructive effects of phallocentric discourse by depicting the failure of male efforts to control women through language, imagery, and larger artistic forms. It is marked by a tendency, says Person, to deconstruct conventional masculine ideology, which expresses itself in objectifying power over women, in order to achieve a 'feminized' creative self, which comes into being through the surrender of power to women, and manifests itself in the production of a 'feminized' masculine poetics. Such a poetics is characterised by the creation of female characters who, codified in terms of 'fluidity' and 'indeterminacy', challenge male perception and resist type. The salient feature of this alternative, 'female' poetics is its transgression of literary boundaries, its shaking of conventional structures, when the marginal is brought into sudden focus, or intelligibility itself refused. It is a writing which is marked by a 'refusal of mastery', 'an opting for openness and possibility'. Even Hawthorne's attraction to romance may be seen as rebellion against various constraints of form, an embracement of more open form that allowed greater freedom of imagination. In all of these ways a new, feminised poetics might hope to challenge the literary structures it must necessarily inhabit. 'It is not surprising in this regard', remarks Person, 'that works of fiction designed to challenge the limitations of artistic form should embody their subversive energy in female characters who challenge the social and moral order'. These subversive or deviant tendencies in Hawthorne's fiction, Person concludes, 'closely resemble the resisting and subversive goals of contemporary feminist writers and critics'. However, as he also stresses, at the same time that Hawthorne's narrative carries the potential for subverting formal order, it illustrates the struggle between 'subversive energy and its repression or containment by social and artistic form'.

■ The letter, upon which all eyes are 'concentred' at the beginning of the novel, is at first an allegorical emblem confidently imposed by the Puritan community. Attending church, Hester often finds herself 'the text of the discourse'; she wears and becomes the community's 'birthmark,' a sign of its liability to sin. From the beginning the community attempts to contain Hester's meaning by 'inclosing her in a sphere by herself' and by 'concentrating' her identity in an art object that eclipses her efforts to define herself. As Baym has so convincingly shown, of course, Hester never entirely conforms herself to the prescribed meaning of the scarlet letter; she embroiders the A even before she first emerges from the prison until it blazons forth manifold symbolic meanings and implicates the whole community, despite the allegorical distance its members would maintain. Her whole attire, Hawthorne notes, is 'modelled much after her own fancy' and 'seemed to express the attitude of her spirit, the desperate recklessness of her mood, by its wild and picturesque peculiarity.' Attempting to make a 'halo of the misfortune,' she is thus partially successful in transfiguring herself through the 'fantastically embroidered' letter.

Eric Sundquist has argued, in fact, that the scarlet letter finally becomes an indeterminate symbol. It 'refuses to assume the function of the thing it symbolizes, that is, so refuses to stand reliably for any one thing and thus draws all significance into itself that all referents disappear into the function of symbolizing.'[9] If that is true, then Hester would succeed in subverting the community's effort to denote her character and make her simply a sign of sin. She would so fragment the power of signification that it would disappear; all signs would be called into question. But in fact, even though the scarlet letter accommodates additional meanings (or readings), it never loses its original meaning entirely – not even for Hester. As she tells Chillingworth, 'Were I worthy to be quit of it, it would fall away of its own nature, or be transformed into something that should speak a different purport.'

Such a conditional statement does look forward to a time when the letter will cease to mark her or at least will change meaning. But Hester despairs of living to see that time, and missing from her expression is any faith that she can actively alter her essential relationship to the letter.

Not satisfied to embody creative energy in a single female character, Hawthorne doubles his heroine; while Hester wears the scarlet letter, Pearl is the letter, the 'scarlet letter endowed with life', a living art object that embodies her mother's creative power and represents an alternative, potential version of her . . . Despite her independence, the letter remains a sign which confers a sense of self. At one point, for example, she fashions her own letter out of seaweed, a material more appropriate to her 'natural' character, but the form she gives that letter – the letter A – is that prescribed by the community. Up until the end of the novel and her removal to England, Pearl as hieroglyphic must be interpreted and must interpret herself in the context of Puritan Boston.

[. . .]

Whereas Pearl's condition improves over the course of the novel (enabling her to escape Boston by the end), Hester's vitality withers under the ignominy of the letter. She suffers a 'sad transformation' under social pressure; temporarily, she accepts the role and identity that the community has assigned her and conforms herself to the parameters of the art object by which she is 'inclosed.' Even though the letter comes to stand for 'Able,' Hester encourages that redefinition largely by conforming to community expectations. As Hawthorne comments, the townspeople's new 'regard' for her arises from the fact that 'She never battled with the public, but submitted uncomplainingly to its worst usage.' In private, of course, Hester does engage in a certain 'freedom of speculation,' but she is content with radical thoughts. She has no need for 'the flesh and blood of action.' She is one of those people 'who speculate the most boldly [but] often conform with the most perfect quietude to the external regulations of society'.

The personal cost of her new status is the repression of her sexuality and the suppression of the kind of verbal passion she had expressed at the Governor's mansion. Some 'attribute had departed from her, the permanence of which had been essential to keep her a woman.' Despite her efforts to embroider the scarlet letter, to 'loosen' that imprisoning form, she seems to harden gradually into the kind of objectified marble form we have seen in previous works. 'Statue-like' in appearance, she becomes a devitalized art object whose 'marble coldness,' Hawthorne says, requires some 'magic touch' to effect her 'transfiguration' into vital womanhood. Hawthorne thereby suggests, of course, that relationship is essential to selfhood, though as we shall see his point is not that only women are so dependent; Dimmesdale, too, loses certain attributes that are essential to keep him a man. In spite of her imaginative and intellectual self-reliance, Hester needs and wants Dimmesdale to provide a 'magic touch' that will restore her womanhood – just as the minister requires a similar gesture from her. Based on their experience in the forest later in the novel, we must assume that both enjoyed a 'transfiguration' before the novel began . . . But if Dimmesdale once offered a 'magic touch' and a 'warm reality,' in place of the 'marble image of happiness' that Chillingworth 'imposed' upon Hester, he clearly has withdrawn such magic from her during the present time of the novel. Indeed, the frequent comparison of Hester to cold marble is often associated with Dimmesdale's refusal to touch or come near her at all.

[. . .]

Unlike Hester, who, in embroidering the letter, partially transcends the identity she has been granted, Dimmesdale can neither say nor feel that what they did 'had a consecration of its own'. According to Hester, they once 'said so to each other' and 'felt it so,' but now she alone has the power to express those feelings. Hawthorne emphasizes Dimmesdale's loss of the power of emotionally informed speech at the same time that he gives Hester increasing responsibility for expressing the 'deep meaning' of the novel. Dimmesdale 'gazed into Hester's face with a look in which hope and joy shone out, indeed, but with fear betwixt them,' he observes, 'and a kind of horror at her boldness, who had spoken what he vaguely hinted at, but dared not speak.' Only briefly, by apparently reenacting his original 'sin' with Hester, can Dimmesdale feel released from public and private censure. He feels 'risen up all made anew'; he experiences the 'exhilarating effect – upon a prisoner just escaped from the dungeon of his own heart – of breathing the wild, free atmosphere of an unredeemed, unchristianized, lawless region.' In telling Hester to 'speak' for him, Dimmesdale reverses their roles at the Governor's house when he spoke for her. In effect, he asks her to re-create him through the power of her speech, and she obliges by imagining his assumption of a new name. Becoming a kind of mirror for woman, Dimmesdale's agreement to Hester's proposal enables her to remove the scarlet letter and, as she lets down her hair, to reclaim her full sexual nature, her identity as a woman. In contrast to her former 'marble coldness,' she reanimates her person with a sacred flame, a measure of the self-creative power Hawthorne attributed to male-female relationships. With her 'bold' speech, she has created the male 'artist' who then creates her. 'Her sex, her youth, and the whole richness of her beauty, came back from what men call the irrevocable past, and clustered themselves, with her maiden hope, and a happiness before unknown, within the magic circle of this hour.' Most important, a scene that began with Dimmesdale deferring to Hester's power of speech ends in an apparent mutuality of voice: 'Then, all was spoken.'

Hawthorne not only allows the two characters a sense of liberation but also comes close to moving his novel into a new path. In freeing Hester from the various forms that confine her character, he is also on the verge of opening up the narrative to the values with which she is identified: in particular, a sexually freer, but still 'consecrated' relationship between a man and a woman. In Hester's suggestion that they escape either to the wilderness or to Europe, of course, he is also on the verge of allowing his heroine to shape the plot, breaking it free from the paradigm of sin-guilt-penitence that governs it. As Terence Martin has pointed out, however, in agreeing to accompany Hester to Europe, Dimmesdale plays the hypocrite, subverting her plot even as he apparently acquiesces in it. In making sure that they will not disembark until after he can preach the Election Sermon that will climax his public career, Dimmesdale tries to 'have it both ways, to leave, but to leave with his duty well performed – which is to say, with the congregation marveling at their saintly, inspired minister.'[10]

Hawthorne does not, therefore, give Hester absolute power to shape the story. Besides his subtle account of Dimmesdale's duplicity, he has Chillingworth book passage on the ship as well, ensuring that all the principle characters and the problems their conjunction embodies will be exported. There can be no escape. Dimmesdale's problem is internal, and only by reconciling his public role and his private self can he experience the exhilaration of full selfhood. And Hester, as Pearl reminds her, can only discover her full humanity by replacing the scarlet letter on her breast, by asserting her character within a social context. A major part of Pearl's function is encouraging her parents to a public acknowledgment of their relationship and thereby of her identity as their daughter. Hence, she will not recognize their reunion in the midnight privacy of the scaffold, nor will she accept their escapist indulgence in the freedom of the forest. When Dimmesdale allows himself the 'mockery of penitence' on the scaffold, Pearl insists that he embrace her and her mother in the same place during the day. Here in the forest, as her parents remove to their 'magic circle,' she stands estranged from them across the brook, on the other side of the 'boundary between two worlds.' In thus straddling this symbolic stream of consciousness, the child and the letter with which she is identified – the sign and its meaning – remain abridged and unintegrated. As the embodiment of all that the scarlet letter means, Pearl demands a full public confession and the assimilation of the letter's meaning into the imaginative life of the future. Not by escaping the implications of the letter, but by researching its meaning, Pearl seems to say, can any of them realize their human potential.

If this is the ideal toward which Hawthorne pushes the novel, he falls just short of its realization. Despite the epiphany of recovered energy and speech in the forest (or perhaps because of it), the balance of power between Hester and Dimmesdale shifts markedly in the last part of the novel. Dimmesdale is finally overwhelmed by his experience in the forest and by the image of himself that it reveals. He 'seemed to stand apart, and eye this former self with scornful, pitying, but half-envious curiosity. That self was gone! Another man had returned out of the forest; a wiser one; with a knowledge of hidden mysteries.' Yet Dimmesdale is unable to reconcile his relationship with Hester and his role as keeper of the public morality. Returning to town, he feels bewildered and 'in a maze.' Unable to discover a viable outlet for his 'knowledge of hidden mysteries,' in his imagination he scandalizes his parishioners with illicit whisperings from his own haunted mind . . . Dimmesdale is terrified by the image of himself that his own language reveals; the devil in the 'manuscript' of his imagination, he recognizes, is himself. The self-image he prefers is the one 'enshrined within the stainless sanctity of [the maiden's] heart,' and rather than jeopardize that objectified figure, he will suppress the linguistic power that creates another self. In repressing the seductive power of language and the masculine self empowered by that language, Dimmesdale moves toward a more feminine discourse, signalled by the almost vampirish transfer of energy from Hester to himself – and to his 'art.'

Dimmesdale's experience in the forest does finally assume a verbal form. Temporarily abandoning his mind to impulses he perceives as evil, he writes his final Election Sermon as a compulsive effort both to express and to exorcise the 'fiend' which possesses his 'foul imagination.' . . . Dimmesdale's sermon comes to him largely unbidden, the product of forces within himself released by his temporary reconciliation with Hester. . . . Dimmesdale gives in momentarily to an 'impulsive flow of thought and emotion' and becomes an inspired, visionary artist. That is, the conflict between those previously buried feelings and the pressure of his professional office generates so much internal energy that he is finally able to write in 'words of flame.' Yet so alien are the impulses which converge upon his soul that he can only view himself through his society's eyes as a madman. . . . In eschewing the seductive power of language on his walk through the 'maze,' however, Dimmesdale does not become more open to the creative potential of relationship. The 'impulsive flow of thought and emotion' that generates his revised sermon is no gushing out of 'warmth and freedom.' Hawthorne does not share the text of that sermon with the reader, but the language he uses to describe its composition certainly implies that, rather than celebrating his 'consecrated' union with Hester, Dimmesdale condemns it. If he resists the temptation to seduce the 'youngest sister' of his congregation with his 'potent' art, in other words, it is largely because he seeks a larger audience. He will seduce the congregation as a whole. Repressing the impulse to scandalize his parishioners one at a time, he sublimates that impulse in a sermon that condemns himself, but in precisely the form that will elevate him to the highest public stature he has yet enjoyed. In the process, of course, he effectively kills himself – ironically, ensuring that he will live on in the community's collective imagination in the form his words have established.

Although he cannot live through the experience, Dimmesdale seems to discover the courage to confess his relationship to Hester and Pearl, to make restitution to the female characters who have been victims in some sense of his timid imagination. Just as Hawthorne had placed the scarlet letter upon his breast and felt its searing heat, Dimmesdale assumes the burden of the letter's meaning in the final scaffold scene. He admits his own experience of the truth which the letter symbolizes; he tells the townspeople that 'it is but the shadow of what he bears on his own breast, and that even this, his own red stigma, is no more than the type of what has seared his inmost heart!'. In so doing, he apparently offers his audience a lesson in interpretation, asking them to review the scarlet letter with minds open to its many meanings. Yet as Hawthorne observes, the townspeople resist Dimmesdale's message. They misread the letter on his breast, just as they have misread the one on Hester's . . . this failure of interpretation is central to the novel's meaning. It suggests a pessimism similar to Melville's in *Pierre* about the power of language to express 'deep meaning and to discover a sympathetic audience, that 'one heart and mind of perfect sympathy.'

Dimmesdale's confession also bears directly on Hester's status in the novel, suggesting, it seems to me, her failure to 'subvert' the meaning of the scarlet letter and use it to express herself. In this scene, Dimmesdale, in effect, has expropriated the letter for his own purposes. Hester may, in some sense, inscribe her letter and the story it represents on her lover's bosom, but the speech he makes before revealing the letter belies its meaning. At best, Dimmesdale's speech and revelation are ambiguous, encouraging a diffusion of understanding; at worst, they are deliberately duplicitous, designed to confirm his canonization in his listeners' hearts. Dimmesdale, in short, writes his own story on the letter over Hester's. He has still not found the words to reiterate what he felt and evidently said in the novel's pre-history: 'What we did had a consecration of its own.' Just as he had turned the reunion in the forest to his own uses, here he uses the letter itself to express something other than the 'consecration' of their relationship. In failing to discover an unambiguous language by which Hester and their relationship can speak through him, he subverts Hester's intentions, in effect, if not in design. Indeed, rather than unambiguously uniting himself with Hester (and with Pearl), he substitutes himself for Hester, feminizing his discourse and himself in order to unite himself – alone – with God.

Hawthorne, moreover, makes very clear Hester's loss of vitality and self-expressive energy. Having undergone a 'sad transformation,' she seemed to regain her identity as a woman in the forest through Dimmesdale's 'magic touch.' In the final scene, too, her stature seems to depend on Dimmesdale's behavior, his willingness to free her from the 'circle' of her self-enclosed and alienated life and to bring her within the 'sphere' of the Puritan community. Yet Hawthorne's description of Hester throughout the scene of this 'New England Holiday' suggests her loss of energy. As she enters the market-place, she has resumed her character as pariah. Her face shows a 'marble quietude' and is like a mask, 'or rather, like the frozen calmness of a dead woman's features.' Dimmesdale, on the other hand, appears to have gained the vitality that Hester has lost. Never, Hawthorne notes, 'had he exhibited such energy as was seen in the gait and air with which he kept his pace in the procession.' The euphoria of their forest walk rapidly dissipates as Hester recognizes that, in so energetically fulfilling his public role, Dimmesdale is estranging himself from her. As she watches him from afar, she feels a 'dreary influence come over her, but wherefore or whence she knew not; unless that he seemed so remote from her own sphere, and utterly beyond her reach.'

As we have seen before, the result of such male distancing from a woman is the woman's increasing objectification. And so it is with Hester. She can scarcely forgive Dimmesdale, Hawthorne says, 'for being able so completely to withdraw himself from their mutual world; while she groped darkly, and stretched forth her cold hands, and found him not.' While Dimmesdale is inside the church preaching his sermon, Hester is relegated to a position outside at the foot of the scaffold – ironically, the very spot where she was first punished. Although she cannot hear Dimmesdale's words, she registers his sermon's underlying meaning 'in the shape of an indistinct, but varied, murmur and flow of the minister's very peculiar voice.' As Hawthorne notes, 'the sermon had throughout a meaning for her, entirely apart from its indistinguishable words.' That meaning inheres in the 'plaintiveness,' the 'expression of anguish,' the 'deep strain of

pathos,' and the 'cry of pain' with which Dimmesdale seeks forgiveness for his sins. . . . If Dimmesdale's energetic pace in the procession
were enough to turn Hester's hands cold, the 'statue-like' appearance
she assumes as she listens to his sermon is a sure indication that,
whatever its power, it does not celebrate its speaker's passionate relationship with her. Hester may have contributed the energy for
Dimmesdale's sermon, in other words, but she obviously has not contributed the text.

After the sermon, moreover, Hester is as alienated from the community as she has ever been. Outward from the 'magic circle of
ignominy' in which she stands there radiates a simultaneously attractive and repulsive power. It is both ironic and prophetic that the same
people who listen to Dimmesdale's 'words of flame' still resist any
implication in Hester's 'sphere by herself.' As they throng around her,
they are 'fixed' at a distance by the 'centrifugal force of the repugnance
which the mystic symbol inspired.' Hawthorne's diction is especially
important here, for he had used the term 'mystic symbol' to express
his own sense of awe (in the Custom-House) at what the scarlet letter
inspired. Here, that sense of openness to various meanings 'streaming'
forth from the symbol has devolved into closed-minded 'repugnance.'
Most important, that revulsion has been inspired at least in part by
Dimmesdale's sermon. There could not be a greater or more tragic
irony for Hester, since the energy that 'wrote' the sermon was inspired
by her forest walk with the author. Thus, whatever her temporary success in expanding or even subverting the given meaning of the letter,
Hester appears in this final scene as the letter's victim. It defines her
more effectively than ever before. 'At the final hour, when she was so
soon to fling aside the burning letter, it had strangely become the centre
of more remark and excitement, and was thus made to sear her breast
more painfully, than at any time since the first day she put it on.'

Even in death, Hester discovers an ambiguous relationship to the
letter. She shares a plot with Dimmesdale marked by a single tombstone on which the scarlet letter is 'one ever-glowing point of light
gloomier than the shadow.' But even though the letter is her literary
legacy, she has not been successful in writing her own personal meaning into it. The letter may glow on the 'simple slab of slate' that serves
as a tombstone, but the 'curious investigator' of its meaning can only
'perplex himself with the purport.' Just as it has been throughout the
novel, the scarlet letter is still without a truly sympathetic reader, that
'one heart and mind of perfect sympathy.' . . . In this final image the
scarlet letter comes full circle, returning, as it must, to the beginning.
The 'deep meaning' that 'streamed forth' from the 'mystic symbol' in
the Custom-House was rigidly contained within the letter-as-emblem
which the Puritans imposed upon Hester. Although Hester was able to

embroider the letter and wear it in such a way that it defied a single interpretation, she was never able to transcend it. Indeed, the letter's appearance on her tombstone had been anticipated by none other than Chillingworth as early as the second scene of the novel. Regarding the letter as a 'living sermon against sin' he also looked forward to the day that 'the ignominious letter [would] be engraved upon her tomb-stone.' In thus fulfilling a prophecy made early in the novel, the letter on Hester's grave has been denied some of its power to suggest inde-terminate meanings. Despite being 'ever-glowing,' its final office is to mark the location of her dead body.[11] □

CHAPTER SIX

Reader-Response, Phenomenological and Poststructuralist Approaches

READER-RESPONSE criticism, which first emerged in the 1960s, is of many different kinds, but they all focus on the role and activity of the reader rather than on the author or the text. Reader-response criticism allowed for differences in interpretation, a plurality of possible meanings in a given text, as opposed to the New Critics' belief that the great challenge facing the critic was to discover the principle of unity which integrated the disparate elements of a text. Reader-response critics believed that the text was not a well-wrought urn, an icon, a complete and self-sufficient, timeless object with a fixed set of characteristics. Texts are full of gaps, blanks, ambiguities, indeterminacies, and it is the reader's job to interact with these as an unfolding temporal sequence, composing meaning as he/she reads. Roland Barthes distinguished between what he called the 'readerly' (realistic) text, which makes of the reader a passive consumer, and the 'writerly' text (usually a modern, avant-garde text) which demands of the reader that he/she actively engage in the process of producing meaning out of the text's plural, diffuse and unsettled signifieds. *The Scarlet Letter* exhibits many of the characteristics of Barthes' 'writerly' text. For example, Hawthorne deals in ambiguous symbols rather than straightforward statements. He resists simple moral categorisation in terms of the rigid polarities so beloved in Puritan culture, refusing to reduce complex reality into simple binary oppositions between absolute terms – good and evil, light and darkness. He follows the Puritans in seeing 'some deep meaning behind the phenomena of the physical world', but he is not nearly so certain about what that 'deep meaning' might be. He deliberately undercuts the reliability of the narrator, foregrounds contradictory points of view, adopts a shifting, speculative, uncertain mode of narration, and always suggests the element of mystery about human motives. The result is a narrative which is profoundly unstable. In releasing us from his narrative authority,

155

he allows us to choose from a variety of interpretations. We are involved in the meaning-making process.

In *Hawthorne, Melville and the Novel* (1973), Richard H. Brodhead's analysis of Hawthorne's dual narrative mode, as at once realistic and symbolic, evolves into a reader-response criticism, where his focus of attention shifts from the fiction to 'our relation to the fiction':

■ One of the most interesting moments of symbolic experience in *The Scarlet Letter*, and one that best shows how Hawthorne complicates our relation to his fiction, is found in 'The Minister's Vigil.' In this chapter Dimmesdale goes to the scaffold at midnight to do public penance for his sin. But even as he does so he is half-aware that his act, like the rest of his rituals of self-scrutiny and self-torture, is a 'vain show of expiation.' By going through the forms of penitence without actually revealing his guilt Dimmesdale only succeeds in renewing his sin of concealment. Each renewal reinforces his imaginative allegiance to the law that condemns him – thus Hawthorne notes that his sin has the effect of binding him more tightly to the categories of Puritan ortho-doxy – so that the fact of his own untruth becomes his only reality and his only identity. 'The Minister's Vigil' provides an extreme close-up of the processes of Dimmesdale's mind. Its noting of his masochistic fantasies of exposure before the townspeople, of his involuntary and perverse attempts to betray himself by laughing and shrieking, and of his recoils of dread from the prospect of discovery gives us the book's richest realization of the compulsive fantasy life in which Dimmesdale's obsession with his guilt imprisons him. In the midst of these fantasies he gains for a moment an opportunity to escape from his unreal world. He stops Hester and Pearl as they pass through the marketplace, making them stand with him on the scaffold. As he joins hands with them he feels 'a tumultuous rush of new life, other life than his own,' an 'electric chain' of vital relatedness. But he refuses to embrace the possibility for release that this moment offers. When Pearl asks him when he will stand with them publicly he replies: 'At the great judgment day!'. And exactly as he states his refusal a version of the judgment day takes place: the sky is illuminated as if by 'the light that is to reveal all secrets.'

At this point Hawthorne does not trouble us unduly about the nature of this light, allowing us to accept, if we like, the plausible explanation that it is 'doubtless caused by one of those meteors.' Doubtless. But to Dimmesdale the light looks like a scarlet A, and in the brief scene that concludes the chapter the sexton informs us that many of the townspeople saw the same thing. The scarlet letter makes, here, its most audacious appearance. And its appearance works here, as in 'The Governor's Hall' and 'The Child at the Brook-Side,' to reverse the direction of our perception. We have been reading a psychological novel, observing the course of a character's perceptions and emotions; even when we watch Dimmesdale seeing the portent we are still considering the symbol in terms of a character's mental experience of it. But with the sexton's second sighting Hawthorne gives the symbol an independent reality and makes us observe the characters under its aspect as it announces itself as an imperious necessity. Under its aspect the relationships that the characters must live through in the book's dramatic plot are revealed, in an instantaneous vision, in their essential nature. Dimmesdale, Hester, and Pearl stand joined together in the place of punishment, and Chillingworth, looking like the 'archfiend,' looks on. And, above them, including them all in its light, is the scarlet letter.

Was it a vision, or a waking dream? Hawthorne does everything he can to make his letter in the sky unsettling for his readers, but correspondingly he does everything he can to afford us ways of coping with it. We might take it as a naturalistic fact, a somewhat oddly shaped and colored meteor. Or we might treat its apparent supernaturalism as really a psychic projection of Dimmesdale's guilty mind; by refusing to pass judgment on himself he compulsively sees that judgment as being passed on him by the world. Or we might join the Puritans, who unblinkingly accept the supernaturalism of the A and read it as a divine message to their community, announcing the accession of Governor Winthrop to the status of Angel. The inclusion of the Puritans' interpretation here clarifies the peculiarity of Dimmesdale's own. He shares their habit of finding symbols latent with divine meaning in nature, but he perverts that practice by finding 'a revelation, addressed to himself alone' rather than to the whole of God's chosen community. In the morbid egotism of his guilt he assumes that 'the firmament itself should appear no more than a fitting page for his soul's history and fate.' His is a further way in which we might read the celestial sign.

As the last paragraph indicates, 'The Minister's Vigil' concludes with a drama of interpretation. We see how the characters understand the letter, and we see their understandings as proceeding from a whole way of making sense of experience. But what is most interesting about this drama is that we are implicated in it. For finally, when the characters are done with it, we have the fact of the A in the sky left over, unexplained. Hawthorne in effect withdraws his narrative's mediating veil and makes us undergo his own and his characters' central experience of direct and unaided encounter with the flaming symbol. And as we are forced to decide what to make of it the characters' modes of vision become the matter not of detached observation but of our own urgent choice. We are left alone to complete the episode's reality and meaning as we may, and as we do so, Hawthorne's demonstration of the implications of the available options ensures that we will be highly self-conscious about our own procedure as an imaginative act of a certain sort. A final purpose of the symbolic mode of *The Scarlet Letter*, therefore, is to complicate our perception of the story in such a way as to turn it in on itself.

An episode like this one illustrates the most important difference between *The Scarlet Letter* and the realistic novels with which it shares some features. Hawthorne includes all the interacting facets of individual and social life that compose their presented reality, but he refuses to exclude from his novel the presence of a magical or supernatural order. This order is seldom entirely absent even in more strictly realistic fiction. Adam Bede's premonition of his father's death and Anna Karenina's prophetic dream of the train are incidents marvelous enough from the point of view of everyday causality. But Hawthorne is unique in the central place he gives to this mode of experience and in the way he engages his readers' perception of it. He strives to make the celestial A not plausible but as spooky as possible; and at the same time, he uses it to worry us, to render the nature of reality problematic and to make us aware of our own assumptions about that nature.

[. . .]

Charles Feidelson notes that Hawthorne carefully sets *The Scarlet Letter* at the historical watershed between the medieval and the modern, and that the novel presents the interaction of these ages as a conflict between two ways of creating and perceiving meaning.[1] One of these sees experience as having meaning within a context of divine truth; within this context its symbolism tends toward fixity of significance, and its moral perception similarly moves to fix the value of characters and acts within rigidly separated categories of good and evil. The other is more secular and indeterminate. It sees meaning and value as generated from within human experience itself, so that its symbolic expressions and moral discriminations are valid to the extent that they emerge from a recognition of the whole complexity of life, including its inseparable mixture of good and evil. The contrast between Chillingworth's determinism and Hester's openness is only one version of this conflict; we see it again in the contrast between the A the Puritans impose on Hester and the A she creates, and between the sense of duty implicit in the Puritan's legal and religious forms and the sense of duty that leads Hester to go to Dimmesdale's rescue.

In its use of different fictional modes *The Scarlet Letter* also reenacts this conflict in its form. By using in his own right the romance form he associates with the Puritans Hawthorne makes us experience

Chillingworth as fixed to his role in a drama of angels and devils; his inclusion of magic throughout the novel encourages us to participate in the imaginative experience of a supernatural conflict between good and evil. The more realistic – in Hawthorne's terms, novelistic – mode of the bulk of his narrative forces us to make sense of the novel's world in another way. Here our understanding emerges gradually, from a careful observation of the twists of motive, thought, and emotion that make up the characters' lives. And our judgments here must always be tentative and open-ended, coming nearer to truth to the extent that they are faithfully responsive to the quality of the characters' whole experience. In effect the book itself illustrates a newer way of imaginatively conceiving of human existence emerging from an older way.

The inclusion of radically incommensurate fictional modes in *The Scarlet Letter* is a final way in which Hawthorne complicates his book's world and our relation to it. Like the inclusion of symbolic and dramatic articulations, it makes us perceive that world alternately under different aspects; and here again Hawthorne's double procedure also works to heighten our awareness of our own activity of perception. As they play against each other in the novel we become aware of each mode as a kind of fiction, as a specific form of imaginative representation. Hawthorne draws our attention to his own art of illusion, and he does so in order that we will be aware of the views of experience we are subscribing to as we accept his illusion as reality. In doing this he does not destroy the illusion his fiction creates or undermine its value; but he does keep its validity from being assumed too readily. Having understood the Puritans' sense of reality as a function of their scheme of perception, Hawthorne cannot but be aware that whatever he creates must be a function of another such scheme. This does not mean that he sees all representations of reality as simply illusory. But it means that their validity is conditional on a clear awareness of the outlook through which we make sense of reality. Thus he allows us to participate in both versions of his novel's experience, and also frankly to recognize each as a version, so that we may decide within the context of that recognition in which terms that experience is better understood.

[. . .]

This final scene brings to a head a conflict of narrative methods that has run all through the book. Dimmesdale's uncovering of his red stigma stands as the culmination of a carefully cultivated line of suspense – Hawthorne has teased and teased us with allusions to this mystery. In constructing his plot around the concealed presence of this physical sign he gives his book the shape of a ghostly romance; it operates by a magical order of causal determinism in which internal conditions are externalized as physical appearances. This line of suspense is the narrative's equivalent to the fictional mode in which Chillingworth is envisioned, and again Hawthorne associates this mode with Puritan mental fictions. As Dimmesdale presents it the symbol is fraught with providential significance, a wonder-working token of God's justice to sinners. And just as Chillingworth's fictional mode plays against Hester's, so too another kind of suspense is set against that of Hawthorne's romance plot. This interests us not in supernatural manifestations, or in what God has wrought, or in anything that admits of a determinate meaning, but rather in what choice Dimmesdale will make, what role his decision will play in his own psychic life, and what effect his choice will have on the other characters. This is the suspense of a more realistic novel; it invites us to see the story's meaning in its drama, in the texture of the characters' experience and in their exercise of their human freedom.

Hawthorne can and does give us the sort of scene that the latter kind of interest demands, but he insists on including a more mysterious and magical drama as well, and he refuses to make it easy for us to ignore it. As in 'The Minister's Vigil,' when the dramatic scene is completed the appearance of the scarlet letter is still to be explained, and here again Hawthorne uses its problematic status to engage us in a self-conscious act of interpretation. In returning to Dimmesdale's revelation in his last chapter he offers no explanation of his own for his story's omitted climax. Instead he reports the explanations of various spectators—that the letter on Dimmesdale's chest was the result of self-inflicted penitential torture, that it was magically produced by Chillingworth's potent necromancy, that it was the work of 'the ever active tooth of remorse, gnawing from the inmost heart outwardly.' There is a fourth account as well, that of certain 'highly respectable witnesses,' according to whom there was no scarlet letter and Dimmesdale had no hidden personal guilt to conceal. To these witnesses Dimmesdale stood on the scaffold with the adulteress and her child to express in parabolic form the lesson that 'in the view of Infinite Purity, we are all sinners alike.'

Hawthorne releases us from his narrative authority and allows us to choose among these, or to adopt whatever other explanation we like. And while at first his multiple choice seems simply to make the meaning and even the factuality of Dimmesdale's revelation ambiguous, the dimensions and the point of the ambiguity are not at all imprecise. Each of these choices gives the scene significance in terms of an implicit view of the nature of human guilt and evil. By absconding with his book's climax and providing these alternate versions of it instead, he allows us to construct our own conclusion, to see something or nothing on Dimmesdale's chest, but either one on the condition that we be aware of the nature of the vision that will make what we see meaningful to us. Our final moment of direct confrontation with the scarlet letter has the same purpose as the earlier ones did, but now that purpose is more obvious: it leaves us alone to complete the novel by determining its reality and its meaning as we think best, and to be conscious of our imaginative procedure as we do so. Finally Hawthorne's multiple choices provide one last clue to the purpose of his use of romance in *The Scarlet Letter*. From what we have seen of the Puritans in the novel the fourth choice sounds less like their reaction than like that of highly respectable readers of a later age. In its unwillingness to admit mysteries like Dimmesdale's letter to its consciousness it partakes of what Hawthorne calls 'our modern incredulity.' And in ceasing to believe in any form of magic it also ceases to adhere to a concept of sin as anything more than a comfortably universal phenomenon, lacking individual manifestations. In its light we see what the first three views have in common. They are all willing to accept the mysterious letter as a reality, and they all accept as a reality the 'deep life-matter' of guilt or evil from which they see it as springing. Hawthorne's own willingness to enter into the enchantments of romance and his eagerness to make us experience romance's magic all through *The Scarlet Letter* is a form of resistance to the trivializations latent in the secularism of an age that places 'gilded volumes on the centre-table' where the Puritans placed more serious literature and an age that makes adultery a matter of 'mocking infamy and ridicule.' It is his way of regaining access to the mysteries of the psychic life, the reality of which both the Puritans and his own more secular fiction attest to in their own ways.[2] □

Kenneth Dauber, in *Rediscovering Hawthorne* (1977) also adopts a reader-response approach in his examination of the way Hawthorne stages the conflict between the 'generic pressure' imposed by the given Puritan structures of signification and the desire for freedom and re-creation afforded by romance. Confronted with a text that is 'fragmented, thoroughly dislocated . . . remarkably unhinged', the reader, says Dauber, nevertheless tries to make sense of what he reads: 'Perception is always conception. We see events only as we order them into conventional structures, what E.H. Gombrich calls schemata':

■ The reader, faced with such contradiction, may choose to see ambiguity or paradox. More properly, however, if he refuses to impose his own world on the world of *The Scarlet Letter*, he is drawn into a point 'between' schemata, the creative heart of the book . . . the heart of *The Scarlet Letter* is the deeper point between alternative potentialities.

Here is a center of pure possibility. It is the beginning of what . . . we called Hawthorne's romance.[3] □

The scene in the forest is, according to Dauber, the last chance for Hester and Dimmesdale to assert their freedom from the repressive Puritan world and for the author to establish creative control over his work and intimacy with his audience.

■ And indeed, here, for a moment, romance more fully embodied is actually achieved. The language of Puritanism is revalued. The 'mystery of joy' replaces the Christian mystery. Dimmesdale's 'transformation' adapts Christian regeneration as, flinging aside his role of suffering sinner, he is 'risen up anew.' The language of theology becomes lovers' discourse, for in Hester's words, 'What we did has a consecration of its own.' We have, in effect, a series of puns or pun-like structures, alternative definitions of language from which the couple must choose. Hester and Dimmesdale are located at the intersection of the pun. Dimmesdale is a 'minister,' but of an 'interior kingdom.' In the equivoke, his social and his solitary selves are dissolved. Similarly, the woman the community has branded an adulteress is, in her personal relations, an 'angel.' Man and his world are one. Private and public are as yet unseparated. Dimmesdale and Hester unite in a universe that is their own extension when, 'as if the gloom of earth and sky had been but the effluence of these two mortal hearts, it vanished with their sorrow.'

It is the Custom-House, however, that ultimately takes control. Celebration is coerced. Reformation has not sufficiently been undertaken, and the pure potential we encounter more often than reformation yields inevitably to the fully formed. . . .

Allegory, a 'typical illusion,' is the destiny to which each character is doomed . . . The allegory is that of the 'first step awry,' the Christian story of the Fall, specifically Hawthorne's favorite story of the fortunate Fall. It is the Puritan history of sin and regeneration. . . .

In contrast to the scene in the forest, then, stands the great scene on the scaffold . . . It fixes as inevitable schemata that earlier were but potential. Character, landscape, events, all are reconceived in the terms the dream-vision provides.

The discontinuous technique of *The Scarlet Letter* thus achieves its supreme formulation. The result is the end of any further discontinuity, a final fixing of all that may transpire. The novel is most authoritatively, indeed almost prophetically, reconstructed. . . . After the action here, all subsequent action proceeds as a matter of course. It but enacts the world now firmly established.[4] □

These concluding chapters, Dauber believes, are marked by an authorial discomfort that he takes as evidence of Hawthorne's creative frustration by allegory's 'final fixing'.

John Carlos Rowe, examining the same material as Dauber, comes to an opposite conclusion in his essay 'The Internal Conflict of Romantic Narrative: Hegel's *Phenomenology* and Hawthorne's *The Scarlet Letter'* (1980). For Rowe the first half of the novel is characterised by a quality of 'allegorical externality', but this is replaced in the second half by a dramatic, temporalised mode, in which narrative events no longer govern the characters but are determined increasingly by intentional acts. For both Dauber and Rowe, allegory refers to a system of fixed, abstract meaning and communal value that is set against intimate experience and full selfhood, but where Dauber emphasises unresolved, and unresolvable contradiction, Rowe discovers an organic interrelation of elements. The internal conflict of romantic narrative, which in *The Scarlet Letter* is taken to be 'the tension between the Puritan and romantic tendencies' is finally resolved in the affirmation of an authentic self-realisation based on a reconciliation of imagination and historical consciousness, the ideal and the actual, the universal and the particular, romance and realism. Rowe demonstrates the phenomenological critic's concern with the sense of self, the state of consciousness, embodied in the text. Presuming the work to be an organic whole, unified by the author's consciousness, he seeks to penetrate to the 'deep structures' of that consciousness in order to grasp its 'essence'. And what he finds in *The Scarlet Letter* is an enactment of the Hegelian paradigm of romantic self-realisation wherein the experiential variety of life is understood as the manifestation of a unified force or spirit which governs the relation of the individual to society and history. Thus, ignoring any possible irony or equivocation in Hawthorne's presentation of Dimmesdale's ministerial 'triumph', Rowe concludes:

■ Dimmesdale's sermon and his confession on the scaffold bring the evanescence of individual self-consciousness into relation with the more enduring values of a social order in which the individual may discover an active, creative role.[5] □

As for Hester:

■ The allegorical simplicity of Hester's social signification is transformed into a symbolic complex of meanings . . . a point of reference for the entire dialectic of self-consciousness that moves from alienation to recognition and ultimate universality.[6] □

And as far as Hawthorne himself is concerned:

■ Hawthorne achieves an historical relation and spiritual identification with Hester by matching her own method of self-consciousness. Describing his own conception of the 'neutral territory' established by the romance, Hawthorne suggests that the primary object of this mediation wherein 'the Actual and Imagination may meet, and each imbue itself with the nature of the other,' is our own self-consciousness.[7] □

Evan Carton, in *The Rhetoric of American Romance* (1985) disagrees with both Dauber's assertion of 'the final victory of allegory' and with Rowe's notion of the final transformation of alienating, abstract allegory.

■ Informed by the structures of language and consciousness, experience is always allegorical, self-divided, at once intimate and abstract, a representation of itself . . . the non-identity of its tokens and values both provides for the production of meaning and prevents the absolute establishment of it. In this view, then, allegory, like Hester's letter, is neither submitted to nor overcome. Rather, it is the medium of experience itself, a medium that holds word and thing, spirit and matter, self and other in mutual indebtedness but not in synthesis.[8] □

Carton's criticism, which concentrates on the 'textuality' of the work, is characteristically poststructuralist in its concern with the novel's speculative threat to foundations, the obliquity of the authorial role, the impossibility of identifying from the signifier (sign) a final signified (that which the sign points toward). The very novel itself, in Carton's analysis, would seem to be about the whole shifting, unreliable process of signification. *The Scarlet Letter*, he says, 'is about representation'. Hester's scarlet letter is the central signifier. At first its meaning seems to be fixed, but the letter refuses to be exclusively bound to a Puritan meaning. Hester is a subjected victim of the Puritan system, but still engaged in a process of transforming the dominant signified. As a figure of the artist, she is capable of redefining the 'A', the single, simple identity of 'Adulterer', which has been assigned her by Puritan patriarchal ideology. Identity is determined by the semiotic system, yet signification is never settled. The (Puritan) attempt to impose meaning cannot eliminate 'desire' and tends to produce resistance. The signifier, the letter 'A', is inescapable throughout the novel, but its original signification is continually being multiplied and complicated, as it comes to include such a range of signifieds as 'able', 'angel', 'Arthur', 'author', 'artist', 'alpha', 'America'. In examining 'the question of control over the letter', Carton shows how Hester becomes 'the battleground of social and personal authority, of determinate and indeterminate meaning, of letter and spirit'. For all her re-interpretations of the letter, they do not free her from the letter or from the Puritan magistrates, but engage her in the play of significances that the magistrates' sentence similarly inaugurates rather than concludes:

■ This is the serious play of the novel, the play on which social order and personal identity are staked and by which each constrains and empowers the other. As Julia Kristeva has noted . . . 'to interpret' means 'to be mutually indebted'; *The Scarlet Letter* observes this definition and rigorously pursues its implications.

[. . .]

If it insists that words and things are not fundamentally joined, it also insists that they cannot be fundamentally disjoined. Such is the equivocal purport of the meteoric letter. . . . Dimmesdale neither projects the 'A' in the sky, as we assume, nor receives it, as he assumes. He interprets it, an act that involves both projection and reception, freedom and constraint. The constraint, moreover, lies not only in the shape of Dimmesdale's object but in the structure of his consciousness, a structure bound to reflect the cultural forms – perceptual, moral, linguistic – of which it is largely composed . . .

At once representative and semantic, language transports history and convention even as it transforms them. This tension manifests itself most elaborately in the lovers' forest rendezvous . . . Their transformations – of social identities to natural ones, of religious meanings to romantic ones, of established truths to subversive ones – are always transportations as well; the terms of their escape are the terms of their return . . . The integration of romantic and religious language, like the union of sexual and spiritual passion that initiates the story, suggests that no choice will constitute an adequate basis for self-definition and moral resolution. . . . Hester's injunction to Dimmesdale – 'Exchange this false life of thine for a true one' – expresses the necessary presuppositions of such a decision: that the entangled impulses (or meanings) which are implicit in the self-parodic vocabulary of the scene may be separated and objectified as alternative lives, and that these two lives may be accurately identified as a true one and a false one. These presuppositions are incompatible with the complexity that Dimmesdale's character and the novel itself have exhibited up to this point.[9] □

The general inclination of Hawthorne's narrative, Carton concludes, is 'to withhold or unsettle all the bases for absolute moral, social, or ontological judgments', and to frustrate 'the attempt to validate them by reference to a reality that exists prior to and independent of their operations'. Hawthorne offers minute descriptions of objects, situations and characters, only to render them problematic by contradiction, equivocation, multiplication, or attribution to tradition, to the community, and to his own or even to the reader's fancy. Pearl is 'mutable and ungovernable enigma', but also 'relentless agent of Puritan order'; Chillingworth a symbol of evil and 'a poor, forlorn creature'; Hester's role is 'one in which bondage and freedom converge'; Dimmesdale, in defending Hester's right to keep her child, performs 'simultaneously orthodox and subversive ministerial service'; in his Election Day sermon his 'sin is inextricable from his saintliness'. Binary oppositions are dissolved, each term traced through with its opposite. There is no transcendental meaning, the possibilities of interpretation are inexhaustible, there is never any final Truth. Carton ends by referring to Hawthorne's own deep suspicion that his romance was 'improper and unhealthy':

■ In Hester's wayward intellect and imagination, which threaten the social order more seriously than does her wayward flesh, Hawthorne finds a model of his own artistry that both attracts and disturbs him. Even as he fulfills the role of artist as intellectual rambler, challenger of conventional systems and meanings, and interweaver of putative opposites, he shrinks from it.[10] □

Finally, two other highly sophisticated and influential poststructuralist analyses of *The Scarlet Letter* are John Dolis's 'Hawthorne's Letter' (1984) and Peggy Kamuf's 'Hawthorne's Genres: The Letter of the Law *Appliquee*' (1985), both of which explore the problematic status of the sign in Hawthorne's narrative. Dolis concentrates on Hawthorne's struggle to assert 'authorship' of his text. By emphasising 'expression' and 'imagination' as well as 'textuality', Dolis considers Hawthorne's writing as constituting 'the play of presence and absence, disclosure and concealment', which is the only available ground of self.

■ When Hawthorne discovers the Letter in the attic of the Custom-House, he does precisely what the technological attitude demands. He seeks to understand the object by means of analysis: 'This rag of scarlet cloth . . . on careful examination, assumed the shape of a letter. It was the capital letter A. By an accurate measurement, each limb proved to be precisely three inches and a quarter in length.' Yet this solitary mark, discovered in the attic, refuses to assign itself to rational design: 'Certainly, there was some deep meaning in it, most worthy of interpretation . . . but evading the analysis of my mind.' For its significance Hawthorne must go from the 'attic,' or head, to what technology would deem the 'cellar,' the heart: 'While thus perplexed, – and *cogitating*, among other hypotheses . . . I happened to *place it on my breast*. It seemed to me, – *the reader* may smile, but *must not doubt my word*, – it seemed to me, then, that I *experienced a sensation not altogether physical*, yet almost so, as of burning heat' [italics mine]. Here Hawthorne clearly opposes the authority of the *logos* to the traditional logic of the head. It is understood – and not to be doubted – from the outset, that the meaning of the sign is excavated from the logic of the heart: the correspondence between subject and object is primordially grounded in expression. Moreover in its initial design, the Letter falls away from its original place, from its location as circumscribed by Surveyor Pue's manuscript: 'In the absorbing contemplation of the scarlet letter, I had hitherto neglected to examine a small roll of dingy paper, around which it had been twisted. This I now opened, and had the satisfaction to find, recorded by the old Surveyor's pen, a *reasonably* complete explanation of the whole affair' [italics mine]. We need not be reminded of the extent to which these half a dozen sheets of foolscap constitute the authority and domain of rationality in its entirety: so much for reason. This too accounts for the emphasis Hawthorne gives to the imaginary which allows the actual to be appropriated by the logic or affective significance of the heart. This is what happens with the Letter. Indeed one might say that in its very fall from the grace of this original manuscript, the Letter itself is inaugurated into si(g)n. In falling out of his-story (Surveyor Pue's), from the place in which its initial inscription is circumscribed, the Letter needs to be recovered in Hawthorne's own story. For in sliding off the page, the Letter itself does nothing less than fall into the white space of a new margin.

We are recalled to Hester's own predicament beside the brook: 'By this time Pearl had reached the *margin* of the brook, and stood on the farther side, gazing silently at Hester and the clergyman, who still sat together on the mossy tree-trunk, waiting to receive her' [italics mine]. When Hester hastens Pearl to retrieve the Letter, and is refused, she remarks to Dimmesdale:

'Was ever such a child! . . . O, I have much to tell thee about her. But, in very truth, she is right as regards this hateful token. I must bear its torture yet a little longer. . . .'

With these words, she advanced to the *margin* of the brook, took up the scarlet letter, and fastened it again into her bosom. Hopefully, but a moment ago, as Hester had spoken of drowning it in the deep sea, there was a sense of inevitable doom upon her, as she thus received back this deadly symbol from the hand of fate. She had flung it into infinite space!—she had drawn an hour's free breath!—and here again was the scarlet misery, glittering on the old spot [italics mine].

Here we stand witness to the return of the repressed: the Letter comes back to Hester once again from out of the other, its original source of meaning. Here too issues the locus of what Lacan refers to as the 'real' – that which always comes back to the same place and before which all symbolic discourse falters. Constantly held in abeyance, it is 'another locality, another space, another scene': the encounter in as much as it is missed. So with the forest scene in general: its significance resides in what is missing. In place of the Letter, Pearl but indicates its absence – as Hester observes: 'Pearl misses something which she has always seen me wear.' Amid a circular round of pointing (Pearl to Hester: 'Pearl stretched out her hand, with the small forefinger extended, and pointing evidently towards her mother's breast'; Hester to the Letter: '"Pearl," she said, sadly, "look down at thy feet! There! – before thee! – on the hither side of the brook!"'; and so in turn to Pearl: 'She extended her hand to Pearl'), amid this encapsulated round of substitution and displacement of the signifier, the margin of the stream again returns the Letter in its absence, reflecting only the margin of the Letter. 'The child turned her eyes to the point indicated; and there lay the scarlet letter, so close upon the margin of the stream, that *the gold embroidery was reflected in it*' [italics mine]. In this reflection the Letter itself is plainly absent. Only with Hester's Letter finally back in place does Pearl acknowledge her as mother: 'Now thou art my mother indeed! And I am thy little Pearl.'

It is further to be remarked, amid this round of nomination in the very presence of Dimmesdale, that the name of the father is here occluded – and this despite the many lessons in catechism in response to which Pearl repeatedly demands her origins . . . Without a history, Pearl lacks a story of her own. And yet it is logically appropriate that she should omit the name of the father, for it is she who – by upholding the (Puritan) law, demanding with her 'singular air of authority' that Hester return the Letter to its place – usurps the very place of the law itself. In place of the father (the law), she presumes to fill the gap – and does so as an impostor, as but 'the freedom of a broken law.' Indeed desire emerges in this very margin where demand becomes separated from need.

For Hawthorne, also, who – on the margin of discourse, upon the threshold of the Custom-House – seeks to father the Letter as his own, there arises the question of authority. In respect to the Letter, which has fallen out of another manuscript, Hawthorne is acutely sensitive to the demands of authorship. When first he broaches this issue in conjunction with the meaning of historical authenticity, he disclaims responsibility for the story by assuming the position of editor . . . The history of the Letter represents an interruption in Hawthorne's story. This false submission to the authorization of another occupies the very place in which we would expect to see the author's signature. But if he disowns the Letter, Hawthorne must disown *The Letter* as well: 'The original papers, together with the scarlet letter itself, – a most curious relic, – *are still in my possession*, and shall be freely exhibited to whomsoever, *induced by the great interest of the narrative*, may desire a sight of them' [italics mine]. Thus in the very next breath he disclaims his initial disclaimer so that he might reclaim the story as his own:

> I must not be understood as affirming, that, in the dressing up of the tale, and imagining the motives and modes of passion that influenced the characters who figure in it, I have invariably confined myself within the limits of the old Surveyor's half a dozen sheets of foolscap. On the contrary, I have allowed myself, as to such points, nearly or altogether as much license as if the facts had been entirely of my own invention. What I contend for is the authenticity of the outline.

What then is the truth of history? . . . Hawthorne's authority is nothing less than the white page which stands before him: it remains to be written. Here he will mark out his own paternity – the authority by which he will transcend laws external to himself, both Puritanical and political.

The entire Custom-House moves away from this oppressive impotence toward manhood. Heretofore, and indicative of his tenure as Custom-House official, Hawthorne's signature has never been his own, but rather the mark of Uncle Sam's seal . . . As an official representative of conventional authority, Hawthorne's very own manhood is shrinking to aught: 'I began to grow melancholy and restless; continually *prying into my mind*, to discover which of its *poor properties were gone*, and what degree of detriment had already accrued to the remainder. I endeavored to calculate how much longer I could stay in the Custom-House, and yet go forth *a man*' [italics mine]. As things stand (or, in this case, fall), he is not even the remainder of himself.

[. . .]

Toward its climax [of 'The Custom-House'] he therefore inserts his own private part: 'The real human being, all this time, *with his head safely on his shoulders*, had *brought himself to the* comfortable *conclusion*, that every thing was for the best; and, *making an investment in* ink, paper, and steel-pens, had opened his long-disused *writing-desk, and was again a literary man*' [italics mine].

Unlike the blissful couple of Edward and Ellen in *Fanshawe*, who, at the end of the romance and the beginning of Hawthorne's career, were content to leave 'no name behind them,' Hawthorne is now committed to the opposite. It is the problem of nomination repeated in Dimmesdale's failure to admit his own paternity to Pearl. Although for Dimmesdale it is a matter of seven years, for Hawthorne it is simply a matter of several pages before he confesses to the lie of editorship and reveals the truth of authorship. Toward the conclusion of the Custom-House sketch Hawthorne is ready both to admit his indebtedness to the other (Surveyor Pue) and to declare the authority of his own name.

[. . .]

In the Custom-House sketch, he clearly seeks to understand the significance of his own existence, but he is divided in his dual role as editor and author. Similarly the ambivalent tone of 'The Custom-House' discloses Hawthorne's ambiguous attitude toward his Puritan ancestry. He would simultaneously recognize and disown both story line and family line. Furthermore he repeatedly delays the fact that he must stand up to this story as his own, that he must at last sign his own name to it. He is, of course, aware from the outset that his story excludes a privileged authorial position, that its beginning, in fact, originates elsewhere and is ultimately inaccessible. 'As regarded its origin, there were various explanations, all of which must necessarily have been conjectural.' We are repeatedly cautioned regarding this genealogy. If he is ever to come into his own, Hawthorne realizes that he must recognize his source of identity in the other. The source of his story is not his own doing; yet if one tries to follow it back to an absolutely certain origin, the trace of its historical inscription becomes irrevocably lost in pre-historical discourse – that is, in gossip, in what is passed down or passed along by word of mouth. Such is his original source of indebtedness: 'The authority which we have chiefly followed – a manuscript of old date, drawn up from the verbal testimony of individuals, some of whom had known Hester Prynne, while others had heard the tale from contemporary witnesses.' And such is the testimony to which Hawthorne's signature at last bears witness: from the beginning his story is inscribed within the other.

If Hawthorne's story immediately obtains from Surveyor Pue's history, history itself nevertheless appears all the more problematic when we recall its intimate resemblance to story. For while Hawthorne initially remarks its status as official, a closer examination reveals 'more traces of Mr Pue's mental part, and the internal operations of his head, than the fizzled wig had contained of the venerable skull itself. They were documents, in short, not official, but *of a private nature*, or, at least, *written* in his private capacity, and apparently *with his own hand*' [italics mine]. Hawthorne undermines that easy epistemology which relegates knowledge to the simple accumulation of facts. In doing so, he also speaks against the authority of his Puritan ancestors whose judgment would condemn him to insignificance: 'an idler like myself. . . .

A writer of story-books.' Indeed, from the beginning, fact is put in doubt for when he measures the letter (three inches and a quarter in length) it tells him nothing. While the proper measurement of a thing gives us its correct form, its meaning remains absent. The signifier considered in and of itself is nothing but the isolated subject taken by itself: the subject objectified. Thus would reason reduce meaning to the integer of self-identity. A fact is therefore meaningless precisely to the extent that it coincides with itself; identity does not give rise to meaning, but rather – like meaning itself – arises from discrepancy . . . It happens as no accident, moreover, that each and every one desires to know the name of the father, in whom there resides the locus of authority as the source of any and all identity. In this regard identity itself is always a fiction; a text whose context, whose very pre-text, needs to be delineated; a story whose knot might 'induce the beholder to attempt unravelling it.' History, too, reveals its origins in story, in fiction, in narration.

[. . .]

By the time that Hawthorne finally signs his name to the work, we are aware that his ironic signification already contains within it the possibility of meaning its opposite. Discourse, by nature, displaces the insignificant correctness of fact with the sign of fiction. Witness, for example, Hawthorne's 'conclusion' regarding the further adventures of the Letter in the transformed shape of Pearl: 'But, in no long time after the physician's death, the wearer of the scarlet letter disappeared, and Pearl along with her. For many years, though a *vague report* would now and then find its way across the sea, – like a shapeless piece of driftwood tost ashore, with the *initials of a name* upon it – *yet no tidings* of them *unquestionably authentic were received*' [italics mine]. Over and against these vague reports bearing but the initials of a name, Hawthorne's final signature commends us to the discursive fabric of all authority.

Regarding its claim to authority the text refers us purely and simply to the domain of good faith and interpretation. So Hawthorne concludes with respect to Pearl's correspondence with Hester, letters that locate Pearl within another story, another context, yet one for which he implicitly claims authority as well: 'In fine, the gossips of that day believed, – and Mr. Surveyor Pue, who made investigations a century later, believed, – and one of his recent successors in office, moreover, faithfully believes,—that Pearl was not only alive, but married, and happy, and mindful of her mother.' Authority therefore displaces the lineage of fatherhood with the discursive knot of textuality. Language constitutes the beginning of another enterprise, an intentional structure signifying a series of displacements: language replaces genesis with paragenesis, origins with beginnings, continuity (the line) with contiguity (the knot). Textuality transforms an original object whose significance is fixed into a beginning intention, whose significance is open and multiple. The emerging intention to mean, when it is bequeathed to language, strays toward multiplicity, permitting the possible forms of discourse to merge one into the other.

Because meaning is grounded in intentionality, authority primordially refers us back to self-expression – the fictive or fabricated correspondence between subject/object, signifier/signified – always against a background of repression. As Freud observes of the *Hexateuch*, there is violence in texts:

> Almost everywhere noticeable gaps, disturbing repetitions and obvious contradictions have come about – indications which reveal things to us which it was not intended to communicate. In its implications the distortions of a text resemble a murder: the difficulty is not in perpetrating the deed, but in getting rid of its traces. We might well lend the word 'Entstellung' [distortion] the double meaning to which it has a claim but of which today it makes no use. It should mean not only 'to change the appearance of something' but also 'to put something in another place, to displace.' Accordingly, in many instances of textual distortion, we may nevertheless count upon finding what has been suppressed and disavowed hidden away somewhere else, though changed and torn from its context.[11]

This textual disruption is due to the discrepancies inherent in the sign itself. Pearl's nature, as the Letter in another form, articulates this broken law of signification: 'It lacked reference and adaptation to the world into which she was born. The child could not be made amenable to rules. In giving her existence, a great law had been broken.' Meaning emerges from this violent gap in signification. A consciousness of the facts can therefore never account for the fact of consciousness: the self-reflexive subject reveals that its identity in no way coincides with itself, but rather is constituted by another in its origin. This otherness represents the boundary of the self as signifier of desire.

It is precisely the missing or absent beginning which presents the crisis of Pearl's identity: she would know the other by whom she has initially been authorized. Lacking this knowledge, she can nonetheless occasion the significance of the lives surrounding her by means of substitution. In respect to her parents, for example, Pearl knots the chain of signification, 'herself a symbol, and the connecting link between those two.' She is the other whose substitution guarantees one's being, the bond of identity for both Hester and Arthur: 'In her was visible the tie that united them. She had been offered to the world, these past seven years, as the *living hieroglyphic,* in which was revealed the secret they so darkly sought to hide, – *all written in this symbol,* – all plainly manifest, – had there been a prophet or magician skilled to read the character of flame! And Pearl has the oneness of their being' [italics mine]. Significance here emerges from the insertion of one signifier in place of another. When Hester discards the letter (Pearl) in the forest, this alters the relationship insofar as Dimmesdale takes its (her) place: 'The stigma gone, Hester heaved a long, deep sigh. . . . O exquisite relief! she had not known the weight, until she felt the freedom.' Here Hester assumes the very freedom she had for so long postponed, 'the freedom of a broken law' which Pearl represents and yet dissembles in herself. Similarly Hester's self-expression occasions the premonition of Dimmesdale's self-repression. Thus, when Hester returns the Letter to its initial place, when Pearl once again occupies the place next to her mother, Dimmesdale is, in turn, recalled to the displacement of himself – the way in which the real, as Lacan defines it, always comes back to the same place:

> As the minister departed, in advance of Hester Prynne and little Pearl, he threw a backward glance; half expecting, that he should discover only some faintly traced features or outline of the mother and the child, slowly fading into the twilight of the woods. So great a vicissitude in his life could not at once be received as real. . . . And there was Pearl, too, lightly dancing from the margin of the brook, – now that the intrusive third person was gone, – and taking her old place by her mother's side. So the minister had not fallen asleep, and dreamed.

By the same token, that is, in the displacement of the Letter by Pearl, Dimmesdale feels 'this indistinctness and *duplicity of impression*' [italics mine] within himself, though it has *yet to be expressed*:

> The *intervening space* of a single day *had operated on his consciousness* like the lapse of years. . . . Before Mr. Dimmesdale reached home, his inner man gave him other evidences of a revolution in the sphere of thought and feeling [italics mine].

In this regard Dimmesdale typifies the Freudian subject and its deter-mination to write itself off.

> . . . He absolutely trembled and turned pale as ashes, *lest his tongue should wag itself,* in utterance of these horrible matters, and plead

his own consent for so doing, without his having fairly given it. And, even with this terror in his heart, he could hardly avoid laughing to imagine how the sanctified old patriarchal deacon would have been petrified by his minister's impiety [italics mine].

And to 'the eldest female member of his church,' who seeks the 'heaven-breathing Gospel truth from his beloved lips,' he once again consigns himself to this other voice.

> On this occasion, up to the moment of putting his lips to the old woman's ear, Mr. Dimmesdale, as the great enemy of souls would have it, could recall no text of Scripture, nor aught else, except a brief, pithy, and, as it then appeared to him, unanswerable argument against the immortality of the human soul. . . . What he really did whisper, the minister could never afterwards recollect. There was, perhaps, a fortunate *disorder in his utterance*, which failed to impart any distinct idea to the good widow's comprehension, or which Providence interpreted after a method of its own [italics mine].

Once Dimmesdale finally reaches home, he is again confronted with this disordered self. His very meaning is disrupted, his significance broken:

> There was the Bible, in its rich old Hebrew, with Moses and the Prophets speaking to him, and God's voice through all! There, on the table, with the inky pen beside it, was an unfinished sermon, *with a sentence broken in the midst*, where his thoughts had ceased to gush out upon the page two days before. He knew that it was himself, the thin and white-cheeked minister, who had done and suffered these things, and written thus far into the Election Sermon! But he seemed to stand apart, and eye this former self with scornful, pitying, but half-envious curiosity. That self was gone! Another man had returned out of the forest. [italics mine]

Dimmesdale's dilemma echoes Hawthorne's predicament in 'The Custom-House.' He too experiences the chiasm of his discourse. What has been hitherto inscribed within the other, he must pen himself, expressing that authority which is his own though still repressed. Thus 'flinging the already written pages of the Election Sermon into the fire, he forthwith began another, which he wrote with such an impulsive flow of thought and emotion, that he fancied himself inspired. And with the first sign of sunrise, he yet subsists the pen still between his fingers, and a vast, immeasurable tract of written space behind him.' What lies ahead, however, constitutes the measurable tract of his own authority. These 'blank pages' which lie before him, and which have heretofore been writing into his very flesh, reveal by concealing: what is absent cannot hide – what is present can.

From the structure of repression, there emerges the lack of meaning in Pearl's existence as well. While she refuses the ideal – 'I have no Heavenly Father' – she nevertheless repeatedly invokes the name of the real father. Without this name, of course, she lacks a 'history': she is a story begun, but anonymous. Until Dimmesdale's final confession, she remains a character in search of an author (Arthur): a letter takes the place of a name, an initial the place of a signature. Though she lives with Hester as her mother, she must hide the Letter in place of the father. This substitution confers upon Pearl the status of an inauthentic document. It happens as no coincidence, then, that the central character in the novel possesses the Letter as the central, though hidden, letter in her name (PeArl); for so long as Dimmesdale refuses to nominate himself as the author of this work, Pearl's missing identity resides purely in the Letter. While Arthur conceals his Letter behind conventional clothes, Hester ironically wears his secret and hypocrisy as her very garment. In this respect Pearl's identification with the Letter is made all too easy: 'She *is* the scarlet letter' [italics mine]. Her own attire mimics this confusion, arrayed 'in a certain velvet tunic, of a peculiar cut, abundantly embroidered with fantasies and flourishes of gold thread.' From birth, Pearl seeks to decipher the enigmatic significance of the Letter as that which holds the very key to her existence; she grasps it, flings flowers at it, embellishes it with burrs, and places eel-grass on her own breast in its form – 'freshly green, instead of scarlet':

> 'I wonder if mother will ask me what it means!' thought Pearl.
>
> 'My little Pearl,' said Hester, after a moment's silence, 'the green letter, and on thy childish bosom, has no purport. But does thou know, my child, what this letter means which thy mother is doomed to wear?'
>
> 'Yes, mother,' said the child. 'It is the great letter A. Thou hast taught it me in the horn-book.'

The Letter takes the place of a denomination which demands to be announced: there is a proper name involved in its sound for which no substitution can bequeath to Pearl her meaning without the loss of significance. As Derrida remarks, 'Every signified whose signifier can neither vary nor be translated into another signifier without loss of significance, suggests a proper-name effect.'[12] Thus while the 'A' appears in different places, different forms, and while it meaningfully inscribes itself into the existence of others, for Pearl it lacks any and all signification proper to herself. She is an unaccomplished work, missing the other letters. In relation to the other, she stands as a meaningless phoneme – although not insignificantly as the first letter both of the alphabet and of Arthur's name. Isolated as 'the great letter "A" of her horn-book,' she implies the missing part of a whole text and subsequently constitutes 'a law unto herself, without her eccentricities being reckoned to her for a crime.' Not until the end, when Dimmesdale discloses his corresponding Letter and gives her his name, is Pearl at last authorized and authenticated.

At the conclusion, moreover, her substitution for the Letter confers upon *The Letter* a significant displacement – a self-reflexive and therefore bifurcated commentary. Pearl's name, in fact, is interchangeable with Hawthorne's title for the book; we might read into her various 'properties,' the status of the art work. Thus from America, where Pearl 'became the richest heiress of her day, in the New World' – a circumstance which 'wrought a very material change in the public estimation' – Hawthorne cleverly dispatches his 'child' (*The Scarlet Letter*) to Europe, where it 'grew into a legend.' The reader is invited to this 'christening,' permitted to witness the birth of American Art. In this beginning there is the promise that others will follow – a situation as pregnant with possibilities as Pearl herself: 'And, once, Hester was seen embroidering a baby garment.' At last, having come into her own authority, Pearl's correspondence with Hester – 'Letters came') – here parallels her correspondence with *The Letter*. Regarding both, the end of Hawthorne's story holds forth the birth of other beginnings. An author in her own right, bequeathed by Dimmesdale's confession the other letters of her full name, Pearl now initiates her correspondence with the other as one who has come into the fullness of the alphabet. Thus, to Hester, *other* 'Letters came' (B, C, D, E, F, G, H, I, J, K, L, M, N, O, P, Q, R, S, T, U, V, W, X, Y, and Z?) And with her signature *The Letter* too begins its round of nomination, the proselytization of American letters in Europe: 'Through the remainder of Hester's life, there were indications that the recluse of the scarlet letter was the object of love and interest with some inhabitant of another land.'

Furthermore Pearl's signature commends the Letter to its authentic assignment. Though Hester is sentenced to wear the sign of the Letter, she nevertheless redeems it by way of embroidery. Indeed, what the pen is to Hawthorne, the needle is to Hester. With it she transforms her subjectivity to discourse. By means of her needlework, Hester confers upon the existent 'a fictitious value even to common or worthless things; . . . Hester really filled a gap which must otherwise have remained vacant': she weaves herself into the status of a text. Her sentence is becoming to her: she becomes a sentence. Upon entering a church, for example, 'it was often her mishap to find herself the text of the discourse'). Indeed she often fancies 'that the scarlet letter had endowed her with a new *sense*' [italics mine]. With her return from abroad, she is at last bequeathed a textuality of her own making on a new threshold in her story:

> But there was a more real life for Hester Prynne, here, in New England, than in that unknown region where Pearl had found a home. . . . She had returned, therefore, and resumed, – of her own free will, . . . the symbol of which we have related so dark a tale. Never afterwards did it quit her bosom. . . . the scarlet letter ceased to be a stigma . . . and became a type. . . . And, as Hester Prynne had no selfish ends . . . people brought all their sorrows and per- plexities, and besought her counsel.

Now given over to dialogue, the Letter thence transforms itself toward its revelation as a sacred scripture of love – a text whose very nature is destined to unknot itself 'in Heaven's own time' and is therefore doomed to remain forever undisclosed . . .

And so the harbinger of the new sexuality must be a woman – one, we might conjecture, who would dismiss the epithalamion as super- fluous. In all of this there is again the ironic bifurcation of significance, for insofar as Hawthorne's own child (*The Scarlet Letter*) is female (Pearl), his book will not perpetuate his paternal name. This suggests that writing does not simply play at childbirth across the abyss of paternity alone, but rather articulates the androgynous abyss across which signs signify, the continually problematic status of being which combines the absence of the dead father with the presence of the living mother. 'Writing leaps back and forth across this impossible interval, doubling, multiplying, with no escape save annihilation'.[13]

Just as the Letter multiplies its meaning across the otherness of itself (adultery, angel, apostle, able, authority, authenticity, alpha, alphabet, american, art, alterity), so too with the subject: the signifier acquires its meaning from the other signifiers, resisting a transcenden- tal signified. The otherness of the Letter always and everywhere returns its bearer to the place in which it inaugurates the subject to the responsibility for language and the inscription of the self upon the margin of another text. As Geoffrey Hartman remarks, 'The word that is given up is not given up: it must inscribe itself somewhere else, as a psychosomatic symptom.' Thus, for example, while Hester is tempted – should Pearl be taken from her – to enter the forest, where souls are consigned to the devil, and sign her name in 'the Black Man's book,' she yet refuses to resign herself to another text. Rather than submit to either this or the Puritan conscription – 'she will be a living sermon against sin' – she chooses to embroider a discourse of her own. Reassigning the Letter of the Puritan law to herself, she thereby returns it to the Puritan community at the very point at which it originated, for her needlework now clothes the community in garments of her own making. By means of her embroidery, Hester rewrites their history as her story, reversing the short circuit: those who would initially write her off are finally written by her, a discourse signed, sealed, and delivered, moreover, with her very signature. It is no wonder then, that the Letter (as symptom) shows up on the blank page of the night sky to (dis)cover the entire community.

Dimmesdale, on the other hand, re( )signs himself to the 'A.' By its absence from consciousness, the Letter is destined to be present elsewhere. Its symptomatic manifestation inscribes itself upon his very body in the form of his psychosomatic illness. When he speaks, the Letter bespeaks him; just as his sermons represent a paranoid form of dictation, the divine writing calls him to remember a dead Letter and thereby forget himself. For Dimmesdale the Letter must be uncovered, laid bare: he must expose himself to self-aversion. Hawthorne's addiction to the truth – 'Be true! Be true! Be true! Show freely to the world, if not your worst, yet some trait whereby the worst may be inferred!' – simply underscores the sentence whereby human existence is called to express the inter-textuality of self and other, the inter-subjective dimension of being oneself. In this context truth knows nothing of fact but rather exposes the facticity of being. To be true is to express one's self as an original, to discover a voice of one's own, to fabricate a version, to rehearse the dialogic interval of existence: 'To open an intercourse with the world.' To be false, on the other hand, is to be missing a version of one's self. To repress a version constitutes the very perversion of being to which Dimmesdale is given over until the end.

Like Hester's Letter, furthermore, Dimmesdale's final revelation allows a multiplicity of versions to figure forth once again. With his disclosure, not only the Letter's significance, but its very appearance, have yet to be discerned. For some it represents his self-inflicted penance; for others it represents the impotence of Chillingworth's necromancy; for still others it represents 'the ever active tooth of remorse, gnawing from the inmost heart outwardly.' A special few, moreover, who 'professed never once to have removed their eyes from the Reverend Mr. Dimmesdale, denied that there was any mark whatever on his breast.' Except for this last, blind version, which obviously misses the mark, Hawthorne permits each version to stand side by side with the others: 'The reader may choose among these theories.' Herein subsists that genuine conversion of consciousness which Hawthorne's oeuvre provokes, the inter-textuality of existence . . . With *The Letter* Hawthorne's openendedness allows us to choose and thereby releases us from the narrative authority: the reader is called upon to authorize the text in terms of its significance to self. And while the narrative announces its desire, once the Letter has done its office, to 'erase its deep print out of our brain,' the trace of this efface-ment must nonetheless remain forever upon the heart. By handing over the potential of this lack, Hawthorne entrusts the reader with the task of further inscription – that in the overabundance of this other-ness, the reader would write himself all the more.

In all of this there is implied the ontological status of language – 'the page of life' – and being itself, as the narrator of *The Marble Faun* observes regarding Miriam's life:

> In weaving these mystic utterances into a continuous scene, we undertake a task resembling, in its perplexity, that of gathering up and piecing together the fragments of a letter, which has been torn and scattered to the winds. Many words of deep significance – many entire sentences, and those possibly the most important ones – have flown too far on the winged breeze to be recovered. If we insert our own conjectural amendments, we perhaps give a purport utterly at variance with the true one. Yet, unless we attempt something in this way, there must remain an unsightly gap, and a lack of continuousness and dependence in our narrative.

Narration occupies both story and history at their points of embarka-tion, that locus of authorization which makes existence into a work. Meaning is born through exposition, the temporal fabrication in which existence is made to stand out. It must have a narrator. Hawthorne's pre-text ('The Custom-House'), Pearl's correspondence, Dimmesdale's confession, Hester's embroidery – each inscribes the story of the self in the context of the other to which it corresponds; each discourse makes the other its own. While Hester, for example, initially rejects her needlework as sin, she learns its joy as '*a mode of expression*, and therefore soothing, the passion of her life' [italics mine]. Both Chillingworth and the Puritans in general, on the other hand, deny being its exposition. Adverse to expression, repression thus cir-cumscribes the subject as an 'impostor' (as not its own), and therefore articulates the very imposition of being. Precisely and ironically to the extent that Chillingworth, for example, entirely subscribes to or underwrites the text of Dimmesdale's life, he serves as but an annota-tion to the authority of another. What is the Letter, if not the cutting edge of this bifurcated, asymmetrical structure: self-other? If at its ori-gin the self is always already written by another, it nevertheless is called upon to inaugurate the manner and meaning of its significance. In its intention to secure a beginning, the self thus authorizes its emergence into the world as an authentic work – one of its own making. With this expressive exposition, being is provoked to itself. Hawthorne's villains, however, revoke the self to the failure of being, entirely spoken for and written by the other – upon this line of resistance to the self at the insistence of another, existence is repressed. Authentic existence would yet tie this original (family) line with a significant knot of its own expression: the subject itself is always a fiction.

Hawthorne's *Letter* exposes this duplicity of being within the very structure of his work. His authorial switch from the first-person 'Custom-House' to the third-person 'romance' enacts the abyss between self and other, subject and object, fiction and fact, individual and community, private and public. Here the personal pronoun not only reveals the reciprocity between subject and object within narration, but also its reciprocal means of being present/absent to itself. The gestalt of a consciousness articulated both within and without implies the very otherness of discourse. Insofar as existence is given over to language, to the irreducible discrepancy between signifier and signified, the subject transacts both speech and writing as separate aspects of the same phenomenon, the otherness of being itself. Each is the horizon of, though neither is ontologically prior to, the other. The narrative discourse comes from the manuscript of Surveyor Pue, although this manuscript, in turn, originates in the gossip of the age; Hester's discourse comes to her from the spoken judgment of the Puritan tribunal; Pearl's discourse comes to her from Dimmesdale's confession; Dimmesdale's discourse, on the other hand, comes to him from the unspoken name – the written mark inscribed upon his very flesh, the host of a divine insignia. In every case discourse is called to assume responsibility both for the discourse of the other as its own and for its own otherness. Hawthorne assumes his pen in order to write his romance; Hester utilizes her needle in order to embroider her garments; Pearl takes up her armorial seals in order to post her letters of correspondence; Dimmesdale employs his voice in order to sing the song of himself. In every case, moreover, the subject is provoked to sign the other with a discourse which encircles the (w)hole of its (in)significance.

Expression redeems the subject from the abyss of nothingness across which the signs signify and for significance itself, just as Hepzibah, for example, is 'redeemed from insignificance' by her scowl. Expression articulates the heartfelt meaning of being in its exposition – the subject's correspondence to the heart of things is the matter of discourse. Dimmesdale's voice suggests this correspondence: 'It breathed passion and pathos, and emotions high or tender, in a tongue native to the human heart.' Within the logic of the head, of course, significance is purely arbitrary: Hawthorne's repetitions and signs function solely as a self-referential system, precluding any and all sense of totality (the A itself is but a fragment). Yet this is not the case within the logic of the heart. While Hawthorne 'undoes meaning' at the level of reason, he nonetheless secures the self to a significance which precedes it and thus occasions the very possibility of self-expression – the greatest danger imaginable to the Puritan community as a whole. Both Dimmesdale's voice and Hester's needle disrupt the communal ratio. As Nina Baym observes: 'Disguised as a social document, the work of art secretly expresses the cry of the heart. Doing this, it covertly defies society in response to hidden but universal needs. . . . *The Scarlet Letter* makes it clear that imagination serves the self.'[14] Imagination interrupts the *ratio* of reason in as much as it returns the subject to an irreducible locus of signification from which all meaning originates. Imagination bestows upon the subject the possibility of exposing what is at the very center of its existence, what inheres as its irreducible *Kern*, to use Freud's term: *a heart of nonsense*. What Hawthorne's narrator in *The Marble Faun* observes of the image in painting articulates the core of textuality in general: '*that indefinable nothing*, that inestimable something, *that constitutes the life and soul*,' [italics mine]. As Lacan suggests, all discourse harbors within it this locus of the imaginary by which means the subject constructs the images both of the real world and of itself: 'The I is not a being, it is a presupposition with respect to that which speaks.'[15]

How else, in fact, are we to account for Hawthorne's final tomb-stone inscription which would efface its very discourse insofar as it substitutes or displaces the symbolic with the imaginary?

> All around, there were monuments carved with armorial bearings; and on this simple slab of slate – as the curious investigator may still discern, and perplex himself with the purport – there appeared the semblance of an engraved escutcheon. It bore a device, a herald's wording of which might serve for a motto and brief description of our now concluded legend; so sombre is it, and relieved only by one ever-glowing point of light, gloomier than the shadow: – 'On a Field, Sable, the Letter A, Gules.'

In one sense, of course, Hawthorne returns this final image to symbolic discourse inasmuch as he translates its significance into the language of heraldry: 'On a Field, Sable, the Letter A, Gules.' In another sense, however, there remains only the image itself or rather its ghost: the after-image of what can now only suggest the presence of a dead Letter. If anything, this reading of the inscription is reinforced by Hawthorne's narrative description: for here the invisible motto –

the visible 'A' – is 'relieved only by one ever-glowing point of light gloomier than the shadow.' The oxymoron expresses what in the register of the symbolic must remain forever unspeakable: existence is a dead end.

It also seems that in the lack of a verse upon the tombstone, there is once again failure in signing a name. The missing epitaph marks the point of origin of this ghost story, that most simple discontinuous space of the Freudian *fort-da* where the presence of the father-to-be – that is, the presence of the father – 'playing' with the absence of the mother engenders a symbolic lack of discourse: 'Writing oscillates between a name that cannot be inscribed and the dead body, a corpse effect whose intrusion into the real is the sign and signature of this impasse. . . . the tomb is the point at which name and body are wed in their common impasse.'[16] It should come as no surprise that in the failure of adequation – the signifier as that which represents a subject for another signifier – death has already taken place, has taken up its place in the end, and has done so from the beginning. His crossing of signifiers constitutes, in effect, the very locus of significance as the gap or void of being itself. As the skeleton at 'The Christmas Banquet' betokens:

> And if, in their bewildered conjectures as to the purpose of earthly existence, the banqueters should throw aside the veil, and cast an inquiring glance at this figure of death, as seeking thence the solution otherwise unattainable, the only reply would be a stare of the vacant eye-caverns, and a grin of the skeleton-jaws. Such was the response that the dead man had fancied himself to receive, when he asked of Death to solve the riddle of his life; and it was his desire to repeat it when the guests of his dismal hospitality should find themselves perplexed with the same question.

The subject comes and goes upon its round of nomination, and reads in advance this ever-unwritten inscription: 'Death . . . is an idea that cannot easily be dispensed with, in any condition between the primal innocence and that other purity and perfection, which, perchance, we are destined to attain, after travelling round the full circle.'

Here reading and writing are one and the same: for in the end, as we have seen regarding its ultimate design, the Letter which goes abroad is finally returned to its initial place. Lacan observes the same of Poe's 'Purloined Letter,' in which the sender receives from the receiver his own message in reverse form: 'Thus it is that what the . . . "letter in sufferance" means is that a letter always arrives at its destination.'[17] Throughout its circular course, in fact, the Letter elicits the reader's response – indeed, repeats the very trauma of interpretation which inaugurates the self to meaning. As Barbara Johnson says of psychoanalysis: it is 'the traumatic deferred interpretation not *of* an event, but *as* an event which never took place as such. The "primal scene" is not a scene but an *interpretive infelicity*. . . . Psychoanalysis has content only insofar as it repeats the dis-content of what never took place.' Similarly, every reader is destined to have the Letter addressed to him precisely to the extent that the Letter's destination is 'wherever it is read.'[18] Hawthorne's Letter assigns the reader to himself. Thus fiction simultaneously conceals and reveals its truth. This open-ended text refers us to the infinite regress of referentiality. The source of a story is always another story. Each and every discourse on/of the Letter bears the trace of another signifier, another letter, a dead letter. We are recalled to Hawthorne's pre-text in 'The Custom-House,' where the Letter turns up as simply one of the innumerable pieces of dead weight which clutter the House itself: the mere ghosts of men who through the repetition and redundancy of bureaucratic scribbling have come to occupy this dead letter office. It is indeed their office to repress – by means of idle chit-chat and procrastination – the very thing bureaucracy perpetually defers: the dead-line. Here it is (mis)construed, of course, that life goes on forever. How else are we to understand the overpowering lethargy that befalls Hawthorne, surrounded by these dead letters, the 'beings-of-no-consequence' who because they are always talking are therefore never able to write a thing, insuring a veritable dead end which by its impotence leaves everything unfinished?

Within this House of dead letters, the subject is provoked to build, to dwell, to construct the text of himself. The Letter serves to distinguish Hawthorne from both the other(s) and himself, as he inaugurates the repetition of its various rounds within the symbolic structure of discourse. Hawthorne's writing is this House of Fiction, which constructs a passageway between self and other, and thereby opens him to intercourse with the world: 'Thoughts are frozen and utterance benumbed, unless the speaker stand in some true relation with his audience.' Upon the threshold of this (Custom) House, Hawthorne's discourse initiates that homecoming of the subject to itself. As he expressed it in a letter to his publisher, James T. Fields, '"The Custom-House" is merely introductory, – an entrance-hall to the magnificent edifice which I throw open to my guests.'[19] Hawthorne's prefaces are thus significant precisely to the extent that they function as various thresholds to this single house. Edgar Dryden brilliantly seizes the significance of this event when he observes that the Custom-House sketch endows the familiar house-of-fiction metaphor with an important ontological dimension.'[20] Indeed, Hawthorne's House of Fiction is nothing less than language itself. Thus he could refer to fiction as the very 'kingdom of possibilities.'

Meaning here constitutes the play of presence and absence, disclosure and concealment, whereby the ghost of substitution assumes its port of entry. Language expresses the otherwise silent correspondence between signifier and signified, subject and object, self and other. The structure of signification plays across a silent abyss in which the Letter is both cutting edge and knot. Regarding all forms of being, there is the gap, the chasm which yawns – waiting for the subject to insert itself, to uncover its meaning, its truth. Being shelters absence within the house of language itself. Discourse implies an ontology wherein both presence and absence equiprimordially obtain: the construction and repetition of a story in which the subject is at all times missing and thereby stands in need of interpretation. Interpretation returns us to Hawthorne's own obsession for masquerade, the persona of textuality – disclosure in concealment: being (exposed or unmasked) in the very face of the masked text. Herein dwells the genuine *work* of Hawthorne's world, the tangle whence emerges its na(rra)tivity. And in this fabrication, this construction, this weaving, is inscribed the magic limen – the thread of a story designed to be, yet from the outset fated to end: the very knot of being itself. When Hawthorne posts his *Letter*, it is for nothing less than this: to send being on its way, its destination – to be more than the k(not).[21] □

Kamuf's essay is an example of the way in which a deconstructionist approach can be made to serve a feminist criticism. Kamuf sets out to unravel the texture of power and authority enmeshed in 'the Letter of the Law', knowledge, meaning, language, and interpretation. Kamuf's critique, beginning with the assumption that the Letter of the Law is not an absolute, transcendent value, participates in the interminable movement of laying bare the unavoidable machinations of (patriarchal) power and authority.

■ I said above that *The Scarlet Letter* may be read as thinking the relation between the text of the letter and the letter of the law, or, in other terms, between the written work and its interpretation according to the laws of genre. Thus, a relation which is generally conceived as subordinating written texts to externally independent rules for the classification of writing by genre cannot be so simply applied in this case. To indicate how Hawthorne's text thinks this relation differently, we'll consider briefly two parallel scenes in which the letter and the law of its interpretation are displayed together but with contrasting effect. Of the many passages in the text where interpretation of the letter is explicitly in question, I have chosen these because they inflect the difference they display with gender. The first scene, following the order of the narrative, is the initial exposure of Hester Prynne's scarlet letter on Boston's public scaffold; the second is Arthur Dimmesdale's self-exposure and reenactment of this first scene when he ascends the same scaffold, but at night. I will take up these scenes, however, in reverse order.

Dimmesdale's watch on the scaffold is marked by an event which, though insignificant in itself, produces an interpretation of significance. As he stood there 'a light gleamed far and wide over all the muffled sky,' which, the narrator conjectures, 'was doubtless caused by one of those meteors . . . burning out to waste in the vacant regions of the atmosphere.' Although the form of this conjecture points to the probable negative material significance of the phenomenon – it is but matter consuming itself in a vacuum – the light produced by the conversion of energy acts as well to transform the scene as described. This transformation is twice marked in the passage as a conversion of the meaningless into the significant by means of figurative language: first when we read that the 'familiar scene of the street . . . (was) visible, but with a singularity of aspect that *seemed* to give another moral interpretation to the things of this world than they had ever borne before' [italics added]; and then again at the end of the same paragraph, where we read that Dimmesdale, Hester, and Pearl 'stood in the noon of that strange and solemn splendor, *as if it were* the light that is to reveal all secrets, and the daybreak that shall unite all who belong to one another' [italics added]. This is only the beginning, however, of a metaphoric conversion or interpretation that will end up going well beyond the narrator's two carefully qualified suggestions. As the passage continues in the next paragraph, the narrator remarks that for the Puritans 'nothing was more common, in those days than to interpret all meteoric appearances . . . as so many revelations from a supernatural source.' Bracketing for a moment the narrator's comments on this customary form of interpretation, we follow the passage as it moves to the zenith of the interpretive movement, the final conversion of nothingness into a fully meaningful sign. It is Dimmesdale who completes the circle, for while 'looking upward to the zenith, [the minister] beheld there the appearance of an immense letter, – the letter A, – marked out in lines of dull red light.'

These paragraphs – like the event they describe – seem to demand interpretation. Not because a hidden sense needs to be uncovered but, as Henry James has remarked, because of an excess of meaning. James singles out parts of this passage to illustrate what he thought was one of the work's few defects – what he calls 'a certain superficial symbolism' [see pages 18–20]. He quotes at length from the narrator's description of the meteoric light in the initial paragraph and judges it 'imaginative, impressive, poetic,' but adds that this admirable effect is lost when, as he writes, 'almost immediately afterwards' Hawthorne goes on to evoke the minister's vision of the letter in the sky. With that, writes James, 'we feel he goes too far' and he comments: 'Hawthorne is perpetually looking for images which shall place themselves in picturesque correspondence with the spiritual facts with which he is concerned, and of course the search is of the very essence of poetry. But in such a process discretion is everything, and when the image becomes importunate it is in danger of seeming to stand for nothing more serious than itself.' Although James is for the most part a sympathetic and careful reader of Hawthorne, I think he has misread this passage – but with an interesting result. By following the letter of Hawthorne's text – but also by restoring the intervening paragraph, hidden behind James's hedging phrase 'almost immediately afterwards' – one may find the terms of this critique well-chosen but poorly aimed. Perhaps this is because Hawthorne is not, as James implies, concerned with only 'spiritual' facts.

First, what James terms 'a superficial conceit' finds an echo in the narrator's remark that Dimmesdale's interpretation could only be the symptom of morbid self-contemplation. There is indeed, as James suggests, a failure of discretion in the search for an image, since in that process Dimmesdale, in the narrator's terms, 'extended his egotism over the whole expanse of nature.' If, as James writes, an 'image' is importunate here and 'in danger of seeming to stand for nothing more serious than itself,' then is it not in the sense of imitation, likeness, or reflection – a mirror image? Perhaps what imposes here – dangerously in James's judgment – is the image as 'nothing more serious than' the mirror of interpretation. The minister's act, which conceives a written sign in the closed narcissistic circle from the guilty subject back to itself, is a failure of discretion in the sense that it does not discern the difference between the interpreter/subject and an exteriority of the material world in which that subject imposes itself as image. At that moment, the whole differentiated expanse of nature becomes the subject's likeness, or, rather, repeats the sign whereby the subject acknowledges his identity to himself, his secret interiority. A is for both Arthur and Adulterer, that other name which signals the corruption of the essence of identity, since to adulter or adulterate is 'to render spurious or counterfeit by the admixture of baser ingredients' (*OED*).

However, the paragraph which James skips over in his summary of the passage links Dimmesdale's interpretive act to the practice of a community which read 'natural phenomena . . . as so many revelations from a supernatural source.' Of this belief in a transcendent meaning of community, the narrator remarks: 'It was, indeed, a majestic idea, that the destiny of nations should be revealed, in these awful hieroglyphics, on the cope of heaven. A scroll so wide might not be deemed too expansive for Providence to write a people's doom upon. The belief was a favorite one with our forefathers, as betokening that their infant commonwealth was under celestial guardianship of peculiar intimacy and strictness.' Dimmesdale's vision of the sign is then measured against this 'majestic idea' and, like a telescope collapsing on itself, the transcendence of meaning is revealed to be a device with which the self addresses itself: 'But what shall we say, when an individual discovers a revelation, addressed to himself alone, on the same vast sheet of record! In such a case, it could only be the symptom of a highly disordered mental state, when a man, rendered morbidly self-contemplative by long, intense, and secret pain, had extended his egotism over the whole expanse of nature, until the firmament itself should appear no more than a fitting page for his soul's history and fate.'

Dimmesdale's symptom is the particularization, the individualiza-tion of the shared belief in the transcendent meaning of the commonwealth. As such, however, it points to the contradiction within communal meaning which the transcendent interpretation turns away from, disregards. This contradiction is put into relief at the end of the chapter whose central scene we've been considering: there, in the aftermath of the meteoric appearance, Dimmesdale is con-fronted with the community of interpretation. Its spokesman, the church sexton, says to the minister 'But did your reverence hear of the portent that was seen last night? A great red letter in the sky, – the let-ter A, – which we interpret to stand for Angel. For, as our good Governor Winthrop was made an angel this past night, it was doubt-less held fit that there should be some notice thereof!' Dimmesdale's reply is an equivocation: '"No," answered the minister. "I had not heard of it."' The "it" here may refer either to the symbol – A – or to the symbolized – Angel, either to the sign or to its interpretation. This equivocation in turn signals Dimmesdale's ambiguous identity within the interpretive community of which he is a privileged representative – both a part of it and outside it. Thus, the sexton's report confirms Dimmesdale's revelation at the same time as it denies what the revela-tion revealed. These several strands of ambiguity converge in the phrase 'the letter A,' which occurs first in the description of the minis-ter's vision ('the appearance of an immense letter, – the letter A, – marked out in lines of dull red light') and is then repeated, set off with the same double punctuation, in the sexton's description ('A great red letter in the sky, – the letter A,– which . . .'). The letter A joins the com-munity in its manifest appearance only to divide it in its apparent significance, which alternates within paired oppositions: Adulterer or Angel, Abject or Adored, Arthur or Another. The letter A thus turns in a mirror of interpretation, its image infinitely reversible without a change in its appearance.

The reversibility of the letter, what the narrator earlier called its lack of 'definiteness,' is resolved in the theocratic Puritan state, as we have seen, by the common belief in the transcendent source of the letter's meaning. Arthur Dimmesdale not only shares this belief, he internalizes it and thus comes to exemplify it. Thereby, however, the minister also becomes in himself the locus of the contradiction which the concept of transcendent meaning seeks to remove from the community's midst. As the guilty subject of equivocation, the identity which hides its difference behind an appearance of sameness, his example to the community of its own belief must itself remain equivocal. Therefore in the penultimate chapter, 'The Revelation of the Scarlet Letter,' when Dimmesdale returns to the scaffold in the full light of day and uncovers his breast before the gathered citizenry, his revelation shatters rather than binds community. Interpretation of what one saw (or did not see) is then a matter of individual sensibility and contradiction is made manifest. When the narrator concludes the description of the final scaffold scene by turning its interpretation over to the reader – 'The reader may choose among these theories. We have thrown all the light we could acquire upon the portent' – it is as if to remind one that, in a world of untranscended appearance, all that remains to give meaning to community is what we call literature.

In *The Scarlet Letter*, this remainder retains the form of the material letter which Hester Prynne, after the shattering dispersal of the last scaffold scene, returns to take up again. To be sure, Hester's letter also marks the place of the guilty subject as determined by the agency of Puritan law. Yet unlike the instances of a transcendent mark which make Arthur the locus of guilty contradiction, the material application of the letter to Hester reveals a contradiction at the very source of judgment. This displacement of the contradiction already appears in the different role assigned to interpretation in the scene of Hester's punishment.

To begin with, there is no question about what anyone saw, as in the above scene. The letter, as 'the point which drew all eyes,' is clearly discerned:

On the breast of her gown, in a fine red cloth, surrounded with an elaborate embroidery and fantastic flourishes of gold thread, appeared the letter A. It was so artistically done, and with so much fertility and gorgeous luxuriance of fancy, that it had the effect of a last and fitting decoration to the apparel which she wore; and which was of a splendor in accordance with the taste of the age, but greatly beyond what was allowed by the sumptuary regulations of the colony.

While interpretation has little role here in the narrator's description, it does obtain in the question of which law is to be applied to the adulteress. Significantly, this question is raised by gossips present at the scene who quarrel about the magistrates' judgment on Hester, one arguing that 'they should have put the brand of hot iron on (her) forehead,' another that she should be put to death: 'This woman has brought shame upon us all and ought to die. *Is there no law for it?* Truly there is, both in the Scripture and the statute-book' [italics added]. When Hester appears with 'that Scarlet Letter, so fantastically embroidered and illuminated upon her bosom,' the gossips are dismayed. Says one to her *commeres*: 'What is it but to laugh in the faces of our godly magistrates and make a pride out of what they, worthy gentlemen, meant for a punishment?'

The judgment on Hester – as strictly interpreted – is simply that of display. In the words of the town beadle who, as we read, represented 'the whole dismal severity of the Puritanic code of law, which it was his business to administer in its final and closest *application* to the offender' [italics added], Mistress Prynne 'shall be set where man, woman and child may have a fair sight of her brave apparel, from this time till an hour past meridian.' And he adds 'A blessing on the righteous Colony of the Massachusetts, where iniquity is dragged out into the sunshine!'.

By means of the counterpoint of the woman's chorus of gossips, which disputes the law as applied to Hester, and the official representation of the law, which drags iniquity out into the sunshine, a question is allowed to surface about the meaning of this punishment as an instance of the law's application. Towards the end of the description of the scene, the narrator suggests that this question can only be answered by the 'solemn presence of men no less dignified than the Governor and several of his counsellors, a judge, a general and the ministers of the town. . . . When such personages could constitute *part of the spectacle*, without risking the majesty or reverence of rank and office, it was safely to be inferred that the infliction of a legal sentence would have an earnest and effectual meaning' [italics added]. In other words, it is the presence of the theocratic state's officials, their self-display on the balcony dominating the scaffold, that dissipates the potential ambiguity of this instance of the law's application of its mark upon the guilty subject. But with this suggestion, we see that the ambiguity has been not so much resolved as displaced upwards onto the personages who both guarantee the meaning of the spectacle as if from some transcendent position, and yet are themselves 'part of the spectacle' they guarantee.

The effects of this displacement of ambiguity, from the guilty subject at the center of the spectacle onto the personages embodying the law at the margins of the scene of its application, can be traced to the letter itself, which, in applying the law of display of guilt to Hester's example, at the same time went 'greatly beyond what was allowed by the sumptuary regulations of the colony.' That is, the letter is an instance of display in two senses of the word, one of which the law invokes as the instrument of righteous truth in this 'land where iniquity is searched out, and punished in the sight of rulers and people'; the other of which the law – as sumptuary regulation – condemns as ostentatious expenditure. Thus, to make an ostentatious display of the law's display of guilt – as Hester's letter does – is to dissociate that law from itself in a fashion (the word is appropriate here) that leaves a doubt about the certain meaning of the symbol by which the law manifests itself to the community. In the face of this uncertainty, one may wonder how the simple presence of these dignified men could guarantee the effectual meaning of a legal sentence and what mark or sign assures the spectator that that presence in fact represents the legality of the law.

Unlike the meteor's immaterial light, which reveals the law to itself as in a mirror of interpretation and leaves no traces, the embroidery of the letter makes known the duplicity within the law itself. As both the prescription and proscription of display, the law shows itself to be infallibly a *scription* – a writing in a certain relation to the material exteriority of the sign. The law cannot take form except in the letter's difference – the very difference which is repressed by the narcissistic interpretation of signs as images of the interpreter. The articulation of the scarlet letter, in other words, discerns and displays the necessary complicity between the outlaw and the law, the design of difference and the sign of identity. To be sure, as John Irwin has observed, the position of the outcast wearer of the letter also figures the alienation of the self-conscious writer – 'the feminine role of the artist in a Puritan, business-oriented society.' But Hawthorne's text, I believe, goes even further in relating the art of the lettered outcast to the central business of the community.

'It was the art – then, as now, almost the only one within a woman's grasp – of needlework.' While Hester's 'delicate and imaginative skill' should have found little use in a society where sumptuary laws restricted rich display, nevertheless we read that the products of her craft had a necessary function there.

> Public ceremonies, such as ordinations, the installation of magistrates and all that could give majesty to the forms in which a new government *manifested itself* to the people, were, as a matter of policy, marked by a stately and well-conducted ceremonial, and a sombre, but yet a studied magnificence. Deep ruffs, painfully

wrought bands and gorgeously embroidered gloves, were all deemed *necessary* to the official state of men assuming the rank of wealth, even while sumptuary laws forbade these and similar extravagances to the plebeian order . . .

By degrees, nor very slowly, (Hester's) handiwork became what would now be termed the fashion . . . Her needlework was seen on the ruff of the Governor; military men wore it on their scarfs, and the minister on his band [italics added].

Here one may pick out, with perhaps more precision than in the scene of Hester's punishment, what Hawthorne terms the *office* of the letter as illuminated by Hester's needlework. It is that which marks the law as law in its manifestation of itself but at the same time in contradiction with itself. As a supplementary device, embroidery designates the law with a sign of its own infraction. Thus we see that it is not the presence of these dignified men which guarantees the meaning of the law as applied to Hester, but the extravagant and extralegal mark on their persons of the law's manifest self-contradiction. There is, in other words, no guarantee of the letter's meaning as an instance of the law.

No formulation we might contrive of this inextricable relation between the manifest state and the extraneous design which is both cast out and 'deemed necessary to the official state' can approach the economy of the text's own language. It was, we read, 'as a matter of policy' that the new government marked its manifestation with a 'studied magnificence' – a matter of *policy*, that is, and not of law. In the word Hawthorne chooses to designate this relation, a crossover has occurred between roots coming from Greek *politeia/polis* (polity, state, political, police) and from the Latin *polītus* (polished, polite, refined, elegant). English has thus been left with a word which straddles a political division designating both 'political sagacity; prudence, skill or consideration of expediency in the conduct of public affairs; statecraft' and 'in a bad sense, political cunning, craftiness, dissimulation; a crafty device, stratagem, or trick' (*OED*).

Thus the office of the letter far exceeds its symbolic function of marking the guilty subject's exclusion from the center of law-governed society. According to the letter of Hawthorne's text, the policy of the mark situates as well a necessary inclusion of the unlawful accessory. The letter cannot be simply in the service of the law whose presence it signals only as an effect of absence. It is the office of the letter or the mark (in its extravagant wanderings over the manifest surface of the state's official aspect) to make known what the law does not, of itself, reveal: the policy of an unequal division and the accumulated disparities of power by which wealth signifies itself on the face of government as the neglected logic of a sociopolitical order.

It is in this sense that Hester's art – the embroidery of the letter – may be read as a necessary difference which exceeds the law of the same. It is a speculation she embroiders on the position of the symbol of the guilty subject, the subject of nonidentity, the 'woman' presented in social spectacle. This speculation of the letter overturns in its movement the narcissistic grounds of interpretation in the self-identical subject – as we may see, in conclusion, by turning to the chapter entitled 'Another View of Hester.' Here the narrator speculates on a certain speculation he ascribes to Hester as an 'effect . . . of the position in respect to society that was indicated by the [letter]'.

> A tendency to speculation, though it may keep woman quiet, as it does man, yet makes her sad. She discerns, it may be, such a hopeless task before her. As a first step, the whole system of society is to be torn down, and built up anew. Then, the very nature of the opposite sex, or its long hereditary habit, which has become like nature, is to be essentially modified, before woman can be allowed to assume what seems a fair and suitable position. Finally, all other difficulties being obviated, woman cannot take advantage of these preliminary reforms, until she herself shall have undergone a still mightier change; in which, perhaps, the ethereal essence, wherein she has her truest life, will be found to have evaporated.

This 'speculation' cannot be specular, since the movement from the position of the thinking subject through 'the whole system of society' back to itself does not close a circle but opens the possibility to thought of a woman who is essentially not a woman, as well as a man who is essentially not a man. If we may call such speculation feminist, then clearly it is only as a place to begin: a place at which to begin to think about both woman and man as other than guilty subjects which phallic law represses in its own midst.[22] □

NOTES

INTRODUCTION

1 Henry James, *Hawthorne* (New York: AMS, 1968), p.109.
2 Arlin Turner, *Nathaniel Hawthorne: A Biography* (New York: Oxford University Press, 1980), p.189.
3 Leo Marx, 'Foreward', *The Scarlet Letter* (New York: Signet Classics, 1959), p.xii.
4 Raman Selden, *Practising Theory and Reading Literature: An Introduction* (Hemel Hempstead: Harvester Wheatsheaf, 1989), p.77.

CHAPTER ONE

1 Letter to W.D. Ticknor, 12 October 1854, 'A Group of Hawthorne Letters', *Harper's Monthly Magazine*, Julian Hawthor ne (March 1904), cviii. 606–7. Quoted in *Hawthorne: The Critical Heritage*, ed. Donald J. Crowley (London: Routledge & Kegan Paul, 1971), p.6.
2 Crowley, p.3.
3 Nathaniel Hawthorne, *Mosses from an Old Manse*. Centenary Edition, vol.10 (Columbus: Ohio State University Press, 1974), p.5.
4 Letter to James T. Fields, 11 February 1860, *Yesterdays with Authors*, James T. Fields (1878), pp.87–8.
5 Letter to Duyckinck, 27 April 1851, Duyckinck Collection, MS Division, New York Public Library.
6 Letter to Horatio Bridge, 4 February 1850, MS. Houghton Library, Harvard University. Quoted in Crowley, p.151.
7 Herman Melville, 'Hawthorne and his Mosses', *The Literary World*, vii (August 17, 1850), p.126.
8 Quoted in Crowley, pp.155–7.
9 Quoted in Crowley, pp.158–9.
10 Quoted in Crowley, pp.160–2.
11 Quoted in Crowley, pp.163–4.
12 Quoted in Crowley, pp.164–7.
13 Quoted in Crowley, pp.168–75.
14 Quoted in Crowley, pp.175–9.
15 Quoted in Crowley, pp.179–84.

16 Henry James, *Hawthorne* (New York: AMS, 1968), pp.113–15.
17 George E. Woodberry, *Nathaniel Hawthorne* (Boston: Houghton, 1902), pp.199–203.
18 D.H. Lawrence, *Studies in Classic American Literature* (Harmondsworth: Penguin Books, 1971), p.89.

CHAPTER TWO

1 Yvor Winters, *In Defence of Reason* (Denver: Alan Swallow, 1947), p.165.
2 Ibid., pp.166 and 168.
3 Ibid., pp.170 and 174.
4 F.O. Matthiessen, *American Renaissance: Art and Expression in the Age of Emerson and Whitman* (New York: Oxford University Press, 1941), p.275.
5 Ibid., p.277.
6 Leland Schubert, *Hawthorne, the Artist: Fine Art Devices in Fiction* (Chapel Hill: University of North Carolina Press, 1944), pp.138–9.
7 Hyatt H. Waggoner, *Hawthorne: A Critical Study* (Cambridge, Mass.: Belknap-Harvard University Press, 1955), pp.127–9 and 138–41.
8 Darrel Abel, *The Moral Picturesque: Studies in Hawthorne's Fiction* (West Lafayette: Purdue University Press, 1988), pp.1–2.
9 Ibid., pp.169–71.
10 Ibid., pp.176–7.
11 Ibid., pp.180 and 186–7.
12 Ibid., pp.193–8.
13 Ibid., p.204.
14 Ibid., pp.207–11.
15 Ibid., pp.225–40.
16 G.R. Thompson and Virgil L. Lokke, eds. *Ruined Eden of the Present: Hawthorne, Melville, and Poe* (West Lafayette: Purdue University Press, 1981), p.x.
17 Roy R. Male, *Hawthorne's Tragic Vision* (New York: Norton, 1957), pp.90–118.
18 Ibid., pp.90–118.
19 R.W.B. Lewis, 'The Return into Time: Hawthorne', *The American Adam: Innocence, Tragedy, and Tradition in the Nineteenth Century* (Chicago: University of Chicago Press, 1955), pp.110–26.

20 Lionel Trilling, *The Liberal Imagination* (Harmondsworth: Peregrine Books, 1970), p. 214.

21 Richard Chase, *The American Novel and its Tradition* (London: G. Bell and Sons, 1957), pp. 12–13, 18–19 and 20–21.

22 Ibid., pp. 81–2.

23 Ibid., p. 80.

24 Harry Levin, *The Power of Blackness: Hawthorne, Poe, Melville* (New York: Alfred A. Knopf, 1967), p. 35.

25 Ibid., pp. 73–8.

26 William Bysshe Stein, *Hawthorne's Faust: A Study of the Devil Archetype* (Gainesville: University of Florida, 1953), pp. 121–2.

27 Leslie A. Fiedler, *Love and Death in the American Novel* (London: Paladin, 1960), p. 400.

28 Ibid., pp. 401–8.

29 Hugo McPherson, *Hawthorne as Myth-Maker: A Study in Imagination* (Toronto: University of Toronto Press, 1969), p. 8.

30 Ibid., pp. 17 and 20.

CHAPTER THREE

1 Charles Boewe and Murray G. Murphey, 'Hester Prynne in History', *American Literature*, 32 (1960), pp. 202–3.

2 Michael Colacurcio, 'Footsteps of Anne Hutchinson: The Context of *The Scarlet Letter*', *ELH*, 39 (1972), p. 461.

3 Michael J. Colacurcio, '"The Woman's Own Choice": Sex, Metaphor, and the Puritan "Sources" of *The Scarlet Letter*', in *New Essays on 'The Scarlet Letter'* (Cambridge: Cambridge University Press, 1985), p. 114.

4 Ibid., p. 123.

5 *The Letters of Ralph Waldo Emerson*, ed. Ralph L. Rusk, IV (New York: Columbia University Press, 1939), pp. 73–4.

6 Margaret Fuller, *At Home and Abroad, or Things and Thoughts in America and Europe*, ed. Arthur B. Fuller (1856; rpt. Port Washington, N.Y.: Kennikat, 1971), p. 380.

7 Arlin Turner, *Nathaniel Hawthorne: A Biography* (New York: Oxford University Press, 1980), p. 181.

8 See Joseph B. Felt, *The Annals of Salem, from its First Settlement* (Salem: W. & S.B. Ives, 1827), pp. 176 and 317.

9 Leland Schubert, *Hawthorne the Artist* (Chapel Hill: University of North Carolina Press, 1944), pp. 137–8.

10 Henry Nash Smith, *Democracy and the Novel: Popular Resistance to Classic American Writers* (New York: Oxford University Press, 1978), p. 25.

11 Donald A. Ringe, 'Hawthorne's Psychology of the Head and Heart', *PMLA*, 65 (1950), p. 129.

12 Michael David Bell, *Hawthorne and the Historical Romance of New England* (Princeton: Princeton University Press, 1971), p. 140.

13 Francis Kearns, 'Margaret Fuller as a Model for Hester Prynne', *Jahrbuch für Amerikastudien*, 10 (1965), pp. 191–7.

14 Thomas Woodson, 'Hawthorne's Interest in the Contemporary', *Nathaniel Hawthorne Society Newsletter*, 7 (1981), p. 1.

15 Larry J. Reynolds, '*The Scarlet Letter* and Revolutions Abroad', *American Literature*, 57, 1, March 1985, pp. 44–67.

16 Arlin Turner, *Nathaniel Hawthorne* (New York: Oxford University Press, 1980), p. v (Page references hereafter incorporated into text).

17 Nathaniel Hawthorne, *The Life of Franklin Pierce*, in *Works*, ed. G. P. Lathrop (Boston: Houghton Mifflin, 1883), 12: 381 (Page references hereafter incorporated into text).

18 Quoted in Turner, p. 373.

19 William Wordsworth, 'The Borderers' (1797), lines 1539–44.

20 David Potter, *The Impending Crisis* (New York: Harper & Row, 1976), pp. 43, 47 and 74.

21 Sacvan Bercovitch, *The American Jeremiad* (Madison: University of Wisconsin Press, 1978), pp. 12 and 170; and *The Puritan Origins of the American Self* (New Haven, Conn.: Yale University Press, 1975), p. 143; Arthur M. Schlesinger, Jr., *The Age of Jackson* (Boston: Little, Brown, 1945), p. 421. 'Paranosic gain' is standard psychoanalytic discourse for the primary advantages gained from illness.

22 See Claude Lévi-Strauss, 'The Structural Study of Myth' in *Structural Anthropology* (New York: Basic, 1963), and Fredric Jameson, *The Political Unconscious* (Ithaca: Cornell University Press, 1981), pp. 46–9, 163–9 and 253–6.

23 Perry Miller, *The Life of the Mind in America from the Revolution to the Civil War* (New York: Harcourt, Brace & World, 1965), p. 132.

24 Ibid., p. 162.

25 Morton J. Horovitz, *The Transformations of American Law, 1780–1860* (Cambridge, Mass.: Harvard University Press, 1977), p. 200.

26 Ibid., pp. 197–8.

27 Jonathan Arac, 'The Politics of *The Scarlet Letter*', in *Ideology and Classic American Literature*, eds Sacvan Bercovitch and Myra Jehlen (Cambridge: Harvard University Press, 1986), pp. 247–66.

28 Michael David Bell, 'Arts of Deception: Hawthorne, "Romance", and *The Scarlet Letter*', in *New Essays on 'The Scarlet Letter'*, ed. Michael Colacurcio (Cambridge: Cambridge University Press, 1985), p. 35.

29 Ibid., p. 37.

30 Ibid., p. 53.

CHAPTER FOUR

1 Richard H. Brodhead, *Hawthorne, Melville, and the Novel* (Chicago: University of Chicago Press, 1973), pp. 53–4.

2 Julian Hawthorne, *Nathaniel Hawthorne and his Wife* (Boston: Houghton Mifflin and Co., 1884), p. 335.

3 Randall Stewart, *Nathaniel Hawthorne* (New Haven: Yale University Press, 1948), p. 95.

4 Mark Van Doren, *Hawthorne* (New York: William Sloane Associates, 1949), p. 143.

5 Van Wyck Brooks, *The Flowering of New England* (London: J. M. Dent & Sons, 1936), p. 224.

6 Van Doren, p. 33.

7 Stewart, p. 11.

8 Joseph Levi, 'Hawthorne's *Scarlet*

Letter: A Psychoanalytic Interpretation', *American Imago*, 10 (1953), pp. 293–7.

9 Frederick C. Crews, *The Sins of the Fathers: Hawthorne's Psychological Themes* (New York: Oxford University Press, 1966), pp. 7–8.

10 Ibid., pp. 16–17.

11 Ibid., pp. 138–53.

12 Stewart, p. 4.

13 Arlin Turner, *Nathaniel Hawthorne: A Biography* (New York: Oxford University Press, 1980), p. 22.

14 Ibid., p. 106.

15 Clay Daniel, 'The Scarlet Letter: Hawthorne, Freud, and the Transcendentalists', *American Transcendental Quarterly*, 61 (1986), pp. 26–34.

16 Sigmund Freud, *The Standard Edition of the Complete Psychological Works of Sigmund Freud*, ed. James Strachey, XXI (London: Hogarth, 1953–74), pp. 152–3.

17 Leo Barsani, *A Future for Syntax* (Boston: Little, 1976), p. 6.

18 Joanne Feit Diehl, 'Re-Reading The Letter: Hawthorne, the Fetish, and the (Family) Romance', in *The Scarlet Letter, Case Studies in Contemporary Criticism*, ed. Ross C. Murfin (New York: Bedford Books, St Martin's Press, 1991), pp. 240–51.

CHAPTER FIVE

1 Nina Baym, 'Thwarted Nature: Nathaniel Hawthorne as Feminist', *American Novelists Revisited: Essays in Feminist Criticism*, ed. Fritz Fleischmann (Boston: Hall, 1982), pp. 60–2.

2 Ibid., p. 73.

3 Nina Baym, 'The Significance of Plot in Hawthorne's Romances', *Ruined Eden of the Present: Hawthorne, Melville, and Poe*, eds G. R. Thompson and Virgil Lokke (West Lafayette: Purdue University Press, 1981), p. 51.

4 Ibid., pp. 51–2.

5 Nina Baym, *The Shape of Hawthorne's Career* (Ithaca: Cornell University Press, 1976), pp. 143–6.

6 Judith Fryer, *The Faces of Eve: Women in the Nineteenth-Century American Novel*

(New York: Oxford University Press, 1976), pp. 72–9.

7 Wayne Booth, *The Rhetoric of Fiction* (Chicago: Chicago University Press, 1961), pp. 178 and 388–9.

8 Mary Suzanne Schriber, *Gender and the Writer's Imagination: From Cooper to Wharton* (Lexington: University Press of Kentucky, 1987), pp. 47–60.

9 Eric J. Sundquist, *Home as Found: Authority and Genealogy in Nineteenth-Century American Literature* (Baltimore: Johns Hopkins University Press, 1979), p. 113.

10 Terence Martin, 'Dimmesdale's Ultimate Sermon', *Arizona Quarterly*, 27 (1971), p. 235.

11 Leland S. Person, *Aesthetic Headaches: Women and a Masculine Poetics in Poe, Melville, and Hawthorne* (Athens: University of Georgia Press, 1988), pp. 126–38.

CHAPTER SIX

1 Charles Feidelson, Jr., 'The Scarlet Letter', in *Hawthorne Centenary Essays*, ed. Roy Harvey Pearce (Columbus: Ohio State University Press, 1964), pp. 31–78.

2 Richard H. Brodhead, *Hawthorne, Melville, and the Novel* (Chicago: University of Chicago Press, 1973), pp. 7–9, 63–5 and 67–8.

3 Kenneth Dauber, *Rediscovering Hawthorne* (Princeton: Princeton University Press, 1977), p. 100.

4 Ibid., pp. 106–10.

5 John Carlos Rowe, 'The Internal Conflict of Romantic Narrative: Hegel's *Phenomenology* and Hawthorne's *The Scarlet Letter*', *MLN*, 95, p. 1222.

6 Ibid., p. 1224.

7 Ibid., p. 1229.

8 Evan Carton, *The Rhetoric of American Romance: Dialectic and Identity in Emerson, Dickinson, Poe, and Hawthorne* (Baltimore: Johns Hopkins University Press, 1985), p. 213.

9 Ibid., p. 196 and 209–12.

10 Ibid., p. 216.

11 Freud, 'Moses and Monotheism', *The Standard Edition of the Complete Psychological Works of Sigmund Freud*, trans. James Strachey (London: Hogarth Press, 1964), XXIII: 43.

12 Jacques Derrida, 'Coming into One's Own', in *Psychoanalysis and the Question of the Text*, ed. Geoffrey H. Hartman (Baltimore: Johns Hopkins University Press, 1978), p. 127.

13 Daniel Sibony, '*Hamlet*: A Writing-Effect', in *Literature and Psychoanalysis: The Question of Reading, Otherwise*, ed. Shoshana Felman (Baltimore: Johns Hopkins University Press, 1982), p. 74.

14 Nina Baym, *The Shape of Hawthorne's Career* (Ithaca: Cornell University Press, 1976), p. 142.

15 Lacan, 'From Interpretation to the Transference', *The Four Fundamental Concepts of Psycho-Analysis*, trans. Alan Sheridan (New York: Norton, 1978), p. 250 ff.

16 Daniel Sibony, '*Hamlet*: A Writing-Effect', in *Literature and Psychoanalysis: The Question of Reading, Otherwise*, pp. 82 and 75.

17 Lacan, *Seminar on the 'Purloined Letter'*, quoted in Barbara Johnson, 'The Frame of Reference: Poe, Lacan, Derrida', in *Literature and Psychoanalysis: The Question of Reading, Otherwise*, p. 476.

18 Barbara Johnson, 'The Frame of Reference: Poe, Lacan, Derrida', in *Literature and Psychoanalysis: The Question of Reading, Otherwise*, pp. 499 and 502.

19 Cited in James T. Fields, *Yesterdays with Authors* (Boston: James R. Osgood, 1874), p. 52.

20 Edgar A. Dryden, *Nathaniel Hawthorne: The Poetics of Enchantment* (Ithaca: Cornell University Press, 1977), p. 149.

21 John Dolis, 'Hawthorne's Letter', *Notebooks in Cultural Analysis: An Annual Review*, ed. Norman F. Cantor (Durham: Duke University Press, 1984), pp. 103–23.

22 Peggy Kamuf, 'Hawthorne's Genres: The Letter of the Law *Appliquee*', *After Strange Texts: The Role of Theory in the Study of Literature*, ed. Gregory S. Jay and David L. Miller (University of Alabama Press, 1985), pp. 75–84.

BIBLIOGRAPHY

Works by Nathaniel Hawthorne

Fanshawe: A Tale, published anonymously and at his own expense. Later withdrawn.

The Scarlet Letter and Selected Tales (Harmondsworth: Penguin, 1986).

The House of the Seven Gables (Harmondsworth: Penguin).

The Blithedale Romance (Harmondsworth: Penguin).

The Marble Faun (Harmondsworth: Penguin).

Selected Tales and Sketches (Harmondsworth: Penguin).

The Complete Works of Nathaniel Hawthorne, 12 vols (Riverside Edition: Boston, 1883).

The English Notebooks of Nathaniel Hawthorne, ed. Randall Stewart (New York, 1941).

Books

Darrel Abel, *The Moral Picturesque: Studies in Hawthorne's Fiction* (West Lafayette: Purdue University Press, 1988).

Nina Baym, *The Shape of Hawthorne's Career* (Ithaca: Cornell University Press, 1976).

Michael David Bell, *Hawthorne and the Historical Romance of New England* (Princeton: Princeton University Press, 1971).

Sacvan Bercovitch, *The American Jeremiad* (Madison: University of Wisconsin Press, 1978) and *The Puritan Origins of the American Self* (New Haven, Conn.: Yale University Press, 1975).

Richard Brodhead, *Hawthorne, Melville, and the Novel* (Chicago: Chicago University Press, 1973).

Evan Carton, *The Rhetoric of American Romance: Dialectic and Identity in Emerson, Dickinson, Poe, and Hawthorne* (Baltimore: Johns Hopkins University Press, 1985).

Richard Chase, *The American Novel and its Tradition* (London: G. Bell and Sons, 1957).

Michael J. Colacurcio, (ed.), *New Essays on 'The Scarlet Letter'* (Cambridge: Cambridge University Press, 1985).

Frederick C. Crews, *The Sins of the Fathers: Hawthorne's Psychological Themes* (New York: Oxford University Press, 1966).

Donald J. Crowley, (ed.), *Hawthorne: The Critical Heritage* (New York: Barnes, 1971).

Kenneth Dauber, *Rediscovering Hawthorne* (Princeton: Princeton University Press, 1977).

Leslie A. Fiedler, *Love and Death in the American Novel* (London: Paladin, 1960).

James T. Fields, *Yesterdays with Authors* (Boston: James R. Osgood, 1874).

Judith Fryer, *The Faces of Eve: Women in the Nineteenth-Century American Novel* (New York: Oxford University Press, 1976).

Julian Hawthorne, *Nathaniel Hawthorne and his Wife* (Boston: Houghton Mifflin and Co., 1884).

Henry James, *Hawthorne* (New York: AMS, 1968).

D. H. Lawrence, *Studies in Classic American Literature* (Harmondsworth: Penguin, 1971).

R.W.B. Lewis, *The American Adam: Innocence, Tragedy, and Tradition in the Nineteenth Century* (Chicago: Chicago University Press, 1955).

Harry Levin, *The Power of Blackness: Hawthorne, Poe, Melville* (New York: Alfred A. Knopf, 1967).

Hugo McPherson, *Hawthorne as Myth-Maker: A Study in Imagination* (Toronto: University of Toronto Press, 1969).

Roy R. Male, *Hawthorne's Tragic Vision* (New York: Norton, 1957).

F.O. Matthiessen, *American Renaissance: Art and Expression in the Age of Emerson and Whitman* (New York: Oxford University Press, 1941).

Leland S. Person, *Aesthetic Headaches: Women and a Masculine Poetics in Poe, Melville, and Hawthorne* (Athens: University of Georgia Press, 1988).

Mary Suzanne Schriber, *Gender and the Writer's Imagination: From Cooper to Wharton* (Lexington: University Press of Kentucky, 1987).

Leland Schubert, *Hawthorne, the Artist: Fine Art Devices in Fiction* (Chapel Hill: University of North Carolina Press, 1955).

William Bysshe Stein, *Hawthorne's Faust: A Study of the Devil Archetype* (Gainesville: University of Florida, 1953).

Randall Stewart, *Nathaniel Hawthorne* (New Haven: Yale University Press, 1948).

G.R. Thompson and Virgil L. Lokke, *Ruined Eden of the Present: Hawthorne, Melville, and Poe* (West Lafayette: Purdue University Press, 1981).

Arlin Turner, *Nathaniel Hawthorne: A Biography* (New York: Oxford University Press, 1980).

Mark Van Doren, *Hawthorne* (William Sloane Associates, 1949).

Hyatt H. Waggoner, *Hawthorne: A Critical Study* (Cambridge, Mass.: Belknap-Harvard University Press, 1955).

Yvor Winters, *In Defence of Reason* (Denver: Alan Swallow, 1947).

George E. Woodberry, *Nathaniel Hawthorne* (Boston: Houghton, 1902).

Articles on *The Scarlet Letter*

Jonathan Arac, 'The Politics of *The Scarlet Letter*', in *Ideology and Classic American Literature*, (eds) Sacvan Bercovitch and Myra Jehlen (Cambridge: Cambridge University Press, 1986), pp.247–66.

Nina Baym, 'The Significance of Plot in Hawthorne's Romances', in *Ruined Eden of the Present: Hawthorne, Melville, and Poe*, (eds) G.R. Thompson and Virgil Lokke, pp.49–70.

Nina Baym, 'Thwarted Nature: Nathaniel Hawthorne as Feminist', in *American Novelists Revisited: Essays in Feminist Criticism*, (ed.) Fritz Fleischmann (Boston: Hall, 1982), pp.58–77.

Michael David Bell, 'Arts of Deception: Hawthorne, "Romance", and *The*

Scarlet Letter', in Michael Colacurcio (ed.), *New Essays on 'The Scarlet Letter'*, pp. 29–56.

Charles Boewe and Murray G. Murphey, 'Hester Prynne in History', *American Literature*, 32 (1960), pp. 202–4.

Michael Colacurcio, 'Footsteps of Ann Hutchinson: The Context of *The Scarlet Letter'*, *ELH*, 39 (1972), pp. 459–94.

Clay Daniel, '*The Scarlet Letter*: Hawthorne, Freud, and the Transcendentalists', *American Transcendental Quarterly*, 61 (1986), pp. 23–35.

Joanne Feit Diehl, 'Re-Reading The Letter: Hawthorne, the Fetish, and the (Family) Romance', in *The Scarlet Letter, Case Studies in Contemporary Criticism*, (ed.), Ross C. Murfin (New York: Bedford Books, St Martin's Press, 1991).

John Dolis, 'Hawthorne's Letter', in *Notebooks in Cultural Analysis: An Annual Review*, (ed.) Norman F. Cantor (Durham: Duke University Press, 1984), pp. 103–23.

Peggy Kamuf, 'Hawthorne's Genres: The Letter of the Law *Appliquee'*, in *After Strange Texts: The Role of Theory in the Study of Literature*, (eds) Gregory S. Jay and David L. Miller (University of Alabama Press, 1985).

Joseph Levi, 'Hawthorne's *Scarlet Letter*: A Psychoanalytic Interpretation', *American Imago*, 10 (1953), pp. 291–305.

Larry J. Reynolds, '*The Scarlet Letter* and Revolutions Abroad', *American Literature*, 57, 1 (March 1985), pp. 44–67.

John Carlos Rowe, 'The Internal Conflict of Romantic Narrative: Hegel's *Phenomenology* and Hawthorne's *The Scarlet Letter'*, *MLN*, 95, pp. 1203–31.

Charles Ryskamp, 'The New England Sources of *The Scarlet Letter'*, *American Literature*, 31 (1959), pp. 257–72.

ACKNOWLEDGEMENTS

The editor and publishers wish to thank the following for their permission to reprint copyright material: Oxford University Press (for material from *American Renaissance: Art and Expression in the Age of Emerson and Whitman, The Sins of the Fathers: Hawthorne's Psychological Themes*, and *The Faces of Eve: Women in the Nineteenth-Century American Novel*); University of North Carolina Press (for material from *Hawthorne, the Artist: Fine Art Devices in Fiction*); Alan Swallow (for material from *In Defence of Reason*); Belknap/Harvard University Press (for material from *Hawthorne: A Critical Study*); Purdue University Press (for material from *The Moral Picturesque: Studies in Hawthorne's Fiction*); Norton (for material from *Hawthorne's Tragic Vision*); Chicago University Press (for material from *The American Adam: Innocence, Tragedy, and Tradition in the Nineteenth Century*, and *Hawthorne, Melville, and the Novel*); G. Bell and Sons (for material from *The American Novel and its Tradition*); University of Toronto Press (for material from *The Power of Blackness: Hawthorne, Poe, Melville*, and *Hawthorne as Myth-Maker: A Study in Imagination*); University of Florida (for material from *Hawthorne's Faust: A Study of the Devil Archetype*); Paladin (for material from *Love and Death in the American Novel*); Cambridge University Press (for material from *New Essays on* The Scarlet Letter, and 'The Politics of *The Scarlet Letter*'); Larry J. Reynolds and *American Literature* (for material from '*The Scarlet Letter* and Revolutions Abroad'); Michael D. Bell (for material from 'Arts of Deception: Hawthorne, "Romance", and *The Scarlet Letter*'); *American Imago* (for material from 'Hawthorne's *Scarlet Letter*: A Psychoanalytic Interpretation'); *American Transcendental Quarterly* (for material from '*The Scarlet Letter*: Hawthorne, Freud, and the Transcendentalists'); Bedford Books, St. Martin's Press/Ross C. Murfin and Joanne Feit Diehl (for material from 'Re-Reading The Letter: Hawthorne, the Fetish, and the (Family) Romance'); Cornell University Press (for material from *The Shape of Hawthorne's Career*); University Press of Kentucky (for material from *Gender and the Writer's Imagination: From Cooper to Wharton*); University of Georgia Press (for material from *Aesthetic Headaches: Women and a Masculine Poetics in Poe, Melville, and Hawthorne*); Princeton University Press (for material from *Rediscovering Hawthorne*); John Carlos Rowe/*MLN* (for material from 'The Internal Conflict of Romantic Narrative: Hegel's *Phenomenology* and Hawthorne's *The Scarlet Letter*'); Johns Hopkins University Press (for material from *The Rhetoric of American Romance: Dialectic and Identity in Emerson, Dickinson, Poe, and Hawthorne*); Duke University Press/John Dolis (for material from 'Hawthorne's Letter', in *Notebooks in Cultural Analysis: An Annual Review*); University of Alabama Press/Peggy Kamuf (for material from 'Hawthorne's Genres: The Letter of the Law *Appliquee*', in *After Strange Texts: The Role of Theory in the Study of Literature*).

There are instances where we have been unable to trace or contact copyright holders before our printing deadline. If notified, the publisher will be pleased to acknowledge the use of copyright material.

Elmer Kennedy-Andrews is Senior Lecturer in English at the University of Ulster at Coleraine. His books include *The Poetry of Seamus Heaney: All the Realms of Whisper* (London: Macmillan, 1988), *Seamus Heaney: A Collection of Critical Essays* (London: Macmillan, 1992), *Contemporary Irish Poetry: A Collection of Critical Essays* (London: Macmillan, 1992) and *The Art of Brian Friel* (London: Macmillan, 1995). He has also published essays on American and Irish writers in various books and journals, and is the editor of the Icon Critical Guide to the poetry of Seamus Heaney.

INDEX